The Dead Hand's Grip

The Dead Hand's Grip

How Long Constitutions Bind States

ADAM R. BROWN

Oxford University Press is a department of the University of Oxford. It furthers
the University's objective of excellence in research, scholarship, and education
by publishing worldwide. Oxford is a registered trade mark of Oxford University
Press in the UK and certain other countries.

Published in the United States of America by Oxford University Press
198 Madison Avenue, New York, NY 10016, United States of America.

© Oxford University Press 2023

All rights reserved. No part of this publication may be reproduced, stored in
a retrieval system, or transmitted, in any form or by any means, without the
prior permission in writing of Oxford University Press, or as expressly permitted
by law, by license, or under terms agreed with the appropriate reproduction
rights organization. Inquiries concerning reproduction outside the scope of the
above should be sent to the Rights Department, Oxford University Press, at the
address above.

You must not circulate this work in any other form
and you must impose this same condition on any acquirer.

Library of Congress Control Number: 2022912046

ISBN 978–0–19–765528–3

DOI: 10.1093/oso/9780197655283.001.0001

1 3 5 7 9 8 6 4 2

Printed by Integrated Books International, United States of America

Contents

Acknowledgments   vii

1. Introducing Constitutional Specificity   1
   Conceptualizing Specificity   3
   Institutional Inflexibility   5
   Policy Inflexibility   7
   Institutions, Policies, and Specificity   9
   Alabama as a Cautionary Tale   10
   Specificity as Length   13
   State Constitutions   14
   Preview of Findings   18
   Appendix: Major Variables   21

2. Contextualizing Specificity   24
   American Constitutionalism   25
   Scholarly Neglect and Revival   28
   Interpretation and Specificity   31
   From Revision to Amendment   37
   Correlates of Modern Length   43
   Summary   48

3. Specificity and Amendments   49
   Democratic Constitutionalism   50
   Pressures to Amend   52
   Amendment Barriers   56
   Analysis and Results   60
   Voter Ratification   64
   Summary   67
   Methodological Appendix   68

4. Specificity and Judicial Review   75
   Four Approaches   76
   Constrained Discretion   78
   Amendment and Revision   81
   Complications   84
   Analysis and Results   86
   Petitioner Claims   88
   A Critical Test   90
   Summary   91
   Methodological Appendix   92

5. Specificity and Prosperity 104
   Cross-National Research 105
   Specificity in the States 108
   Analysis and Results 111
   Granger Causality 116
   Summary 117
   Methodological Appendix 119

6. Evaluating State Constitutions 127
   Founding Feuds 128
   Different Frames for Different Constitutions 130
   Experiment and Results 133
   Summary 136
   Methodological Appendix 138

7. Conclusion 142
   What Is Not Shown 144
   A Benign Alternative? 145
   Endurance and Performance 147
   The Burden of Constitutional Specificity 149

Notes 151
References 165
Index 181

Acknowledgments

Portions of this manuscript were presented in draft form at the 2015 State Politics and Policy Conference (Sacramento); the 2015 annual meeting of the American Political Science Association (San Francisco); the June 2016 workshop of Brigham Young University's Center for the Study of Elections and Democracy; the 2016 State Politics and Policy Conference (Dallas); the 2016 meeting of the Western Political Science Association (San Diego); the November 2016 "Changing Constitutions" symposium sponsored by the Kaliste Saloom Chair Speaker Series at the University of Louisiana, Lafayette; the 2017 meeting of the Midwest Political Science Association (Chicago); the 2018 meeting of the Western Political Science Association (San Francisco); the 2019 State Politics and Policy Conference (College Park, Maryland); and on several occasions at my department's brownbag research workshop.

This book has benefited from advice and comments provided by discussants and workshop participants at these venues and elsewhere. At risk of missing someone, I thank Michael Barber, Celeste Beesley, Chris Bonneau, Allen Brierly, Nathan Brown, Craig Burnett, Richard Davis, Adam Dynes, Elizabeth Fredericksen, Jay Goodliffe, Stephen Griffin, Josh Gubler, Kirk Hawkins, John Holbein, Chris Karpowitz, David Magleby, Jason Maloy, Chad Nelson, Janine Parry, Kelly Patterson, Jeremy Pope, Jessica Preece, Joel Selway, Yvonne Tew, Dick Winters, and Jeff Yates. I have also benefited from correspondence with John Dinan, Alan Tarr, George Tsebelis, and Robert Williams. Three former students provided diligent research assistance: Matthew Beck, Justin Chang, and Steven Torgesen.

I owe a special debt to Jeremy Pope, who collaborated in fielding the survey discussed in chapter 6, which draws partially from our coauthored article, "Measuring and Manipulating Constitutional Evaluations in the States: Legitimacy versus Veneration," *American Politics Research* 47 (5): 1135–61 (2019).

Chapter 4 draws partially from my essay "The Role of Constitutional Features in Judicial Review," *State Politics and Policy Quarterly* 18 (4): 351–70 (2018).

My greatest thanks go to my wife, Janelle, and our sons for their love and support.

1
Introducing Constitutional Specificity

In *Gulliver's Travels*, the eponymous hero washes ashore shipwrecked on an unknown island. Seeing no one, he lies down exhausted and sleeps. He wakes the next morning shocked to find himself tightly bound. Fearing Gulliver's gigantic size and strength, the island's tiny inhabitants conquered him not with a single rope but with thousands of thin strands. Later these Lilliputians would form an alliance with Gulliver, dispatching him against their foes—only to seek once again to assert their control when he proved more headstrong than they hoped. The Lilliputians' efforts to control and unleash Gulliver illustrate the challenges surrounding citizens' delegation of authority to democratic governments. An overly constrained government will lack the power to act on behalf of its constituents, yet an unleashed leviathan can turn on its would-be masters. James Madison once articulated this dilemma in Federalist 51:

> What is government itself, but the greatest of all reflections on human nature? If men were angels, no government would be necessary. If angels were to govern men, neither external nor internal controls on government would be necessary. In framing a government which is to be administered by men over men, the great difficulty lies in this: you must first enable the government to control the governed; and in the next place oblige it to control itself. (quoted in Rossiter 1961, 319)

Often, political science places one individual Lilliputian strand under a microscope rather than consider the aggregate effect of so many cords. That is, most political science research examines presidents, legislatures, courts, referendums, electoral systems, or other individual institutions more than it examines Madison's broader dilemma about how much authority citizens should delegate to the state and how much to restrict that authority. With Madison's dilemma in mind, this book contemplates a new way to step back and consider the authority citizens delegate to their governments—especially the restrictions placed on that authority. Conceptually, this new measure is constitutional specificity; operationally, it is the constitution's length.

There are, of course, dysfunctional governments scattered around the globe that have yet to muster sufficient power to fulfill even the most basic functions. This book does not examine these failing states, as it serves little purpose to consider the effects of Lilliputian bonds when there is no Gulliver to begin with. Rather, this book considers established constitutional democracies. Put differently, this book concerns itself with the latter half of Madison's dilemma, showing how citizens' efforts to "oblige [their state] to control itself" can go too far, undermining the state's ability to govern in the first place.

This book makes a straightforward claim: detailed constitutions bind states. A state burdened by a single ill-conceived constitutional provision could correct the problem easily enough by amendment, but a state burdened by hundreds of seemingly minor provisions will flail, unsure how to begin freeing itself from its Lilliputian bonds. Excessive constitutional specificity restricts officeholders' ability to respond quickly, completely, and appropriately to new circumstances. States tinker endlessly with their constitutions, leading them to wax and wane in length, but much of the variance in modern constitutional specificity has roots in the past. Legal scholars often speak of the "dead hand problem" as they debate how to apply a constitution written by dead hands to modern concerns.[1] Constitutional specificity exacerbates this problem. Detailed constitutions bind states to a dead generation's solutions to a dead generation's problems. The more detailed a constitution, the tighter the dead hand's grip on modern states.

This book will show that constitutional specificity has three major effects. First, constitutional specificity compels policymakers to rely more often on extraordinary amendment procedures relative to routine statutory or regulatory processes, hindering policy flexibility. Second, constitutional specificity leads state appellate courts to enforce narrower limits on policymakers' authority, so that judicial invalidations increase with constitution length. Third, constitutional specificity hinders policy performance, resulting in lower incomes per capita, higher unemployment rates, greater economic inequality, and reduced policy innovativeness generally. The first two findings suggest that policymakers feel so burdened by a detailed constitution that they grow increasingly desperate to escape its constraints; they tug one Lilliputian strand at a time, whether by pursuing onerous amendment procedures or by enacting policies that risk judicial scrutiny. The latter finding suggests that policymakers are correct to feel so burdened.

I detail these three major effects in chapters 3, 4, and 5, respectively. For now, I will proceed by developing a conceptual definition of constitutional specificity and previewing a theory of how excessive specificity harms states, leaving subsequent chapters to develop hypotheses connecting this theory to specific outcomes. I then present constitution length as an operational measure of constitutional specificity and introduce American state constitutions as an ideal setting for evaluating my claims. Though my argument is general enough to apply to any well-established polity, state constitutions not only offer wonderful statistical properties but also resemble typical national constitutions more closely than the unusual US Constitution does. I conclude this chapter by previewing the remainder of the book.

Conceptualizing Specificity

Political scientists study every sort of institution, yet in so many studies of presidentialism, federalism, and bicameralism it can be difficult to see how these institutions aggregate into a coherent whole. Just as biologists must occasionally step back from individual species to consider entire ecosystems, political scientists must occasionally step back from individual institutions to consider entire political systems. After all, a constitutional convention plants not a tree but a forest.

Madison's dissertation on checks and balances in Federalist 51 illustrates this ecological approach. Preserving liberty, Madison wrote, requires "so contriving the interior structure of the government as that its several constituent parts may, by their mutual relations, be the means of keeping each other in their proper places," for "ambition must be made to counteract ambition." The "different branches" must be "as little connected with each other as the nature of their common functions and their common dependence on the society will admit" (quoted in Rossiter 1961, 317–19). Applying and evaluating this logic requires attention to the entire political system, not to one part of it. The federal convention planted a forest, not a tree.

Like the federal convention, state constitutional conventions also erect complete systems, not isolated institutions. Dinan's (2006, 4) review of dozens of state convention records reveals that constitution writers after 1787 were "fully aware of the reasons why federal convention delegates had chosen to design national institutions in a particular fashion," but they also "benefited from institutional knowledge and experience that was unavailable to the eighteenth-century federal founders." With time, state constitutions increasingly departed from the federal model—but with reasoned intent. As a result, "state convention debates are in many ways a better expression of the considered judgement of the American constitutional tradition than can be found in the eighteenth-century federal sources" (5), and their records "are at least entitled to be placed alongside the arguments in *Madison's Notes*, *Elliot's Debates*, and *The Federalist*" (4).

Ambitious scholars have made several fruitful attempts to step back and view the constitutional forest rather than the institutional trees. Consider a few major examples. Lijphart (1969, 2012) differentiated majoritarian from consensus democracies, showing the implications of allowing a bare democratic majority to govern as opposed to a consociational system forcing competing groups to cooperate. Taking a different approach, Tsebelis (2002) generalized from institutions to veto players, considering the total number of actors capable of impeding reform as a critical systemic variable. And Bueno de Mesquita et al. (2003) turned our attention to nominal selectorates, real selectorates, and winning coalitions, emphasizing how the size of the constituency that keeps leaders in power influences their incentives. Acemoglu and Robinson (2012) made related claims about the inclusiveness of political and economic institutions. Each of these pathbreaking works identified a systemic feature of political systems that operated at a more basic level than any one specific institution. That is, each of these pathbreaking works looked to the forest rather than the trees.

Taking inspiration from these scholars, this book proposes constitutional specificity as a new way to look beyond individual institutions to capture something broader about a political system. A constitution's specificity suggests something important about the political system it erects. Cross-nationally, constitutions are lengthier in nations with greater respect for civil rights, with more complex political institutions, and with higher levels of democracy.[2] All this makes intuitive sense; adding specificity to a legal document is costly (Ehrlich and Posner 1974), a claim that extends to constitutions (Elkins, Ginsburg, and Melton 2009; Ginsburg 2010). As Versteeg and Zackin (2014, 1667–68) write:

> Of course, working out all the details of government up front entails substantial negotiation costs. Constitutions are like incomplete contracts—in an ever-changing political environment, it is impossible to foresee all contingencies of governing. Yet constitution makers can strive for various

degrees of completeness.... Specificity is likely to increase negotiation costs because it is easier for parties to reach agreement on broad principles than on specific rules.

Adding constitutional detail incurs negotiation costs. Constitution writers are more willing to bear those costs when they wish to delegate authority more deliberately (cf. Kiewiet and McCubbins 1991; Huber and Shipan 2002; Versteeg and Zackin 2016). Constitutional specificity comes with a price, though, beyond these short-term negotiation costs. Adding detail to a constitution also locks in current political compromises, making it harder for future generations to adapt to new circumstances. Political compromises that may have been expedient a century or more in the past can outlive their usefulness if they are written into the constitution instead of being left to statutory or regulatory discretion. For example, the US Constitution guaranteed two senators per state at a time when Virginia had only 12 times Delaware's population, failing to foresee that California would one day have almost 70 times Wyoming's population. As another example, the US Constitution addressed a right to bear arms in a time of single-shot flintlock muskets, failing to foresee weapons enabling a lone shooter to inflict mass casualties. The question contemplated here is neither Senate malapportionment nor American firearm policy. Rather, it is whether to handle those matters in the Constitution or in statute—and especially the aggregate effect of giving an increased number of issues constitutional stature. This sort of constitutional specificity binds states to past compromises. The more detailed a constitution, the more it binds to the past.

Institutional Inflexibility

Consider a first way specificity binds states: institutional inflexibility. It takes more constitutional detail to create a bicameral than a unicameral legislature, a plural executive than a unitary governor, or a three-tiered than a two-tiered judiciary—all of which are found among the 50 states. It takes more constitutional detail to create transportation commissions, agricultural commissions, boards of education, and insurance commissions with constitutional authority independent of the legislature and governor.[3] Speaking generally, it takes more constitutional detail to empower more veto players, and empowering more veto players reduces the state's ability to change course.

In this sense, constitutional specificity is, in part, an application of Tsebelis's (2002) veto players model—but constitutional specificity goes further. A detailed constitution can also increase institutional inflexibility by specifying complicated procedures for the bodies it establishes. The US Constitution broadly asserts that the "House of Representatives shall choose their Speaker and other officers," saying nothing further about committees, parliamentary procedure, or legislative process. This terse approach preserves broad flexibility, allowing each chamber of Congress to freely choose its officers, structures, rules, and processes. Because congressional procedure is largely extraconstitutional, congressional majorities are free to suspend internal rules or adopt other ad hoc procedures when necessary to reach a workable compromise—and they resort to unorthodox procedures often (Sinclair 2016).

Rather than follow this flexible example, many state constitutions impose detailed structural or procedural constraints on state legislatures. State constitutions may require, for example, that each proposed bill receive three readings in each chamber, that no amendment conflict with a bill's original purpose, that bills be heard in the order introduced, that every bill receive a committee hearing prior to floor consideration, or that bills address only a single subject (Townsend 1985; Binder, Kogan, and Kousser 2011; Williams 2009, 257–67; Miller, Hamm, and Hedlund 2015). As one legal scholar observed, "Commonly, state constitutions provide that the legislature shall determine its own rules of procedure, and then deny it the effective exercise of that right by providing for the conduct of legislative business in such detail as to leave very little to rulemaking" (Grad 1968, 963).

State constitutions can also impose institutional or procedural inflexibility on other branches of state government. The US Constitution gives the president broad authority to appoint cabinet secretaries, judges, and other executive officers, but state constitutions routinely detail more complicated alternatives (Beyle and Ferguson 2008). Nearly all state constitutions deny governors authority to choose the attorney general, lieutenant governor, treasurer, or other critical officials; instead, voters elect these officials, who then wield independent authority (Beyle and Ferguson 2008; Kousser and Phillips 2012). Many states allow governors to appoint judges, but with their discretion constrained in practice by judicial nominating commissions or other structures (cf. Hall 2008). And many state constitutions modify the executive veto in ways that complicate legislative-executive bargaining, disrupting the legislature's ability to build broad coalitions by empowering the governor to strip individual provisions from a bill (Brown 2012).

Constitutional specificity can also impose institutional inflexibility on the judicial branch. At the federal level, the terse US Constitution declares generally that a US Supreme Court will exist but leaves Congress to define the Court's jurisdiction, set the number of justices, and establish lower courts. As a contrasting example, the New York state constitution leaves little to legislative or judicial discretion, defining in detail the jurisdiction, organization, processes, and appointment scheme for the New York State Supreme Court as well as various appellate divisions, county courts, family courts, New York City courts, and town courts. The New York constitution also addresses judicial expenses, judicial administration, child custody criteria, and more. All this detail means the New York constitution devotes 40 times more space to its judiciary than the US Constitution does (Hammons 2001, 1330).

States vary in the legislative, executive, and judicial structures they erect, but most important for this book, they vary in whether those differences have constitutional stature. Extraconstitutional structures and processes developed within an institution, such as the US House's committees and rules, are easier to modify or circumvent than constitutionalized structures and processes. As a first implication of constitutional specificity, then, a detailed constitution indicates institutional inflexibility, whether through an increase in the number of actors or through an increase in the procedural restrictions placed on those actors.

Policy Inflexibility

Consider now a second way constitutional specificity binds states: constitutionalized policies. Many states limit statutory and regulatory discretion, locking in policies on "ski trails and highway routes, public holidays and motor vehicle revenues" (Tarr 1998, 2). Critics see in these constitutionalized policies "simply a frivolous people who are unable to distinguish between things that are truly important and things that are not" (Gardner 1992, 820). Whether frivolous or not, such provisions reduce the people's grant of authority to the state.

Constitutionalizing a policy places it beyond the reach of officeholders unless they pursue extraordinary processes to amend the constitution.

Such restrictions are common: "States devote an average of forty percent of their constitutions to these types of issues—matters that most political scientists and constitutional experts consider extraneous at best" (Hammons 2001, 1333). As examples, consider Florida's constitutional restrictions on marine net fishing, Oklahoma's constitutional provisions for interoperability of telephone and telegraph lines, Alabama's constitutionalized protections for peanut farmers, and Vermont's constitutional protection of the estates of those who die by suicide (1351). Some state constitutions specify processes for the "assessment, taxation, and rules of incorporation" for corporations; the "regulation, attendance, textbooks, land use, funding, boards of regents, religious regulation, and school districts" for public education; or detailed regulations concerning livestock, railroads, labor, student loans, workers' compensation, prison labor, and internal improvements (Hammons 1999, 847). In 1978, California's Proposition 13 imposed constitutional restrictions on state and local governments' collection of property taxes. State constitutions may also mandate certain actions by articulating positive rights, such as a right to a free public education (Zackin 2013). Gardner (1992, 818–19) adds more examples:

> [A]lmost every state constitution contains lengthy and explicit provisions about financial matters—how taxes are to be assessed, how revenue bills are to be enacted, how revenues are to be collected and spent. Some state constitutions contain detailed provisions relating to aspects of transportation such as highways, railroads, or levee construction and maintenance. Other constitutions contain provisions dealing with corporations, mines, interest rates, lotteries and bingo, and prisons. These are, of course, concerns entirely absent from the US Constitution that are handled on the federal level exclusively as legislative matters. . . . [T]he New York Constitution contains a provision specifying the width of ski trails in the Adirondack Park. The California Constitution specifies the way in which taxes are to be assessed on golf courses. The Texas Constitution provides for banks' use of "unmanned teller machines."

Again, this book takes no stance as to whether ski trails, golf courses, or unmanned teller machines are appropriate arenas for government action. This book considers only the aggregate effect of addressing these matters through the constitution rather than by statute.

Institutions, Policies, and Specificity

Conceptually, then, by "constitutional specificity" I refer not to any specific constitutional provision but to the aggregate effect of increasing the number of provisions in a constitution generally. Some provisions complicate a state's institutional machinery, whether by dividing power across more actors or by imposing more procedural hurdles on existing actors. Other provisions elevate specific policies from statutory to constitutional law. Either way, adding constitutional specificity increases inflexibility.

This understanding of constitutional specificity combines two types of state constitutional provision that have traditionally been examined separately. Hammons (2001, 1338, emphasis removed), for example, defines "framework provisions" as "those provisions that deal exclusively with the principles, institutions, powers and processes of government," while "policy provisions" are "those provisions that deal with 'statute law' or 'public-policy' type issues, do not relate to the establishment of the government, [and] are rather specific." After the preamble, essentially every line in a typical state constitution is either a framework provision or a policy provision.

There can be value in distinguishing framework provisions from policy provisions as Weberian ideal types.[4] Still, the distinction can be overwrought, as Williams (2009, 364) reminds us: "[W]hat constitutes a policy-oriented provision rather than a framework-oriented provision can be in the eyes of the beholder, and neutral, academic observers may not appreciate the important historic and political reasons why state constitutions contain certain detailed provisions." After all, states have plenary rather than enumerated power—a point I expand on in chapter 2—and "as plenary governments, the states automatically possess all powers not specifically denied them" (Elazar 1982, 15). Accordingly, those who insert seemingly trivial "policy" provisions into state constitutions may well see them as essential to defining the citizenry's grant of power to the legislature, equal in importance to "framework" provisions. Dinan (2006, 274) concurs: "[S]tate constitution makers have determined that such [policy] provisions deserve to be placed in the constitution."

In a larger sense, all constitutional provisions are framework provisions, even so-called policy provisions. Because constitutions can be amended, policy provisions do not lock in unalterable policies. Rather, they designate certain policies as requiring extraordinary procedures to amend. As policy provisions multiply, their practical effect is that legislators must more often follow constitutional amendment procedures rather than statutory procedures. Policy provisions are therefore framework provisions, since they designate a special set of procedures applicable to certain policies. Following this logic, this book will not typically differentiate between framework and policy provisions in its conceptual understanding of constitutional specificity. Either type of provision makes it harder for government officials to respond quickly, completely, or appropriately to changing circumstances. Either type of provision binds states to a past compromise. Constitutional specificity thus empowers the dead hand of the past to restrict the living generation.

To reiterate an earlier point: adding provisions to a constitution is not always bad. There have been and are now many autocratic polities that would benefit from greater restrictions on state power. But within established constitutional polities like the American states, where federal courts and democratic tradition place a floor on states' bad behavior, the concern lies with restrictions that go too far. As later chapters will elaborate, we can see evidence of excessive restrictions if a state resorts frequently to constitutional amendment procedures, if a legislature routinely enacts statutes that press constitutional limits, or if a state's economic and policy performance worsens as its constitution grows more detailed.

Alabama as a Cautionary Tale

Alabama adopted its current constitution in 1901. Alabama's leaders made no secret that they were revising their constitution to strengthen segregation and ensure white supremacy, at a time when those were the foremost concerns of the governing elite. The convention's president, John B. Knox, made these racist motivations clear in his opening remarks to the delegates:

> "[T]he people of Alabama have been called upon to face no more important situation than now confronts us, unless it be when they, in 1861 . . . were forced to decide whether they would remain in or withdraw from the Union. Then, as now, the negro was the prominent factor in the issue. The Southern people, with this grave problem of the races to deal with, are face to face with a new epoch in Constitution-making . . . which, if solved wisely, may bring rest and peace and happiness. If otherwise, it may leave us and

our posterity continuously involved in race conflict. . . . These [segregationist] provisions are justified . . . because it is said that the negro is not discriminated against on account of his race, but on account of his intellectual and moral condition. . . . There is in the white man an inherited capacity for government, which is wholly wanting in the negro.[5]

Knox's words were prescient, but not in the way he intended. Because the convention worked to strip Black Alabamians of their few remaining rights, delegates did not solve their "grave problem of the races" wisely, and "race conflict" half a century later was indeed the result. Federal intervention eventually ended racial segregation in Alabama and elsewhere, but Alabama has yet to amend Jim Crow provisions out of its constitution. True, Alabama removed a constitutional prohibition on interracial marriage in 2000, 33 years after the US Supreme Court rendered it inoperative in *Loving v Virginia*. Nevertheless, Alabama's constitution retains (inoperative) provisions designed to bar Black Alabamians from voting, including a poll tax and a literacy test. It also retains a grandfather clause exempting voters from the ostensibly race-neutral literacy test if they or their "lawful" ancestor fought in certain 18th- or 19th-century national conflicts or in the Confederate armed forces. In addition, the Alabama constitution retains to this day a provision that "separate schools shall be provided for white and colored children, and no child of either race shall be permitted to attend a school of the other race," rendered inoperative by the US Supreme Court's 1954 decision in *Brown v Board of Education*.

The endurance of these offensive provisions illustrates a broader point: constitutional provisions often outlive the circumstances that birthed them. Federal action may have rendered these openly racist provisions inoperative, but the Alabama constitution also retains countless other antiquated provisions written to deal with long-dead concerns—including many written to maintain white supremacy less explicitly. Some of these provisions originated in 1901, but the 1901 convention also "kept much of the anti-Reconstruction provisions of the 1875 Constitution" designed to limit centralization of authority, "carrying forward, for example, its prohibition against the state's building roads, bridges, and docks, or making other internal improvements" (Thomson 2006, 117). The 1901 revision also preserved "the prohibition against local governments' entering into economic partnerships with corporations" (117), one of many provisions that was "profoundly distrustful of democracy, especially when exercised at the local level" (125). Much of this distrust of local democracy reflected Jim Crow fears that a certain class of white Alabamians might lose control of local government to a concentrated majority of Black or even poor white voters. Unlike Alabama's explicitly segregationist provisions, these constitutional provisions remain operative and continue to constrain state action today, reflecting the sort of institutional racism left untouched by federal civil rights interventions.

These numerous provisions restricting state and local authority make Alabama's constitution by far the nation's longest. Moreover, Alabama's endless flailing against its Lilliputian bonds gives it by far the nation's highest amendment rate, with 711 amendments in its first 100 years and another 181 in the next 14 years alone.

Still, the Alabama constitution retains so much specificity, binding it so securely to political compromises forged by long-dead segregationists, that even this prodigious amendment rate cannot keep pace. The dead hand of the past has a tight grip on modern Alabama. As early as 1949 Governor James Folsom declared in a radio address, "I believe the progress we have made in the past 50 years will be many times surpassed during the half century ahead if we do not remain hide-bound by old-fashioned laws. And certainly the greatest single need toward that progress is a new constitution" (quoted in Thomson 2006, 121). Despite a diligent effort, Folsom failed to get that new constitution. Another half-century later, Governor Bob Riley pressed in 2003 for a constitutional convention, arguing that century-old provisions prevented critical government reform and contributed to Alabama's economic lag behind its southern neighbors (Thomson 2006, 113). Riley's efforts, too, failed.

Alabama is such an extreme case that I omit it from most of the book's statistical analysis, as explained in this chapter's methodological appendix. Still, Alabama's experience illustrates this book's central argument. Evidence supports Governor Folsom's and Governor Riley's intuition that an excessively detailed constitution inhibits policy innovativeness and economic performance. Just as the Lilliputians bound Gulliver with hundreds of small cords, constitutional specificity binds states to the past with hundreds of small provisions. Each provision might pose little problem in isolation, but hundreds of minor provisions can combine to prevent a state from adapting to ever-changing circumstances.

Specificity as Length

Conceptually, then, this book examines constitutional specificity. Operationally, I measure each state constitution's length in words. (See this chapter's appendix for technical details.) In some ways, this approach follows the lead of Huber and Shipan (2002), who used the length of the statute creating a particular bureaucratic agency to measure the amount of discretion delegated from the legislature to the bureaucracy. Their study had to grapple with diverse challenges that do not arise here. For example, they had to consider which parts of a wide-ranging bill to count as relevant to a particular agency, how to count provisions incorporated into a statute by reference, and, in the cross-national portion of their analysis, how to control for linguistic differences. With state constitutions, the connection between conceptual specificity and operational length is more straightforward. All state constitutions are written in English, and there is no guesswork about which parts of the constitution to include.

Length is not the only possible operationalization of specificity. Perhaps a better approach would be to count the number of provisions in each constitution rather than the number of words, as Hammons (1999) did. Of course, provisions themselves can vary in specificity. The Utah constitution contains only one provision addressing firearm rights, for example, but this one provision contains twice as many words as the US Constitution's Second Amendment. The extra detail found in the Utah constitution avoids the Second Amendment's ambiguity about whether it protects an individual's right to self-defense rather than a state's right to organize a militia. Word counts alone, then, are a more direct indicator of specificity than provision counts. Writing from a legal scholar's perspective, Curtis (1950, 425) concurs on the link between words and specificity:

> Words in legal documents . . . are simply delegations to others of authority to give them meaning by applying them to particular things or occasions. . . . And the more imprecise the words are, the greater is the delegation, simply because then they can be applied or not to more particulars. This is the only important feature of words in legal draftsmanship or interpretation.

As it happens, Hammons's (1999) provision counts correlate with word counts almost perfectly ($r = 0.92$, $p<0.0001$), so the distinction is largely academic.[6] Though Hammons counts framework provisions and policy provisions separately, both have a similar statistical relationship with the constitution's length in words, supporting my decision not to distinguish between the two types.[7] As a practical matter, it is also much easier to count words than provisions. Counting provisions requires so much expert labor that Hammons did so only at a few moments in time for each state. Using word counts facilitates the biennial analysis used in much of this book.

State Constitutions

American state constitutions offer an excellent setting to evaluate the effects of constitutional specificity. For starters, the states provide tremendous variance in constitution length. The states have adopted 144 constitutions since 1776. The 50 current documents contain a median of 27,000 words, compared to 16,000 for the 190 current national constitutions. State constitutions vary in length by two orders of magnitude, from under 9,000 words to almost 400,000. The lengthiest (Alabama's) is more than 45 times longer than the shortest (Vermont's) and 3 times longer than the lengthiest national constitution (India's).[8]

State constitutions also vary over time. The 94 retired state constitutions endured an average of 32 years before replacement. As discussed in chapter 2, the eventual development of streamlined amendment processes enabled states to update their constitutions incrementally rather than replacing them entirely (Dinan 2006, 2016, 2018; Kogan 2010). As a result, the 50 current documents have survived an average of 116 years, albeit with 6,603 combined amendments. The median state constitution received more amendments in the past 20 years (18) than the US Constitution has received in 200 (15). These amendments are not distributed evenly, of course. Over the past two decades, 6 states adopted fewer than 5 amendments, and 7 adopted more than 40.

Unlike the US Constitution, states generally amend by inserting, changing, and deleting text within the body of the constitution rather than appending new language at the end. All this amendment activity therefore allows for a study of constitution length not only cross-sectionally across states but also within states over time. Over the past decade, 15 states added more words to their constitutions than were in the 1787 US Constitution (4,400), and another 4 trimmed their constitutions by at least the same amount.

INTRODUCING CONSTITUTIONAL SPECIFICITY 15

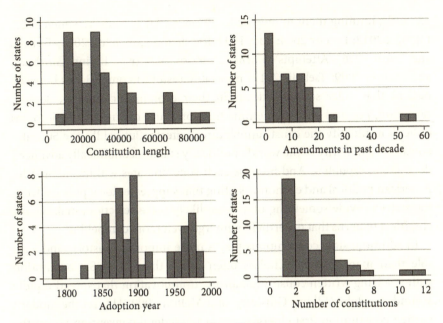

Figure 1.1 Features of Current State Constitutions.

The histograms in Figure 1.1 summarize trends in current state constitutions, omitting Alabama. The upper-left panel depicts their length, with bins 5,000 words wide; one constitution has 5,000 to 9,999 words, 9 have 10,000 to 14,999 words, and so on, with one (Texas) having 85,000 to 89,999 words. The upper-right panel depicts their amendment rates, with bins 3 amendments wide. Thirteen states adopted 0, 1, or 2 amendments in the past decade; 6 states adopted 3, 4, or 5; and so on, up to Louisiana's 55 amendments. The lower-left panel depicts their adoption years, with bins 10 years wide. Two were adopted in the 1780s, one in the 1790s, and so on, up to the 2 revisions adopted in the 1980s. And the lower-right panel depicts the cumulative number of constitutions adopted by each state, with 19 retaining their initial constitution and the rest having adopted at least one revision, up to Louisiana's 11 constitutions.

Not only do state constitutions offer rich variance in length and amendment rates, but they do so within a common linguistic, cultural, and economic setting that reduces or eliminates the effects of many confounding variables that complicate cross-national research. Comparative studies of national constitutional amendment rates, for example, have generally focused on economically advanced democracies that take constitutionalism seriously, limiting them to only 22 to 39 cases (Anckar and Kavonen 2002; Lijphart 2012; Lorenz 2004; Lutz 1994; Rasch and Congleton 2006; Tsebelis and Nardi 2016). Attempts to bring in more cases (e.g., Elkins, Ginsburg, and Melton 2009; Tsebelis 2017) inevitably result in comparisons between nations that differ so dramatically in their economic condition, democratization, political structure, ethnic harmony, and culture that it becomes difficult to identify the constitution's direct effects. Put baldly, the 50 states constitute a majority of the world's politically stable, economically advanced democratic republics. And because each state operates within the broader American political and economic setting that suppresses local policy effects, the states provide something of a "least likely" case selection, making any empirical patterns that nevertheless emerge even more compelling.

In addition, state constitutions play a more important historic and legal role than many realize. Scholars often credit the 1787 US Constitution with inspiring written constitutionalism, an innovation that spread rapidly around the globe (Elkins, Ginsburg, and Melton 2009, 41). Yet the modern written constitution first emerged not at the federal convention but in the states, reflecting their revolutionary experiments with popular sovereignty (Wood 1969; Adams 1980; Morgan 1988; Lutz 1994). Experience with these state constitutions informed debates at the 1787 federal convention, which drew on them heavily (Morey 1893; Wood 1969; Lutz 1980, 1988, 1998; Kincaid 1988; Williams 2009; Sutton 2018).

For 150 years these state constitutions drove American jurisprudence, until the twin crises of the Depression and World War II solidified federal dominance of US politics, followed by a civil rights movement that leaned on federal authority to override discriminatory state laws. After a generation of neglect, however, legal scholars and jurists began in the 1970s to rediscover state constitutions as independent sources of law. State courts today strike down more laws for state constitutional violations than for federal violations.[9] Still, state constitutions remain far from the minds of those outside legal circles. Polls show that only half of Americans know that their state even has its own constitution, as detailed in chapter 6. Levinson (2012, 29) chastises Americans for overlooking their state constitutions: "Many have written in recent years about American provincialism regarding other countries . . . [b]ut it is important to recognize a more important provincialism, which is the almost willful ignorance of what we might learn by looking at our own country and its extraordinarily rich constitutional experiences instead of remaining fixated on the singular US Constitution."

Woodward-Burns (2021, 1) concurs: "In ignoring state constitutional politics, we risk misinterpreting national politics."

Beyond their historic role, state constitutions serve a legal role similar to most national constitutions—even more so than the US Constitution does. As Versteeg and Zackin (2014, 1643, emphasis in original) have argued, "The federal Constitution may indeed be exceptional, but American constitutional*ism* is not confined to the text of the federal Constitution." To the contrary, "Americans have participated in extensive and ongoing constitution making at the state level, in the course of which they have evaluated and updated the choices reflected in the US Constitution" (1644; cf. Dinan 2006).

State constitutions play the same role within the United States that national constitutions play elsewhere, protecting Americans' positive rights (Zackin 2013) and providing a workable, adaptable foundation for modern governance. "When state constitutions are included in characterizations of American constitutionalism, it becomes clear that Americans have participated in forms of constitutional politics that look very similar to those in the rest of the world" (Versteeg and Zackin 2014, 1652). The similarities are many: "Like most foreign constitutions, state constitutions tend to be highly specific, to grant plenary rather than enumerated powers, to be amended or replaced frequently, and to be fairly unfamiliar to their publics" (Versteeg and Zackin 2016, 660). Analysis of state constitutions is therefore an exercise in comparative constitutionalism.

State constitutions also enable us to consider counterfactual scenarios for the US Constitution. Try as they might, political scientists cannot find a parallel universe where everything is the same except, perhaps, the US Constitution's level of detail or its Article V amendment procedure. The 50 state constitutions come awfully close to this ideal, however.[10] Each state has the same general institutional model while immersed in the same American culture, yet each state ornaments itself with a unique assortment of peripheral features. With respect to amendment procedures, states vary in whether the legislature proposes amendments by majority vote, supermajority vote, or votes spread across consecutive sessions; whether voters must ratify new amendments, and by what margin; and whether citizens may propose amendments directly by initiative.

State constitutions have shaped American constitutional development since the founding. They fill in the many gaps left by the terse US Constitution, making American constitutionalism resemble global constitutionalism.

And, conveniently, they provide tremendous statistical variance within a common legal, linguistic, economic, and cultural environment.

Preview of Findings

This introductory chapter has provided a conceptual definition of constitutional specificity, proposed constitution length as an operational measure of specificity, and sketched out a general theory of specificity's effects, arguing that a detailed constitution implies a narrower grant of authority from the people to the state. Because it takes more constitutional specificity to erect more political institutions that introduce more veto players subject to more procedural hurdles, and because it takes more constitutional specificity to impose greater restrictions on the state's plenary power by placing certain policies beyond the legislature's statutory reach, a detailed constitution implies a state less able to react to changing circumstances. A lengthy constitution indicates more than logorrhea. When a detailed constitution endures, one generation binds the next. I will develop this theory further chapter by chapter.

Chapter 2 contextualizes specificity by exploring the history, development, and law of state constitutions, expanding on the preceding section's overview of American state constitutionalism. After pairing legal and historical scholarship with statistical analysis, national historical circumstances at the time of each state constitution's adoption emerge as the primary driver of modern constitution length. Distrust of concentrated government authority peaked nationwide in the late 19th century. States that happened to adopt new constitutions between roughly 1870 and 1900—whether because they were first admitted to the union or had cause to revise an existing constitution—have lengthier constitutions today than states that adopted their current constitutions at other times. These differences have endured through decades of subsequent amendment activity. Though there is a strong correlation between constitution length and adoption era, there is essentially no correlation between constitution length and modern political variables that may plausibly affect it, including partisanship and amendment procedures. Later chapters therefore treat modern constitution length as exogenous, an idiosyncratic product of past circumstances.

The next three chapters explore the effects of constitutional specificity and form the empirical core of this book. Chapter 3 shows that specificity has a more powerful influence on amendment rates than anything else does. Restrictive amendment procedures do less to slow amendment rates than constitution length does to increase them. Detailed constitutions constrain state action so severely that even the costliest procedures cannot dam pressures for reform. This finding affirms legal scholars' intuition: "Every detailed constitution thus develops certain sore points that become the foci for veritable clusters of constitutional amendments," becoming "constitutional amendment breeders" (Grad and Williams 2006, 28).

Chapter 4 links constitutional specificity to increased judicial invalidations. State supreme courts strike down more policy actions where constitutions are lengthy than where they are brief, suggesting that lengthy constitutions genuinely bind policymakers. Frequent constitutional amendments can counteract the problems of constitutional specificity and reduce the invalidation rate, but only partly. As Grad and Williams (2006, 26) write, "The heavy sanction of invalidity of inconsistent legislation is one measure of constitutional inflexibility and the consequent loss of freedom to deal with new problems."

These findings imply that constitutional specificity causes real harm. If policymakers working under lengthier constitutions find it worthwhile to repeatedly bear the extraordinary costs of amending the state constitution, and if policymakers working under lengthier constitutions repeatedly press the limits of their authority by taking actions likely to attract judicial scrutiny, then we can infer that constitutional specificity meaningfully restricts the state's ability to govern.

Chapter 5 demonstrates this harm directly, showing that constitutional specificity hurts economic and policy performance. Because detailed constitutions erect an inflexible government endowed with a narrower grant of authority, governments built on detailed constitutions have less ability to react quickly or completely to changing circumstances, reducing the state's adaptability and impeding economic performance. Time-series cross-sectional analysis reveals that lengthening a state constitution leads to lower income per capita, higher unemployment, and greater income inequality. Constitution length also has a negative relationship with Boehmke and Skinner's (2012) measure of general policy innovativeness, suggesting that states with lengthy constitutions are less likely to adopt new policies that break with the past. Frequent amendments do not mitigate these harmful effects.

Importantly for chapter 5's analysis, past constitution length is negatively associated with future performance, but past performance has no relationship with future constitution length, implying causation and not just correlation (cf. Granger 1969). Moreover, the federal government's dominant economic role limits the impact of any state-level variable on economic performance, making the powerful effects reported in chapter 5 even more compelling; those effects would presumably be even stronger among national constitutions. This finding runs counter to claims that "the specific and flexible constitutions currently populating the globe are not simply failures to achieve brevity and entrenchment, but represent a plausible alternative solution to some of the agency problems associated with constitutional design" (Versteeg and Zackin 2016, 661). This chapter's finding that constitutional specificity significantly burdens state performance is the book's most important contribution.

Chapter 6 supplements the findings from preceding chapters by considering public opinion and knowledge about state constitutions. Only half of voters know their state has a constitution, and far fewer know anything about its substance. Exploiting this ignorance, I report a survey experiment (administered with Jeremy C. Pope) evaluating how voters react to information about their state constitution's length, age, and amendment rate. James Madison once articulated a vision of constitutionalism wherein brief, stable constitutions would naturally develop popular veneration; Thomas Jefferson retorted that no constitution should outlive those who wrote it, and that citizens would show greatest devotion to a constitution their generation helped shape. Despite Madison's obvious victory at the federal level, this experiment's results suggest that Jefferson prevailed in the states. Respondents prefer state constitutions that are recently adopted or frequently amended—with a marginal preference for lengthier constitutions.

Chapter 7 concludes the book and considers its broader implications, grappling particularly with two arguments from the literature that seem to challenge my findings. First, smart scholars have defended constitutional specificity as a benign alternative means of defining citizens' delegation of authority to the state, at least in the abstract (Versteeg and Zackin 2014, 2016). As it happens, my findings suggest that the conditions required in the abstract are not met in practice. Specificity is not benign but causes measurable harm. Second, previous scholarship has shown that lengthier constitutions endure longer than shorter ones, both in the states (Hammons 1999, 2001) and especially abroad (Elkins, Ginsburg, and Melton 2009), which may seem to conflict with my finding that lengthier constitutions harm economic and policy performance. Rather than conflicting, however, I show in the conclusion a logical relationship between these findings. Just as the Lilliputians bound Gulliver with countless thin strands, lengthy constitutions bind states with countless minor provisions. Those who invested the costs to tie these knots have a strong incentive to preserve them, contributing to constitutional endurance—but any incentive to protect the constitutional status quo is also an incentive to tolerate economic and policy underperformance. Stated differently, specificity promotes endurance for the same reason it impedes performance, a tension I consider in the concluding chapter.

Appendix: Major Variables

This appendix provides technical details about a few major variables used throughout the book. I introduce other variables in the chapter where they become relevant. Many variables come from various editions of *The Book of the States*, published biennially by the Council of State Governments until 2001 and annually thereafter. To create a consistent data series, I collapse post-2001 annual data into biennial sums or means as appropriate. Except where specified, the resulting series spans 11 biennia from 1994–95 through 2014–15. References to "current constitutions," "the past decade," and so forth are relative to the end of 2015. When the analysis states that a variable was logged, it was incremented and natural logged to reduce rightward skew. I group variables here by topic. I first discuss measurement of three major constitutional variables: constitution length, amendment rate, and age. After explaining Alabama's exclusion from the analysis, I then discuss measurement of three major legislative variables: "legislative complexity" (a measure of each state's amendment procedure), partisan control of the state legislature, and the length of each state's legislative session.

Constitution length: The number of words in each state constitution is measured biennially from *Book of the States*, but with two corrections. First, *Book of the States* shows a curious jump in Minnesota from 9,500 to 23,700 words in 1996, despite a lack of adopted amendments, reverting to a more consistent estimate in the following edition. Treating 1996 as an error, I correct it to 9,500 words. Second, *Book of the States* shows an unsupported one-year drop in Texas from 90,000 to 80,000 words in 2004, reverting thereafter;

I correct this apparent error to 90,000 words. For a data source providing 550 state-biennia, these are low and forgivable error rates.

Amendments adopted: Each edition of *Book of the States* reports the cumulative number of amendments since each constitution's adoption. I infer the number of new amendments by subtracting the cumulative number in one edition from the cumulative number in the previous edition. (This is a measure of the total number of amendments adopted; chapter 3's separate measures of amendments referred, initiated, and defeated come from a different source.) Occasional errors and recoding decisions produce inconsistencies requiring manual correction. As reported in *Book of the States*, New Jersey's cumulative number of amendments inexplicably drops by 20 in 2004, for example, then increases by 20 in 2015.[11] North Carolina drops by 6 in 2012. Pennsylvania is miscoded as 56 rather than 20 cumulative amendments in 1994. Rhode Island's 1986 amendment package was recoded as a revision beginning in 2002, resulting in a drop in the cumulative amendment count to eliminate pre-1986 amendments from the total. South Dakota's cumulative amendments jumps by 100 beginning in 2005. Wyoming jumps by 22 in 2003. I correct all these inconsistencies prior to my analysis.

Constitution age: Age is calculated from adoption year in *Book of the States*. For reasons discussed in chapter 2, *Book of the States* revised the Rhode Island constitution's adoption year from 1842 to 1986 beginning with the 2002 edition; I apply this change retroactively to previous editions. Outside this exception, *Book of the States* generally codes changes made through a state's amendment process as amendments, and changes made through a convention process as revisions (that is, as complete replacement of the constitutional text), a coding rule I discuss in chapter 2.

Alabama's exclusion. I omit Alabama throughout this book except where specified. The Alabama constitution serves as much as a local charter as a state constitution, containing many provisions pertaining to only one county. Some 70 percent of its amendments are local (Council of State Governments 2014). The Alabama constitution "is profoundly distrustful of democracy, especially when exercised at the local level" (Thomson 2006, 125). State micromanagement of local affairs was once widespread outside Alabama, especially in the mid-19th century, but other states eventually added prohibitions on special or local legislation to their constitutions (Williams 2009, 278). Alabama remains a holdout, interfering in local governance not only by statute but by constitutional provisions. This qualitative difference makes Alabama quantitatively extreme. Its 2015 constitution contained

389,000 words, 4.5 times more than the next longest. Between 1994 and 2015, Alabama adopted 310 amendments; the next state adopted less than half as many. Alabama's constitution plays a different role than other state constitutions, forcing its exclusion.

Legislative complexity. This variable indicates whether the state constitution requires the legislature to follow "complex" procedures to propose a state constitutional amendment. Some states allow the legislature to propose an amendment by simple majority vote, the same as for routine legislation. Other states impose more complicated procedures, such as a supermajority vote or separate simple majorities spread across consecutive sessions with an election intervening. Because several states allow the legislature to choose between the latter two mechanisms when proposing an amendment, "legislative complexity" combines them into a dichotomous indicator coded 0 for states requiring only a simple majority and 1 otherwise, relying on *Book of the States*. Ferejohn (1997) first proposed this measurement strategy. This variable does not address the state's ratification requirements, nor does it address whether a state has an initiative procedure for amending the constitution. Chapter 3 discusses state amendment procedures more fully.

Republican or Democratic seat share. The percentage of state legislators who are Republican or Democratic is calculated from counts in *Book of the States*. This source does not provide partisan counts for Nebraska, where the unicameral legislature is officially nonpartisan. For Nebraska only, I rely on estimates from online sources back through 2007, with no estimates for prior years.[12]

Session length (total legislative days). The total number of days the state legislature spent in any kind of session over the course of each two-year period is compiled from *Book of the States*.[13]

2
Contextualizing Specificity

To contextualize this book's argument that specificity harms states, this chapter sets aside the book's primary thesis, pausing to introduce state constitutions generally and consider the origins of constitutional specificity. State constitutions operate differently from the US Constitution. The US Constitution begins from a presumption that the federal government may do nothing beyond what the Constitution expressly empowers it to do, but state constitutions begin from a presumption that the state may do anything unless the state constitution provides otherwise. That is, state constitutions confer plenary (complete) power, while the US Constitution enumerates powers. State constitutions also are more easily amended than the US Constitution. These critical differences have caused state constitutions to follow a different evolutionary path than the US Constitution.

Because political science has largely overlooked state constitutions, the first several sections in this chapter provide an introductory overview of the relevant legal, historical, and political scholarship. State constitutions shaped the 1787 federal convention and dominated American jurisprudence into the 20th century. After a period of relative neglect, the so-called New Judicial Federalism revived legal and scholarly attention to state constitutions beginning in the late 1970s. Meanwhile, state constitutions themselves changed. Their plenary nature meant that reformers seeking to limit government power added diverse framework and policy provisions. For decades, states made these changes not by amendment but by revision—that is, by holding a new convention to propose a new state constitution. As states increasingly adopted streamlined amendment procedures, revision conventions became rare. Few states have adopted a revision in the past half-century.

After providing this overview, this chapter's final section lays a foundation for the remainder of the book by asking why modern state constitutions vary so widely in length. Legal historians have argued that late 19th-century distrust of concentrated authority caused state constitutions adopted at that time to be much longer than those adopted earlier or later. This chapter concludes by showing statistically that those differences endure today.

The Dead Hand's Grip. Adam R. Brown, Oxford University Press. © Oxford University Press 2023.
DOI: 10.1093/oso/9780197655283.003.0002

Individual amendments have led state constitutions to wax and wane in length, but only from baselines established when each constitution was adopted. State constitutions adopted between 1870 and 1900 remain lengthy today. Constitution length correlates strongly with adoption era but only minimally with modern variables, allowing subsequent chapters to treat length as an exogenous independent variable.

American Constitutionalism

Before drafting the Declaration of Independence or Articles of Confederation, the Second Continental Congress passed a May 10, 1776, resolution directing the 13 colonies to prepare for self-governance:

> Resolved, That it be recommended to the respective Assemblies and Conventions of the United Colonies, where no Government sufficient to the Exigencies of their Affairs, hath been hitherto established, to adopt such Government as shall in the Opinion of the Representatives of the People best conduce to the Happiness and Safety of their Constituents in particular, and America in general. (quoted in Butterfield 1961, 382)

Though Connecticut and Rhode Island operated under their colonial charters until 1818 and 1842, respectively, the other 11 states set to work writing and rewriting constitutions. By the time of the 1787 federal convention, these 11 states had already adopted 13 different constitutions, and courts in at least 7 states had engaged in judicial review under this new constitutional authority (Prakash and Yoo 2003, 933). Adopted "before the surrender of Cornwallis at Yorktown," these documents "were the chief connecting links between the previous organic law of the colonies and the subsequent organic law of the Federal Union," forming "the basis of the Federal Constitution, and furnish[ing] the chief materials from which [it] was derived" (Morey 1893, 2). These documents birthed "a constitutional tradition that was mature by the time the national Constitution was framed in 1787" (Lutz 1998, 24), giving weight to John Dickinson's remark to his fellow delegates at the federal convention: "Experience must be our only guide."[1] State constitutions "are not footnotes to the American history of constitutional thought but rather central components of it" (Versteeg and Zackin 2014, 1649).

The Pennsylvania and Massachusetts constitutions were especially influential (Wood 1969, 435). The 1776 Pennsylvania constitution took revolutionary fervor to its extreme. Placing great faith in democratic majorities, it vested almost unchecked power in a unicameral legislature. Its supporters called it "a model, which, with a very little alteration, will . . . come as near perfection as anything yet concocted by mankind."[2] Its radicalism made it "influential during the founding decade but not necessarily in positive ways" (Williams 2009, 44).

Reacting to Pennsylvania's excesses, the 1780 Massachusetts constitution catered to those who "feared . . . unchecked democracy . . . and denounced the various reformist demands for a unicameral legislature and no governor" (Patterson 1981, 39). Its author, John Adams, would later boast, "What is the Constitution of the United States . . . but that of Massachusetts, New York, and Maryland! There is not a feature of it which can not be found in one or the other" (quoted in Bowen 1966, 199). Concurring, Lutz (1980, 129) calls the Massachusetts constitution "the most important" at the federal convention "because it embodied the Whig theory of republican government," while "the 1776 Pennsylvania Constitution was the second most important because it embodied the strongest alternative."

State constitutions' importance continued past 1787. Americans have grown so accustomed to the federal government's modern visibility that they forget that states dominated American politics for well over a century— and that states today continue to have primary control over most government outcomes besides national defense, Social Security, and Medicare. Along with the Declaration of Independence and critical Supreme Court precedents, state constitutions remain part of the small-c "constitution outside the Constitution" (Young 2007).[3] The "operational American constitution consists of the federal Constitution and the 50 state constitutions," which together "comprise a complex system of rule for a republic of republics," one historian writes. "Compared to most national constitutions, the Constitution of the United States is . . . incomplete," and its success "is due in no small part to the fact that [it] is not the only constitution in the United States" (Kincaid 1988, 13). The US Constitution "assumes, in fact requires, the existence of state constitutions if it is to make any sense" (Lutz 1988, 96). Williams (2009, 18–19) lists several places where the federal Constitution requires the existence of state constitutions:

[T]he Guarantee Clause of the federal Constitution mandates a "republican form of government" for the states' structures of government, or constitutions. The Supremacy Clause makes specific mention of state constitutions in its unequivocal declaration that federal law is the "supreme law of the land." ... Article I, Section 2 adopts voting and citizenship qualifications of the states for the US House of Representatives. ... Article I, Section 4 leaves the "Times, Places, and Manor of holding Elections for Senators and Representatives" to the state legislatures, which are, in turn, governed by the state constitutions. ... The Full Faith and Credit clause requires each state to enforce the "Public Acts, Records, and judicial Proceedings of every other State." ... Article II, Section 1, clause 2 requires the state legislatures to determine how the electors for President will be chosen—a clause made famous in *Bush v. Gore*.

The Ninth Amendment's protection of unstated rights "retained by the people" also assumes the existence of state constitutions, since "we must also look at the state constitutions to see what kind of liberty they are committed to protecting and fostering" (Elazar 1988, 169; cf. Williams 2009, 30). After all, the familiar protections listed in the US Constitution's Bill of Rights did not originally limit state power in any way, protecting Americans only from federal overreach. State constitutions, not the US Constitution, erect state governments, and state bills of rights, not the US Bill of Rights, limit that power. Only in 1925 did federal courts consistently begin interpreting the Fourteenth Amendment, ratified in 1868, as requiring states to respect rights protected in the federal Bill of Rights.[4] State constitutions therefore contain their own lengthy declarations of rights that routinely extend well above the federal floor. For this reason, "[v]irtually all of the foundational liberties that protect Americans originated in the state constitutions and to this day remain independently protected by them" (Sutton 2018, 1).

State constitutions also complete the US Constitution by providing "positive rights, such as a right to free education, labor rights, social welfare rights, and environmental rights"—rights common to most national constitutions but absent from the US Constitution (Versteeg and Zackin 2014, 1645; cf. Zackin 2013). State constitutions complete the US Constitution in many ways: "The writers of the Constitution intended for us to read the state constitutions as well. Without the state constitutions, the national Constitution ... was an incomplete text" (Lutz 1998, 31–32). When we fail to include state constitutions in our legal discourse, our "underappreciation of state constitutional law [hurts] state *and* federal law and [undermines] the appropriate balance between state *and* federal courts in protecting individual liberty" (Sutton 2018, 6, emphasis in original).

Scholarly Neglect and Revival

Serious scholarly attention to state constitutions began with an influential 1868 treatise by Thomas Cooley, with six editions over four decades. Cooley took a general approach, avoiding consideration of matters unique to individual states. His approach inspired the National Municipal League (now the National Civic League) to craft a model state constitution, reflecting an assumption that a single well-drafted document could serve any state.[5] The League revised their model six times over the years but abandoned the effort after their 1963 edition. By then, the New Deal and the civil rights movement had shifted scholarly and legal interest from state to federal constitutionalism, and work on the model state constitution ceased.

In 1977, Supreme Court Justice William Brennan called for renewed attention to state constitutions after the conservative Burger Court succeeded the progressive Warren Court. Fearing a reversal of recent civil rights gains rooted in the Court's interpretation of federal law, Brennan urged jurists and scholars alike to search state constitutions for protections exceeding the US Constitution's minimums:

> State constitutions, too, are a font of individual liberties, their protections often extending beyond those required by the Supreme Court's interpretation of federal law. The legal revolution which has brought federal law to the fore must not be allowed to inhibit the independent protective force of state law— for without it, the full realization of our liberties cannot be guaranteed. (491)

Brennan inspired a resurgence of state constitutional analysis, the so-called New Judicial Federalism. A study of over 2,800 state supreme court decisions issued between 1981 and 1985 found that "when state supreme courts base their decisions solely on state grounds, laws are more often declared unconstitutional" (Emmert and Traut 1992, 37; see also Emmert 1992). "Paradoxically," then, "the activism of the Warren Court, which was often portrayed as detrimental to federalism, was a necessary condition for the emergence of a vigorous state involvement in protecting civil liberties" (Tarr 1994, 73).

At first, ideology rather than sincere interest in state constitutions motivated this New Judicial Federalism, since Brennan's "disagreement with the conservative majority . . . gave him reason to encourage the development of state constitutional law" (Tarr 1994, 73). Gardner (1992) therefore leveled a fierce critique, arguing that for New Judicial Federalism to have a jurisprudential rather than ideological basis we must take states and their varying constitutions seriously as separate polities—a project that, in his view, required untenable assumptions. Gardner wrote, "The central premise of state constitutionalism is that a state constitution reflects the fundamental values, and ultimately the character, of the people of the state that adopted it. This premise, however, cannot serve as the foundation for a workable state constitutional discourse because it is not a good description of actual state constitutions" (764). Instead, he saw in state constitutions "a vast wasteland of confusing, conflicting, and essentially unintelligible pronouncements" (763).

To be sure, some scholars had long argued precisely the point that Gardner challenged—namely, that states do have different political cultures (Elazar 1966) that inspire different constitutional traditions (Elazar 1982). Scholars have argued for the distinctiveness of western (Bridges 2015), southern (Herron 2017), mountain (Bakken 1987), and midwestern (Siddali 2015) state constitutions, as well as the distinctiveness of individual constitutions, such as Utah's (White 1996). Nevertheless, Gardner (1992, 766) felt such approaches relied on "inadequate and outdated assumptions concerning the nature of state and national identity." To Gardner, modern differences among the states are insufficient to justify their differing constitutions: "[R]egardless of whether such regional differences existed in the past, they no longer exist and we may for the most part disregard them as viable elements of state constitutional discourse" (828). He concludes that we cannot build meaningful jurisprudence on these flawed documents:

> When we turn upon state constitutions the narrative devices we use to create constitutional meaning on the federal level, we find state constitutions wanting. The stories to which they lend themselves are not stories of principle and integrity, but stories of expediency and compromise at best, foolishness and inconstancy at worst. And the poverty of state constitutional discourse merely reflects the limited narrative possibilities that state constitutions offer to erstwhile interpreters. (822)

Gardner's (1992, 832) argument rests on an assumption that, however reasonable from his legal perspective, is unfathomable to a political scientist: "The idea that state constitutions result from political bargaining and opportunism rather than deliberation and choice is an idea that conflicts with the premises of constitutionalism." This assertion is frankly puzzling. Even with respect to the celebrated US Constitution, scholars have long acknowledged the role of economic, regional, and ideological self-interest at the federal convention, challenging popular notions of "an assembly of demigods" (Beard 1913; Jillson and Eubanks 1984; Jillson 2002; Pope and Treier 2020).[6] As Levinson (2012, 12, emphasis in original) reminds us, "*all* constitutions necessarily involve tradeoffs and compromises." He adds, "There simply would never have been a Constitution without the two especially important compromises involving slavery and the Senate" (41). If, to use Gardner's language, we cannot lend a document constitutional stature unless it rests on "principle and integrity" and "deliberation and choice," lacking "expediency and compromise" or "bargaining and opportunism," then we will find no constitution worthy of the name. Instead, "the very features of state constitutions that have drawn such derision from American legal scholars are standard features of constitutions around the world" (Versteeg and Zackin 2014, 1706).

In any event, Gardner's critique forced an improvement in state constitutional scholarship—efforts that long ago moved past the ideological motivations of New Judicial Federalism into careful inquiry, led especially by Tarr and Williams (Tarr 1998; Grad and Williams 2006; Tarr and Williams 2006a, 2006b; Williams 2009). Cogan's (1994, 1353) assessment remains more apt than ever: "The legal literature of state fundamental law was, but is no longer, sparse." This literature often emphasizes the point Gardner once challenged: that each state constitution represents the accumulation of a distinct polity's historical, legal, and political experience. One of the most important works on state constitutionalism makes this goal explicit, declaring, "[A]lthough [this book] had its origins long before Professor Gardner's article, it is intended to provide a partial refutation to Professor Gardner" (Williams 2009, 4–5).

This paradigm leads modern scholars to reject the idea of a model state constitution: "[T]here is no 'ideal' state constitution" (Williams 2009, 360). "No one should believe that there are 'perfect' constitutions waiting to be written. There are not" (Levinson 2012, 12). "State constitutions necessarily reflect diverse state constitutional traditions, historical developments within individual states, and the particular political complexion of each state," Tarr (2006b, 4) writes. "As a consequence, no single model is appropriate for all states, and this volume [featuring nine contributors] eschews the creation of a 'model state constitution.'" Instead, detailed volumes have appeared offering individual commentary on each state constitution's history and law (e.g., Connor and Hammons 2008; White 2011).[7]

Moreover, these differences among state constitutions did not arise by accident. Dinan's (2006, 4) review of state constitutional convention debates finds that when "state delegates ultimately decided to reject the federal approach," they did so conscious of experience since the founding, taking "account of the different circumstances in which state constitution makers found themselves." It was intentional, for example, that states moved away from the US Constitution's strict amendment procedures, unitary executive, executive appointment of the judiciary, and so on.

Despite his concerns, Gardner (1992, 830) concedes that "state constitutions do differ, and those differences can have significant legal effects." This book takes the stance that a constitution's legal and practical effects are of sufficient interest to warrant examination regardless of any self-interest or gamesmanship at the constitution's drafting. After all, a "convention is a political body, the process of amendment and revision a political process . . . and a constitution a political document" (Grad and Williams 2006, 18).

Interpretation and Specificity

State constitutions present interpretative challenges different from those of the federal Constitution, and these differences help explain why state constitutions vary in specificity. For example, originalism looks different in the states. State courts have ample resources for understanding how people understood a particular provision while writing or ratifying it, including revision convention transcripts, legislative debates about proposed amendments, and information pamphlets prepared for ratification votes (Williams 2009, 318–19). As such, "the critique of federal original-intent jurisprudence does not apply—or at least does not apply with equal force—to a state original intent jurisprudence" (Tarr 1991, 851).

Stare decisis, or adherence to precedent, also looks different in the states. The US Constitution erects such high barriers to amendment that it offers little recourse to those wishing to reverse a US Supreme Court ruling, forcing the Court to police itself by revisiting its own precedents on occasion. By contrast, states can amend their constitutions so readily that a legislature's failure to propose a corrective amendment can be understood by future courts as tacit endorsement of past interpretations, even of flawed interpretations. "Herein lies a basic difference between the US Constitution and the state constitutions," Kincaid (1988, 13) observes. "Federal constitutional law is changed by acts of interpretation by the US Supreme Court, the Congress, and the president. State constitutional law is changed primarily by amendment."

Justice Louis Brandeis argued that state supreme courts should therefore adhere more rigorously to their precedents than the US Supreme Court, especially in "those States whose constitution may be easily amended." New York's prompt action after a flawed state court ruling "shows how promptly a state constitution may be amended to correct an important decision deemed wrong," he continues. At the federal level, by contrast, only twice "has the process of constitutional amendment been successfully resorted to, to nullify decisions of this Court," referring to the Eleventh and Sixteenth Amendments, the latter of which "required eighteen years of agitation."[8] Federally, the burden falls on the US Supreme Court to correct its own flawed rulings; in states, the burden falls on the amendment process (Williams 2009, 350–51).

Most important, state constitutions differ from the US Constitution by conferring plenary power. The US Constitution purports to erect a government possessing no powers except those expressly enumerated, but state constitutions (like most national constitutions) erect governments possessing all powers except those denied them. Plenary power changes the interpretive environment in ways that create a motivation to add detail to state constitutions. Thus, Williams (2009, 20) writes, "State constitutions are not miniature versions of the federal Constitution, nor are they clones of it"; instead, they "are longer, more detailed, and cover many more topics: taxation and finance, local government, education, and corporations. The constitutional conversation at the state level is considerably different from the federal constitutional conversation."

Because it enumerates powers, the US Constitution must expand to confer more authority; because they confer plenary power, state constitutions must expand to restrict it. Adding provisions to a plenary constitution cannot expand government authority, since a plenary constitution starts from a baseline of limitless authority.

Even provisions that apparently expand state power can restrict it. Following the maxim *expressio unius est exclusio alterius*—expression of one is exclusion of another—state judges can read seeming affirmations of state authority as restrictions. When interpreting a state constitution, judges assume that each provision has a purpose, so that the constitution would mean something else without it. A plenary constitution vests in the legislature all authority not specifically denied. Since no provision can add to this unlimited authority, any provision that seems to do so must have the actual purpose of precluding alternative courses of action.

To illustrate, imagine a hypothetical provision creating a commissioner over skilled trades: "The commissioner shall license practitioners of the skilled trades, including welders, plumbers, machinists, and carpenters." Lay readers might understand "including" as introducing an illustrative rather than exhaustive list, but a judge applying *expressio unius est exclusio alterius* would read it as precluding the commissioner's authority over pipefitters, riggers, electricians, and other unlisted trades. To rule otherwise would imply that the constitution's drafters referenced welders, plumbers, machinists, and carpenters with no purpose.

This illustration turns out not to be purely hypothetical. An Oklahoma court used this logic to bar the state's transportation commissioner from regulating airlines, since the state constitution's list of transportation industries under the commissioner's authority omitted air travel (Grad and Williams 2006, 27). State courts have long applied *expressio unius est exclusio alterius* in this way. Writing almost a century ago, Clifton Williams (1931) recounted a Wisconsin dispute over the legislature's attempt to create and fund an auditor's office. A legislature with plenary power has implicit authority to take this sort of action. However, the state court interpreted a provision granting audit authority to the secretary of state as preventing the legislature from funding any additional auditor. Williams emphasized, "[T]his rule of construction is so strong and was applied with such vigor here that the Court held that the expression that the secretary of state should be the auditor excluded the idea that anybody else could be an auditor" (192).

State constitutional declarations of positive rights operate in a similar way. The negative rights in the federal Constitution prohibit government from infringing speech, establishing a church, quartering soldiers in private homes, conducting warrantless searches, and so on. State constitutions generally go further by articulating positive rights that mandate certain actions, like providing free public schools. Many state constitutions declare positive rights regarding education, health, labor, or environmental quality (Zackin 2013). Some address rights to grain elevators or certain railroad rates (Versteeg and Zackin 2014, 1662; see also Versteeg and Zackin 2016, 665–66). As plenary governments, states have the authority to establish public schools, protect the environment, and take these other actions without specific constitutional authorization, but state constitutions that declare the state's obligation to act limit the state's discretion by precluding alternatives. As Versteeg and Zackin (2014, 1661, emphasis in original) explain, "amending a state constitution can *ensure* that a state government will perform those responsibilities, and astute interest groups routinely push for amendments to that effect, thereby increasing the scope of state constitutions" while narrowing the state's plenary discretion.

These principles illustrate how adding specificity to a state constitution can only reduce the legislature's otherwise unlimited authority. Reform movements motivated by distrust of those currently in power have therefore tended to expand state constitutions, employing constitutional specificity as a defensive weapon against unreliable politicians. These efforts began as early as the Jacksonian era, when "growing popular demands for broader and more direct democracy and an even denser web of social and economic interests produced . . . a wave of state constitutional creation and revision" (Keller 1981, 70). Constitutions adopted at this time "reflected popular pressures for broader representation, more direct democracy, and fuller support (and then governmental restraint) for a booming economy" (70). Beyond expanding the franchise and reworking government structures, reformers also found they could restrict future legislatures by writing "a mass of codelike specifications" into state constitutions (70). Constitutions thus began their evolution from lofty outlines to practical documents that detoured into the nitty-gritty: "By the 1830s it was clear that state constitutional revision was deeply mired in party politics and changing social and economic interests," one historian writes. "Constitutional conventions were arenas for the working out of particular, ongoing conflicts rather than for restating fundamental principles" (71).

These efforts to restrict the state's plenary authority resumed and accelerated after the Civil War. Even in the North, many were startled at Lincoln's centralization of power and revised their state constitutions to prevent similar activism closer to home. "The Civil War unleashed the potential of active, centralized government; the end of the war and the passage of time allowed the strong currents of localism and suspicion of active government in nineteenth century America to reassert themselves" (Keller 1981, 74). Versteeg and Zackin (2014, 1662–63) concur:

> This practice was particularly conspicuous in [late] nineteenth-century state constitutional conventions, which were often a direct response to state legislatures' disastrous experiments with deficit spending. These conventions moved quickly and decisively to craft new constitutional limits on legislatures to prevent them from being drawn back into risky speculation or from being corrupted by corporate wealth. These constitutional conventions placed new restrictions on the gifts and benefits that legislators could receive from corporations, established relatively low caps on state indebtedness, and forbade states from financing internal improvement projects.

Pennsylvania, for example, adopted a revised 1873 constitution wherein "a wide-ranging coalition of interests" who were "unhappy with the wave of particularistic laws emerging from the postwar legislature . . . joined with small-government Democrats to secure a constitution whose primary purpose was to check legislative activism" (Keller 1981, 75–76). Similar efforts followed around the country, as "Illinois forbade its legislature to act in twenty items of local or private concern . . . California in thirty-three" (Keller 1977, 112). Western states began experimenting with positive rights to preclude legislative inaction.[9] Southern states too rewrote their constitutions, but with "different sectional emphases. In the North it was aimed at an interlocking system of boss-led party machines and corporate interests; in the South at black and to some extent poor white voters" (Keller 1981, 77).

One contemporary boasted, "The great design of most that has been done by us in constitution-making for the past ten or twenty years, has been to reduce the field of statute law, and withhold from it every subject which it is not necessary to concede" (Baldwin 1879, 140). Americans commonly conceptualize (federal) constitutional rights as protecting political minorities from tyrannical majorities. This view arises at least in part from Madison's famous argument in Federalist 10 that a larger republic safeguards liberty by preventing any one faction from capturing the government's machinery. Yet efforts to embed specific policies in state constitutions suggest a different view of constitutional rights. Rather than protect political minorities from callous majorities, these state constitutional reforms sought to protect a perceived political majority from legislative malfeasance by placing guardrails on legislative discretion (Marshfield 2022).

These efforts peaked from the 1870s through the 1890s, so that "by the century's end it was clear that state constitutions had a very different place in the polity than their federal counterpart," serving "more as codes than as charters" (Keller 1981, 71). Late 19th-century delegates saw little difference between what Hammons (1999) later called framework provisions and policy provisions. Instead, "there was common agreement that the . . . object of [state] constitutions extended beyond fundamental principles to what delegates called constitutional legislation" to "constrain the powers of the government and the legislature in particular" (Fritz 1994, 964–65). State constitutions adopted from around 1870 through 1900, "at the height of the distrust of the legislature" (Grad and Williams 2006, 19), "became instruments of government rather than merely frameworks for government," specifying "what state legislatures could not do and how they would conduct their business" (Tarr 1998, 132–33).[10]

To be sure, voters rejected many of these proposed revisions, including in Michigan, Nebraska, New York, and Ohio. Their 19th-century ratification decisions still echo today: as the next section will show, states that adopted late 19th-century revisions have lengthier constitutions today than states that retained older constitutions. They also have lengthier constitutions today than states that adopted 20th-century revisions, after state legislatures reemerged as "relatively democratic and representative bodies" (Henretta 1991, 839). Compared to late 19th-century constitutions, "the relative spareness of early state constitutions and of the more recently drafted ones indicates greater confidence in the legislature and in the workings of the representative process" (Grad and Williams 2006, 19). State constitutions thus preserve a snapshot of American political development. An early 20th-century writer made this point in more florid prose:

> One might almost say that the romance, the poetry, and even the drama of American politics are deeply embedded in the many state constitutions. . . . For in them are recorded the growth in the notion of rights, irrespective of race, sex, or economic status; the rise of manhood suffrage, its extension to women and modern reactions against the principle of unrestricted voting; and the developing emphasis on morals in provisions about dueling, lotteries, divorce, polygamy, and the prohibition of the manufacture and sale of liquor. One may cynically note the earlier belief that legislators were men of "wisdom and virtue,"

followed by a conviction expressed in most [late 19th-century] constitutions that they are likely to be corrupt and incompetent. (Dealey 1915, 11)

From Revision to Amendment

The 50 states have held 233 constitutional conventions and adopted 144 constitutions.[11] Nineteen states retain their original constitutions (as amended), but the rest have revised (that is, replaced) their constitutions at least once. At the extreme, Georgia is on its 10th constitution and Louisiana on its 11th. Figure 2.1 shows the number of conventions per decade, with the southern (Confederate) states separated; 8 non-southern states held conventions in the 1770s, 3 in the 1780s, and so on. The figure presents all conventions, including those that did not result in a ratified constitution, using data from Dinan (2006, 8–9), updating Sturm (1982).[12]

Figure 2.2 depicts the number of constitutions actually adopted each decade, with southern states again separated, using data from the Council of State Governments (2016). Bars in Figure 2.2 are stacked, with lighter shading for initial constitutions and darker shading for revisions. The combined light

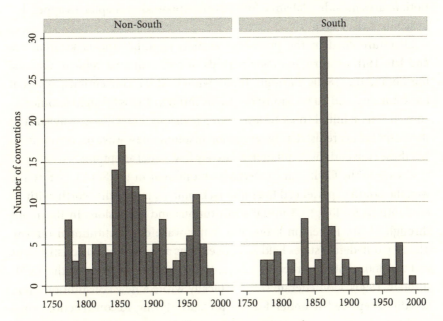

Figure 2.1 State Constitutional Conventions per Decade.

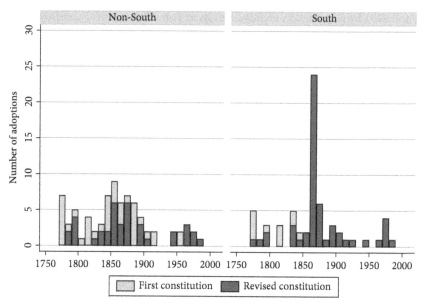

Figure 2.2 State Constitutions Adopted per Decade.

and dark bars depict the total number of constitutions adopted per decade. Both figures include Alabama; for reasons explained in chapter 1's appendix, I exclude it elsewhere.

Literature cited in the preceding section identifies the Jacksonian era and late 19th century as major periods of constitutional reform. Outside the South, the 1830s through 1850s witnessed 21 conventions, 9 initial constitutions, and 10 revisions; the 1870s through 1890s brought another 27 conventions, 8 initial constitutions, and 9 revisions. Later, Progressivism and the *Baker v. Carr* redistricting revolution inspired a new wave of conventions, but these conventions resulted in relatively few actual adoptions.

Owing to the Civil War, patterns look different in the South. Before the war, the South experienced the same Jacksonian surge as the North, with 13 conventions leading to 3 initial constitutions and 6 revisions in the 1830s through 1850s. Rebellion brought a major wave of constitutional reform. The 11 Confederate states held 30 conventions and adopted 24 constitutions in the 1860s, with another 11 conventions and 10 revisions in the 1870s through 1890s. Confederate states typically wrote a new constitution upon seceding, replaced it under federal pressure during Reconstruction, then adopted a "redemption" constitution as federal supervision ceased; several revised their constitutions again in subsequent decades to strengthen white supremacy (Herron 2017).

These figures also document the gradual extinction of conventions and revisions. No state has held a convention since Louisiana in 1992; no state has adopted a revision since Rhode Island in 1986. When the original 13 states adopted their first constitutions, only three included an amendment procedure; in the remaining states, changing the constitution would require a revision convention (Dinan 2006, 32).[13] Amendment provisions gradually became more common and more workable as successive state convention delegates rejected the more rigid approaches of the past. By the late 19th century, "delegates determined that a flexible amendment process was necessary to overcome entrenched geographic interests and thereby bring about a more equitable distribution of power"; later, "an even more flexible amendment process was seen as necessary to . . . secure the enactment of popular reform legislation" (31–32). By 1912 William Jennings Bryan could declare to an Ohio revision convention, "[T]he state constitutions bear witness to a growing confidence in the people; they are much more easily amended as a rule than the federal constitution, and the later state constitutions are more easily amended than the earlier ones" (quoted in Dinan 2006, 56).

In 1964 New Hampshire became the final state to authorize its legislature to propose amendments (Dinan 2016, 286). Conventions have since all but disappeared. Thirty years ago May (1992, 2) observed, "The use of formal . . . revision processes to amend state charters [continues] to decline. Constitutional revision of a comprehensive or general scope [is] conspicuous by its absence." No state has held a convention or adopted a revision since that time. Fourteen state constitutions make it especially easy to do so, mandating a periodic ballot question asking voters whether to call a constitutional convention, but even in these states the amendment process has been sufficient to prevent voters from authorizing a convention. Voter support for these automatic ballot questions rises and falls with economic and political conditions (Blake and Anson 2020), but support has not risen high enough to trigger an actual convention for decades.[14] As later chapters will show, voters readily ratify individual amendments. But when it comes to comprehensive reform, they exhibit "constitutional conventionphobia" (Benjamin and Gais 1996).

The decline of conventions does not mean, as some have supposed, that "as comprehensive reform has decreased, the pace of constitutional amendment has surged" (Tarr 2014, 12). To the contrary, Figure 2.3 shows a steady decline

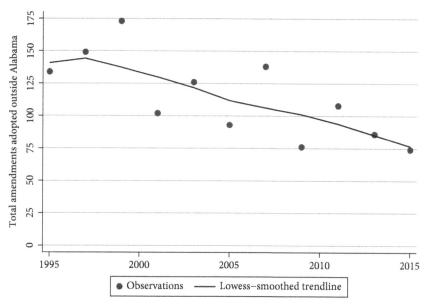

Figure 2.3 Aggregate Amendments Adopted, by Biennium.

in amendment activity. Each point shows the aggregate number of state constitutional amendments adopted nationwide (excluding Alabama) in each two-year period; the line uses Lowess smoothing to depict the overall trend. Half as many amendments were adopted at the end of this series as at the beginning. In the late 1990s, the average state adopted almost 3 amendments per biennium. By 2015, the rate had dipped below 1.5.

Some lament the disappearance of revision conventions. Levinson (2012, 5) dedicated an entire book to "America's 51 constitutions and the crisis of governance," arguing "that there is a connection between the perceived deficiencies of contemporary government and formal constitutions," including "many state constitutions." Tarr (2006b, 3–4) pins these problems on the shift from revision to amendment:

> How effectively individual states respond to the challenges facing them will depend to a significant extent on the quality of their state constitutions.... This, however, is a cause for concern. More than two-thirds of the states now operate under constitutions that are more than a century old, that were designed to meet the problems of another era, and that are riddled with piecemeal amendments that have compromised their coherence as plans

of government.... Many state constitutions would benefit from substantial changes designed to make state governments more effective, equitable, and responsive, and to equip them to deal with the challenges of the twenty-first century.

As later chapters will show, Tarr is correct to fret about obsolete provisions lingering in state constitutions long after they cease to be useful. However, Tarr's lament about the shift from revision to amendment overlooks two points. First, he is too pessimistic about amendments. Most amendments originate in the legislature, where staff advise legislators as to an amendment's effects on other parts of the constitution, and where consideration in committee and across two chambers provides ample opportunity to deliberate these impacts.[15] Concurring, Dinan (2018, 265–66) concludes his book-length assessment of "the consequences of relying on amendments [rather than revision] as instruments of governance" by observing, "The determination to proceed through amendments . . . is often the product of significant deliberation, with arguments for and against proceeding via the amendment process considered at some length." These debates focus "on the virtues of stability and legitimacy, the relative weight to be placed on these virtues, and how they are best secured" (274). Legislatures do not refer amendments for voter ratification ignorant of their impact on the broader constitutional scheme. Subsequent chapters in this book will support this claim by showing that frequent amendments mitigate some of the deleterious effects of constitutional specificity.

Second, Tarr is too optimistic about wholesale revision, expecting what Kogan (2010) labels a "logroll" rather than a "poison pill" revision process. In a logroll revision, convention delegates come to repeated small compromises, resulting in a grand compromise that a supermajority finds acceptable overall despite minor inconveniences. Because the 1787 federal convention achieved this result, Tarr can be forgiven for expecting a modern convention to reach a similarly agreeable outcome. Today, however, partisan polarization and other features of modern politics make such a grand compromise unlikely to win ratification as critics harp on the "poison pills"—the small losses—to sink the entire endeavor. "In short, given voter propensity to cast 'defensive no' votes, a constitutional revision [today] is likely to be only as popular as its least popular component" (Kogan 2010, 886). Sorauf (1981, 126) agrees: "The Fathers of Philadelphia viewed these deliberative assemblies in the context of the elite politics of the eighteenth century. We see them in the context of mass politics, even in the plebiscitary politics of our century." Anticipating these problems, the few successful revisions observed since 1965 have typically split their proposals into a series of sweeping amendments, with the most controversial provisions presented separately to voters (Kogan 2010, 888; Versteeg and Zackin 2014, 1673). Today's polarized climate may doom any revision convention from the start, regardless of the need. Tarr is correct to worry about dated provisions overly constraining modern officeholders, but there is little evidence that reverting from piecemeal amendments to wholesale revisions would help.

Moreover, the occasional blurring of revision and amendment can create difficulties for those concerned with distinguishing between the two. Sixteen years passed after Rhode Island's 1986 adoption of a package of sweeping amendments before the respected *Book of the States* retroactively recoded them as a revision. Occasionally the distinction between amendment and revision has legal effect. For example, the California constitution authorizes voters to amend but not revise their constitution by initiative. The California Supreme Court therefore struck down part of Proposition 115 (in 1990), an initiated amendment dealing with criminal procedure, for having such broad ramifications that it smacked of revision (Williams 2009, 403). California courts have mostly been lax about this distinction, though, viewing change accomplished through the amendment process as presumptively an amendment: "When, for instance, Proposition 140 imposed term limits on the state legislature and cut its budget by 40 percent, the state Supreme Court did not even seriously review . . . the argument that this was a revision" (Cain 2006, 59).

Scholars tend to apply the same standard as California courts. A major study of constitutional survival—an enterprise where "the distinction between an amendment and a replacement is important . . . mistaking one for the other is literally fatal"—draws this line: "We call a constitutional change an amendment when the actors claim to follow the amending procedure of the existing constitution and a replacement when they undertake revision without claiming to follow such procedure" (Elkins, Ginsburg, and Melton 2009, 55). The distinction is less important in this book—partly because nothing approaching a revision has occurred in any state in the period this book examines, but mostly because the book's focus is on constitutional specificity rather than survival.

Table 2.1 Median Duration of State Constitutions

	Non-Southern States	Southern States
Adopted before 1800	45 years	39 years
1800–1849	45 years	24 years
1850–1899	126 years	9 years
1900–1949	87 years	53 years
Adopted since 1950	49 years	43 years

The shift from revision to amendment has had one unambiguous effect: state constitutions endure longer than in the past. In their study of national constitutions, Elkins, Ginsburg, and Melton (2009, 207) observe that Jefferson's "proposed expiration date of nineteen years matches the predicted life expectancy for national constitutions since 1789."[16] The same cannot be said for state constitutions. Table 2.1 gives the median duration of America's 144 state constitutions by their adoption date. Constitutions still in effect had their age calculated as of 2015; others had their age calculated at replacement. The Civil War's effects on southern state constitutions are unmistakable. Outside the South, most constitutions adopted since the rise of flexible amendment procedures in the late 19th century have remained in effect. The median state constitution was adopted in 1890; outside the South, three-quarters are at least a century old.

Correlates of Modern Length

The preceding review of legal and historical scholarship emphasizes a repeated claim: late 19th-century reformers expressed their distrust of elites and of centralized authority by adding specificity to their state constitutions to limit the state's plenary power. Many of those late 19th-century constitutions remain in effect today. This literature implies a straightforward hypothesis, using constitution length as an operational measure of constitutional specificity: state constitutions adopted in the late 19th century should be lengthier than state constitutions adopted at other times.

Unfortunately, I do not have longitudinal data on state constitutions back to the founding, so I cannot examine the length of each state constitution when originally adopted. I can, however, consider the length of each state

44 THE DEAD HAND'S GRIP

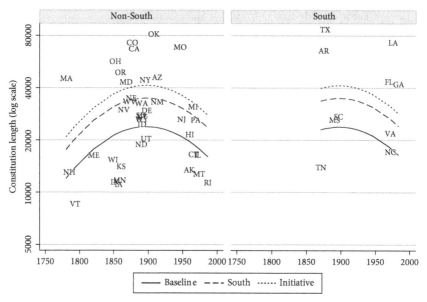

Figure 2.4 Constitution Length by Adoption Year.

constitution today to see whether historical effects have endured. Figure 2.4 plots each constitution's length (in 2015, on a log scale) against its adoption year, with southern states separated. For example, the Vermont constitution, adopted in 1793, currently contains 8,565 words; the Colorado constitution, adopted in 1876, currently contains 72,860.

Overlaid on the scatterplot are three curved lines plotting predicted values from an ordinary least squares regression, with full statistical results shown in the first column of Table 2.2. The statistical model regresses each state constitution's length (incremented and logged) on four variables: the constitution's age, the square of its age (allowing the line to curve), a dichotomous indicator for the 11 Confederate states, and a dichotomous indicator for the 18 states allowing citizens to propose amendments by initiative. This simple model explains 33 percent of the variance in modern constitution length. The solid line plots the baseline relationship between age and length; the dashed line shifts the intercept for southern states; the dotted line shifts it for initiative states. The model's maximum predicted length is for state constitutions adopted in 1897—the tail end of the 1870–1900 period identified in the historical and legal literature. The standard deviation of constitution age for observations in this model is 54 years. The model

Table 2.2 Correlates of Constitution Length

	(2.2a)	(2.2b)	(2.2c)	(2.2d)
Constitution age	0.012*	0.012*	0.015*	0.012*
	(0.0061)	(0.0061)	(0.0063)	(0.0060)
Constitution age squared	−0.000050*	−0.000050*	−0.000063*	−0.000050*
	(0.000024)	(0.000025)	(0.000024)	(0.000024)
Initiative option	0.55*	0.55*	0.57*	0.54*
	(0.16)	(0.18)	(0.16)	(0.16)
South	0.38	0.38	0.44*	0.37
	(0.23)	(0.24)	(0.25)	(0.23)
Legislative complexity		0.0030		
		(0.20)		
Republican share			−0.0071	
			(0.0043)	
Corruption				0.057
				(0.13)
Constant	9.4*	9.4*	9.6*	9.2*
	(0.35)	(0.40)	(0.38)	(0.48)
Observations	49	49	48	49

*$p \leq 0.05$ (one-tailed). The dependent variable is the logged length of each state constitution in 2015. Rounding to two significant digits. Robust standard errors in parentheses. Alabama omitted.

predicts that constitutions will be 13 percent shorter if adopted 54 years earlier (in 1845) and 14 percent shorter if adopted 54 years later (in 1951). Constitutions adopted in the late 19th century remain much longer today on average than other state constitutions. A century of amendment activity has surely weakened this relationship, yet the persistence of late 19th-century adoption remains striking.

Table 2.2 presents variants on this model controlling for modern variables that may plausibly affect a constitution's current length. Model 2.2b controls for legislative complexity, a measure of the procedural difficulty of proposing an amendment, as described in the appendix to chapter 1. Among national constitutions, the lengthiest also have the strictest amendment procedures (Tsebelis and Nardi 2016, 469). We do not observe this pattern in the states; instead, the model shows no relationship at all between length and amendment difficulty.

Model 2.2c adds a control for the average Republican share of legislative seats in each state over the preceding decade, omitting Nebraska, with its nonpartisan legislature. Measurement details appear in the appendix to chapter 1. Legislative partisanship appears to have no relationship to constitution length.

Model 2.2d adds corruption rates, a major predictor of national constitution lengths (Tsebelis and Nardi 2016; Tsebelis 2017).[17] It is easier to measure corruption among states than among nations. Cross-national studies rely on Transparency International's survey-based corruption measure, but state-level analysis uses reports from the Federal Bureau of Investigation, since its Public Integrity Section prosecutes federal, state, and local officials under a uniform set of standards (Goel and Rich 1989; Meier and Holbrook 1992; Glaeser and Saks 2006; Alt and Lassen 2008, 2010). Model 2.2d measures corruption as each state's total number of corruption convictions per million residents over the decade preceding 2015, finding no relationship whatsoever between corruption and constitution length in the states.

Constitutions grew lengthier in the late 19th century because both framework provisions and policy provisions became more common. Hammons (1999) coded each sentence in each state constitution as either a policy provision or a framework provision, for a median of 623 provisions per state constitution. Figure 2.5 plots the number of framework provisions (left panel) and policy provisions (right panel) against each constitution's

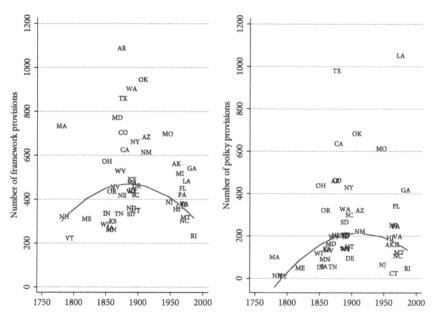

Figure 2.5 Framework and Policy Provisions by Adoption Year.

adoption year. Solid lines depict the relationship between the respective number of provisions and each constitution's adoption year, based on a separate quadratic regression for each panel. Framework provisions crest sooner than policy provisions, but both types of provision are most common in constitutions adopted in the late 19th century.[18] Moreover, the number of framework provisions correlates strongly with the number of policy provisions ($r = 0.61$, $p < 0.01$).[19] These patterns support my decision to operationalize specificity as a single variable—constitution length—rather than treat each type of provision separately.

Some caution is due in interpreting all this statistical analysis. Correlating modern variables to the current length of documents that have evolved over centuries is fraught with pitfalls both obvious and subtle. For example, the regression results in Table 2.2 imply that the initiative option leads to an ever-lengthening state constitution. Perhaps this is true, but a causal relationship seems dubious. First, the regression may be detecting nothing more than the constitutional language used to define the initiative procedure itself rather than language subsequently added by initiative. States with an initiative option may have lengthier constitutions if for no other reason than it takes additional constitutional language to describe the initiative process. Second and more subtly, the regression may also be detecting the historical circumstances that led states to adopt the initiative process in the first place. Nearly every state with an initiative option adopted it between 1900 and 1912. Progressive advocates of the initiative shared the same distrust of elites that motivated many states to lengthen their constitutions just a few years earlier. Thus, the "initiative" effect in Table 2.2 may reflect no more than a state's receptiveness to anti-elite appeals around the turn of the century. If so, the initiative's relationship with constitution length is spurious. Chapter 3's analysis of amendment rates will cast further doubt on the initiative's role in lengthening state constitutions.

More generally, this point highlights the difficulty of using modern variables to understand historical ones. To reiterate, this book seeks to understand the effects of constitutional specificity *today* on political outcomes *today*. This chapter detours into specificity's historical origins only to contextualize this contemporary argument. For this reason, this section's examination of the origins of constitution length is more limited than the statistical analysis used in subsequent chapters to examine the effects of length. In particular, this chapter has not attempted to model any selection process that may explain why some states adopted new constitutions in the late 19th century, why other states convened conventions without ultimately ratifying a new constitution, or why still other states took no action at all. Within this book's broader context, this section's most important finding is that modern variables have little relationship with constitution length, allowing subsequent chapters to treat it as a true independent variable. This section's limited empirical analysis is less about fully explaining the origins of constitutional specificity than about demonstrating its modern exogeneity.

Summary

This chapter has reviewed the origin and development of state constitutions since 1776. State constitutions adopted prior to 1787 provided both a legal and intellectual foundation for the US Constitution, which assumes their existence repeatedly. State constitutions confer plenary power, meaning that adding specificity can only restrict the government's otherwise unlimited authority. As a result, revisions adopted amid late 19th-century concerns about centralized authority and corrupt elites contain more detail than constitutions adopted earlier or later in the nation's history. Constitution makers added this specificity in "a deliberate attempt to constrain those in power" (Versteeg and Zackin 2014, 1647).

Even through a century of amendments, an unmistakable cohort effect endures in modern state constitutions. State constitutions today contain more words, reflecting both framework provisions and policy provisions, if they were adopted between 1870 and 1900. By contrast, there is no relationship between constitution length and modern variables likely to affect it, including legislative partisanship, corruption, or difficult amendment procedures.

One can fairly conclude that modern variations in constitutional specificity are mostly relics of the past. State constitutions today reflect "political forces prevailing nationally at the time they were adopted."[20] Because this book's focus is on constitution length as an independent variable, this finding presents a happy accident: subsequent chapters can treat modern constitution length as statistically exogenous. Constitution length is a valid indicator of the constraints placed on government action—whether through institutional inflexibility or constitutionalized policy—that does not unintentionally proxy for another variable.

3
Specificity and Amendments

Constitutional specificity leads to constitutional obsolescence, binding states to past solutions to past problems. Chapter 1 identified two ways that specificity binds states. First, specificity curbs institutional flexibility by multiplying veto players and procedural rules. Second, specificity curbs statutory flexibility by adding policies to the constitution itself. This chapter examines the first of several observable implications of this argument: if detailed constitutions bind states, then constitutional specificity should lead to elevated amendment rates as states seek to free themselves from their bonds.

Most literature on state and national amendment rates fixates on the effect of varying amendment procedures. This "relatively recent and underinvestigated" literature (Rasch and Congleton 2006, 536) has yet to establish "a satisfactory general theory on constitutional change" (Lorenz 2012, 32). Different authors have drawn "different [empirical] conclusions [about] . . . the rate or difficulty of constitutional amendment" (Dixon 2011, 105). Ultimately, this chapter shows that constitution length affects amendment rates much more powerfully than amendment procedures do. Constitutional specificity creates greater pressure for reform than burdensome amendment procedures can restrain.

Though this book's focus is on constitutional specificity, this chapter makes both conceptual and empirical contributions to the broader literature on constitutional amendment. Conceptually, it brings variables scattered across previous work into a single analysis that pits constitutional and societal pressures for change against procedural barriers to amending. Empirically, it reevaluates the literature's findings about constitutional amendment rates using longitudinal analysis of 49 state constitutions over 11 biennia. Previous research on amendment rates has been almost exclusively cross-sectional,[1] typically examining anywhere from 22 to 39 democratic constitutions (Anckar and Kavonen 2002; Lijphart 2012; Lorenz 2004; Lutz 1994; Rasch and Congleton 2006; Tsebelis and Nardi 2016) or the 50 US states (Besso 2005; Dixon and Holden 2012; Ferejohn 1997; Hammons 1999; Lutz 1994). This chapter finds that procedural barriers do reduce amendment rates, but not as much as constitution length increases them. As a sidelight, this chapter also shows that voters are more likely to reject initiated than referred amendments.

Democratic Constitutionalism

Democratic constitutions must balance opposing ideals of democratic responsiveness and constitutional stability. As for stability, constitutions establish the boundaries and rules governing the governing process, providing a sure arena for the otherwise unsure game of politics. To provide this sure arena, constitutions must be so written as to ensure their own permanence. We often credit James Madison for promoting this ideal of stable constitutionalism. Madison praised the US Constitution's difficult Article V amendment procedure, asserting in Federalist 43 that anything simpler "would render the Constitution too mutable" (quoted in Rossiter 1961, 275). He brushed off critics worried that the 1787 Convention had produced too brief and vague a document; these critics "would have formed a digest of laws, instead of a Constitution."[2] Madison would concur with Tsebelis and Nardi (2016): "A long constitution is a (positively) bad constitution."

Madison's perspective prevailed at the federal convention, which produced the sort of short, broad governing framework he championed. There, Edmund Randolph drove home the point: "In the draught of a fundamental constitution" one must "insert essential principles only, lest the operations of government should be clogged by rendering those provisions permanent and unalterable which ought to be accommodated to times and events."[3] Chief Justice John Marshall later agreed that a constitution should address only the "great outlines" and "important objects" of governance, omitting the "minor ingredients" more appropriate to "the prolixity of a legal code."[4] More recent writers have favorably compared a stable constitution to Ulysses's voluntary bonds as he passed the Sirens (Elster 1979) or to a compact between a monarch and the nobility (North and Weingast 1989), revealing a preference for what Versteeg and Zackin (2014, 2016) label an "entrenched" constitution.

Conflicting with this ideal of stability, democratic constitutions must also submit themselves to the same whims of popular sovereignty that motivated their original creation. Jefferson chided Madison in 1789, "[N]o society can make a perpetual constitution, or even a perpetual law. . . . Every constitution, then, and every law, naturally expires at the end of 19 years. If it be enforced longer, it is an act of force and not of right."⁵ He renewed this argument in 1816:

> I am certainly not an advocate for frequent and untried changes in laws and constitutions. I think moderate imperfections had better be borne with; because, when once known, we accommodate ourselves to them, and find practical means of correcting their ill effects. But I know also, that laws and institutions must go hand in hand with the progress of the human mind. As that becomes more developed, more enlightened, as new discoveries are made, new truths disclosed, and manners and opinions change with the change of circumstances, institutions must advance also, and keep pace with the times. We might as well require a man to wear still the coat which fitted him when a boy, as civilized society to remain ever under the regimen of their barbarous ancestors.⁶

Jefferson here manifests the same impulse that motivated him to assert so forcefully in the Declaration of Independence an inherent right "to alter or to abolish" a flawed regime. To Jefferson, it is as undemocratic to foist a new constitution on living people without their consent as to foist an existing one on generations yet unborn. It is also risky; a nation that inherits a too rigid constitution, impervious to alteration, may resort to ignoring it, reinterpreting it by fiat, or abandoning it. Thus, Jefferson writes, "The real friends of the Constitution . . . if they wish it to be immortal, should be attentive, by amendments, to make it keep pace with the advance of the age in science and experience."⁷ After all, "when constitutional documents are sufficiently difficult to change, political development often occurs outside and around the formal constitution" (Versteeg and Zackin 2016, 660; cf. Griffin 1996; Levinson 1995).

A democratic constitution is therefore an oxymoron, pitting democratic responsiveness against constitutional stability, permanence against change (Woodward-Burns 2021, 2). "Some theorists worry that democracy will be paralyzed by constitutional straightjacketing," Holmes (1993, 196) writes. "Others are apprehensive that the constitutional dike will be breached by a democratic flood." But "both sides agree that there exists a deep, almost irreconcilable tension between constitutionalism and democracy" (196), so much that "no part of a constitution is more important than the procedures we use to change it" (Albert 2019, 2).

Constitutions strike this balance between democracy and stability in diverse ways. The US Constitution leans hard toward stability, requiring a two-thirds bicameral supermajority for Congress to propose an amendment, followed by ratification in three-fourths of the states. Granted, the US Constitution's brevity renders this difficult procedure less problematic than it might be for a more detailed document. Still, the amendment process is burdensome enough that Americans have all but given up on it, tacitly choosing to update the Constitution through judicial fiat rather than formal amendment.[8]

No state constitution erects such high amendment barriers as the US Constitution does, but some come close. New Hampshire, for example, requires three-fifths of legislators to propose an amendment, then two-thirds of voters to ratify it; South Carolina requires two-thirds of legislators to propose an amendment, then ratification by a majority of voters, affirmed by one more (majority) legislative vote. At the other extreme, seven states require only a simple legislative majority to propose an amendment and a simple majority of voters to ratify it, while also allowing voters to propose amendments by initiative. In recent decades, these latter seven states adopted almost twice as many amendments as New Hampshire and South Carolina—and the US Constitution received none.[9]

These differences tempt one to conclude that amendment procedures alone determine the amendment rate. Then again, perhaps amendment procedures play no role at all. Perhaps those seven constitutions contained twice as many flaws as the New Hampshire and South Carolina constitutions, and the US Constitution contained no flaws at all.[10] After all, the US Congress overrode 69 vetoes in the past 100 years but proposed only 12 amendments, even though both actions require a two-thirds supermajority—so perhaps it is the Constitution's substance and not its procedure that results in so few amendments. Nor is ratification as impossible as it seems, with nearly half of presidential elections over the past 100 years finding three-quarters of states on the same side (cf. Jackson 2015; Velasco-Rivera 2021). A complete theory of constitutional change must consider pressures to reform separately from barriers to amendment—and the greatest pressure to reform arises from constitutional specificity.

Pressures to Amend

As much as Madison and others (e.g., Sartori 1994) may have hoped that wise founders can craft good institutions from the start, "any people who believe in constitutionalism will amend their constitution when needed" rather than resort to "extraconstitutional means" like judicial or executive reinterpretation (Lutz 1994, 357). Societies, economies, and polities change, and these changes can cause a people and their constitution to grow apart (Thelen 2003; Elkins, Ginsburg, and Melton 2009). A constitutional provision is obsolete if it lingers only through inertia rather than popular support. The more obsolete provisions that a constitution contains, the more amendment activity we should observe.

Past work on constitutional change has flirted with this concept of obsolescence but struggled to attach it to specific constitutional features. Some have supposed that a constitution's age signals its obsolescence, implying that older constitutions should attract more amendments than younger ones, yet this prediction finds mixed empirical support (e.g., Hammons 1999; Roberts 2009; Reutter and Lorenz 2016). There are two flaws with this approach, though—flaws that should lead us to look elsewhere to understand constitutional obsolescence.

First, equating obsolescence with age assumes that all societies change at the same rate, yet some societies experience more rapid demographic, economic, or cultural change than others. Analysis that substitutes constitution age for direct consideration of social, economic, and political variables therefore misses the mark. Cross-national analysis especially struggles with this problem, owing to a "lack of adequate operationalizations and comparable data" about political culture (Lorenz 2012, 38)—a problem Ginsburg and Melton (2015) claimed to solve, but not without criticism (Tsebelis 2021). This book's focus on the American states mutes concerns about varying political cultures, since there is less difference among Idaho, New York, and Virginia than among Japan, France, and Botswana. Moreover, the longitudinal analysis below has the luxury of including socioeconomic variables omitted from past cross-sectional work, allowing for direct consideration of societal change that may place distance between a society and its constitution.[11] Failure to adequately account for different rates of social, economic, and political change may have produced misleading estimates of the effect of constitution age in past work.

Second, and more to this book's point, equating obsolescence with age assumes that constitutions themselves are equally prone to obsolescence. To the contrary, some constitutions avoid fleeting concerns, sticking to relatively timeless structural matters, while others delve into immense institutional or policy detail. Democratic constitutions, after all, must balance democratic responsiveness and constitutional stability. The more detailed a constitution, the more targets it will have for democratic reform. Each additional provision in a constitution is an additional opportunity for obsolescence. If constitutional specificity binds states to the past, then additional specificity binds more, since "a polity that includes elaborate and detailed policies in its constitution will continue to tinker with the document in a process of trial and error and in response to changing economic and social conditions" (Versteeg and Zackin 2014, 1668). Small wonder, then, that statistical analysis identifies constitution length as "the strongest and most consistent" predictor of amendments (Lutz 1994, 359; see also Ferejohn 1997; Hammons 1999; Tsebelis and Nardi 2016). Constitutional specificity "invites frequent amendment and early obsolescence" (Howard 1996, 393).

Examination of recently adopted amendments affirms this intuition. Of 50 amendments ratified nationwide in November 2016, 60 percent merely updated or modified existing constitutional provisions without adding fundamentally new material to the constitution. That is, 60 percent of these amendments would not have been necessary if previous generations had left material to statutory discretion rather than adding it to the state constitution.

For example, Arkansas clarified how its election code—part of the state constitution—applies to single-candidate elections (Issue 1). California extended the sunset date on a constitutionalized income tax reform (Prop. 55) and extended constitutionalized tobacco regulations to include e-cigarettes (Prop. 56). Colorado adjusted its minimum wage, which had previously been enshrined in the state constitution (Amendment 70). Louisiana tightened constitutionalized qualifications for registrars of voters (Amendment 1). Missouri extended an expiring conservation tax previously added to the constitution (Amendment 1). Nevada updated constitutionalized gasoline tax provisions (Question 2). New Mexico revised constitutionalized bail procedures (Amendment 1). North Dakota changed constitutionalized oil extraction taxes (Measure 2). Oklahoma rewrote constitutionalized regulations on beer and wine (Question 792). Oregon changed the constitutionalized allocation of lottery proceeds (Measure 96). South Dakota revised the constitutionalized control structure for technical schools (Amendment R). Utah modified the constitutionally prescribed oath of office (Amendment A). Wyoming changed constitutionalized provisions for investing state funds (Amendment A).

These policies about bail, technical schools, alcohol, gasoline taxes, tobacco, oil extraction, the minimum wage, the registrar of voters, and investment of state funds could have been updated by statute rather than amendment if a previous generation had not written its preferences into the state constitution. Perhaps these amendments should have removed these provisions entirely rather than merely updating them, freeing the legislature to address them by statute going forward. Such constitutional pruning is rare, though. States typically update restrictive provisions rather than remove them, kicking the problem down the road for yet another generation to confront when those provisions once again grow obsolete.

Moreover, states continue to add restrictive provisions to their state constitutions, as illustrated by the remaining amendments ratified in November 2016. Several of these amendments are examples of multistate interests pushing proposals nationwide. Indiana and Kansas added near-identical guarantees of the right to hunt and fish; North Dakota, South Dakota, and Montana enacted "Marsy's Law," a statement of victims' rights; and Florida, Louisiana, and Virginia enacted provisions exempting surviving spouses of first responders and soldiers killed in action from certain property taxes. Beyond these multistate movements, other amendments adding new provisions to state constitutions included Florida's medical marijuana amendment; Georgia's earmark of firework tax revenues; Idaho's authorization of its legislature to review administrative rules; Illinois's restrictions on the use of transportation funds; Maine's creation of an independent board to set legislators' salaries; Missouri's limits on campaign contributions; and Nevada's restrictions on new regulations affecting energy development. These new provisions create new opportunities for obsolescence that future generations will need to address.

Adding specificity to a constitution launches a vicious cycle of amendment after amendment. In states "where literally hundreds of [provisions] have been added . . . for many purposes the act of amending the constitution has supplanted much normal lawmaking" (Cornwell 1981, 11). The constitutional amendment process "has become hopelessly cluttered and divorced from its proper function," having been "geared down to the level of the making of ordinary legislative determinations" (13). Specificity promotes obsolescence, which creates pressure to amend the constitution. Operationalizing specificity as length, with socioeconomic considerations as a control, we arrive at the following hypothesis:

H1. Lengthier constitutions will attract more amendments.

I have argued that it is a constitution's specificity rather than its age that promotes constitutional obsolescence, prompting corrective amendments. What, then, of age? After accounting for specificity and socioeconomic conditions, constitution age may have the opposite effect on amendment rates than some have supposed. The US Constitution needed only 25 years for its first 12 amendments but another 160 years for its next 12. A new constitution may require amendments correcting provisions that did not translate well from contemplation to practice, like the US Constitution's Twelfth Amendment. It may require amendments addressing unforeseen problems, like the US Constitution's Eleventh Amendment. It may require amendments revisiting a compromise that was acceptable to those who negotiated the constitution but not to a broader audience, like the US Constitution's Bill of Rights. After taking account of a constitution's length, we may well expect young constitutions to attract more amendments than old ones. Failure to consider this interaction between constitutional age and specificity may have contributed to the mixed effects of constitution age reported in previous work.

> H2. Younger constitutions, especially if lengthy, will receive more amendments.

Amendment Barriers

Complicated amendment procedures may reduce the supply of amendments (Lutz 1994; Ferejohn 1997; Rasch and Congleton 2006; Lupia et al. 2010; Tsebelis 2021; but see Ginsburg and Melton 2015). To be sure, institutions are themselves a product of politics, and burdensome processes that stand in the way of desired reforms can be set aside or changed. After all, the federal convention proposed a new US Constitution without clear authority under the Articles of Confederation. Similarly, some early state constitutions lacked any amendment or revision procedure, yet all these states eventually found ways to update their constitutions (Tarr 1998). Likewise, the burdensome Article V amendment process has led most Americans to tacitly accept the US Supreme Court's role in updating the federal Constitution through acts of interpretation.

All the same, if institutions matter at all, then constitutions imposing difficult amendment procedures should receive fewer amendments than constitutions with simpler ones. This theoretical expectation is straightforward and hardly novel, but empirical findings have been mixed—largely because so many diverse amendment procedures exist, complicating comparative analysis. Just within the American states, amendment procedures vary widely. Some states allow the legislature to propose an amendment by simple majority; others require a legislative supermajority; some require the legislature to approve a proposed amendment more than once, with an election intervening; and four limit the number of amendments the legislature may propose per election. As for voters' role, all states but Delaware require voters to ratify amendments proposed by the legislature, usually by simple majority but sometimes by supermajority, and 18 states allow voters to bypass the legislature and propose amendments by initiative. Even more amendment procedures arise when examining national rather than state constitutions, as most research on amendment rates has done.

With so many possible procedures and so few cases for study, research gets so difficult that the "question may well be unanswerable" (Albert 2019, 97). In a groundbreaking study, Lutz (1994) constructed an index of amendment difficulty comprising some 68 possible procedures—a number exceeding the actual number of observations in his statistical models. Constructing index variables is common in small-sample cross-sectional analysis, but indices invariably hide a degree of arbitrariness behind a veneer of precision, which "makes the exactness of [index] scores fictitious" (Lorenz 2005, 342). Measures developed by Lutz (1994), Anckar and Kavonen (2002), Lorenz (2004), and Lijphart (2012) correlate only modestly with one another (Lorenz 2005; Rasch and Congleton 2006, 557). Developing a valid measure of amendment difficulty is so "challenging, and perhaps even impossible" (Ginsburg and Melton 2015, 693), that some advocate giving up entirely, relying on amendment rates themselves rather than amendment procedures as the best measure of constitutional rigidity (Marshfield 2018, 80; Versteeg and Zackin 2016, 661). Indeed, some chapters in this book take this latter approach.

These measurement challenges lead to competing findings about the effect of amendment procedures on amendment rates. Using his broad index, Lutz (1994) concluded generally that procedural difficulty reduces amendment rates. Disaggregating Lutz's index, Ferejohn (1997) found that most of its components had no independent effect. Instead, Ferejohn found a simpler pattern that placed state amendment procedures in only two categories: states where the legislature may propose an amendment by simple majority vote had higher amendment rates than states requiring other, more complex legislative procedures. By contrast, Rasch and Congleton's (2006) analysis of national constitutions found effects for procedures increasing the number of veto players (e.g., bicameralism, an executive veto over proposed amendments, voter ratification, and concurrent majorities over consecutive sessions) but not for other procedures, such as supermajority requirements. Meanwhile, Ginsburg and Melton (2015) later found that amendment procedures appear to have no effect at all after controlling for a nation's "amendment culture"—that is, the nation's amendment rate under its previous constitution—a finding contested by Tsebelis (2021), whose analysis reaffirmed Rasch and Congleton's conclusion: that amendment rules that multiply veto players reduce amendment rates. In any event, this debate produces this testable hypothesis:

H3. Burdensome amendment procedures reduce amendment rates.

In the states, legislative amendment procedures vary in three ways relevant to this hypothesis. First, "legislative complexity." This is Ferejohn's term for states that have a supermajority requirement, a concurrent session requirement, or any other procedure more complicated than a majority vote for the legislature to propose an amendment. (Supermajority requirements and concurrent session requirements must be combined empirically, since several states allow legislators to choose either procedure when proposing an amendment.) Ten states allow the legislature to propose an amendment by simple majority; Ferejohn's "legislative complexity" variable is simply a reverse coding of these states. Second, voter ratification requirements. All states but Delaware require voter ratification of proposed amendments, usually by simple majority but sometimes by supermajority. And third is the presence of a constitutional limit on the number of amendments that the legislature may propose per election. Only four states have amendment limits: Arkansas (3 per election), Illinois (3), Kentucky (4), and Kansas (5). States seldom reach their limits, but a limit may deter legislators from proposing amendments all the same.[12] To test H3, I include variables addressing all three procedural variations.

The literature has focused on formal amendment procedures like these, but this chapter's focus on the American states—with all their similarities and opportunities for comparison—allows us to go further. In particular, nearly all successful amendments originate in a state legislature. Even in the

18 states allowing initiated amendments—a procedure addressed shortly—73 percent of amendments between 1994 and 2015 were legislatively referred. If most amendments originate in a legislature, then anything that lowers the legislature's general productivity should also lower its propensity to propose constitutional amendments. During the 2014–15 biennium, 10 state legislatures enacted fewer than 300 bills (excluding resolutions), while 13 enacted over 1,000. We arrive at an additional hypothesis:

H4. Barriers to legislative action generally will also reduce amendment rates.

This book makes no attempt to model legislative productivity generally, but it does use overall bill passage numbers as a proxy for any underlying factor influencing legislative output. It will also include a few other indicators of legislative capacity. For example, it will consider the state's total number of legislators, under the premise that passing legislation (or proposing an amendment) will be more difficult with more legislators competing for time. Some specifications include three additional variables. First, an indicator for whether the majority party holds enough seats in both chambers to unilaterally meet whatever supermajority threshold is required to propose an amendment, with legislatures with a unilateral majority expected to propose more amendments. Second, a measure of the percentage of legislative seats held by Republicans, included as a control variable without a directional prediction. And third, a measure of the total number of days the legislature spends in any type of session. These considerations of the general legislative environment are new to the study of constitutional amendments.[13]

Eighteen states allow initiated amendments, with varying qualification requirements. In these states, 25 percent of the 538 amendments adopted from 1994 to 2015 were initiated.[14] Research on citizen initiatives has focused mostly on initiated statutes, without addressing initiated amendments as a distinct class. A major concern within this literature has been whether the threat of an initiated statute promotes legislative responsiveness, so that legislatures in initiative states feel pressured into producing policies more consistent with citizen preferences (Gerber 1996; Lascher, Hagen, and Rochlin 1996; Lax and Phillips 2012). Such work makes no prediction about initiated statutes affecting the number of bills considered by the legislature; as such, there is no implied prediction about initiated amendments affecting the number of amendments proposed by the legislature. On the one hand, an initiative option provides an end run around legislative supermajority requirements, possibly increasing the amendment rate. On the other hand, it may leave legislators feeling free to defer thorny questions to citizens, possibly decreasing the amendment rate. I make no hypothesis about the initiative option's effect on the amendment rate, but I do control for its presence.

Analysis and Results

A democratic constitution must balance democratic responsiveness against constitutional stability. Lengthier constitutions bind states to the past, boosting amendment rates as states seek to adapt to new circumstances (H1). Younger constitutions are especially likely to contain delicate compromises or other problems requiring corrective amendments, especially if the constitutions are lengthy (H2). Amendment rates slow under burdensome amendment procedures (H3) or where there are barriers to legislative action generally (H4). In general, states will amend their constitutions more when indicators of demand increase (H1, H2) and less when barriers to supply increase (H3, H4).

I use random effects negative binomial regression to predict the number of amendments within each state biennium, then reduce the model using the Akaike information criterion. Like all regression analysis, this approach allows me to estimate the effect of each independent variable on amendment rates while holding other variables constant. Details of the statistical analysis appear in this chapter's appendix, including raw regression results for several models that lead up to a final one. Here, I will focus on presenting the most important findings rather than wading through the raw statistical output. This discussion draws on the final specification from Table 3.3 in this chapter's appendix. All variables interpreted below have statistically significant effects ($p < 0.05$ two-tailed) unless stated otherwise. The model includes 522 state-biennium observations.

State constitution length turns out to have a stronger relationship with amendment rates than any other variable—and the relationship changes depending on a constitution's age. Figure 3.1 plots amendment rates per biennium (vertical axis) against constitution length in words (horizontal axis).[15] The figure plots longitudinal data, with one dot for each state-biennium. The overlaid lines depict predicted values from the regression analysis, with separate lines for young, average, and old constitutions. "Young" and "old" are defined as one standard deviation below or above the mean—52 or 159 years old, respectively.[16] In plotting these lines, other variables are held constant at

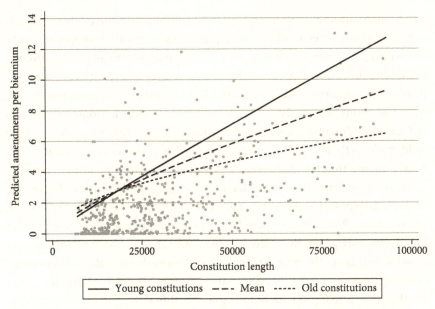

Figure 3.1 Effects of Constitution Length and Age on Amendment Activity.

their median values. To see the effect of constitution length, move along one of the lines; to see the effect of constitution age, chose a point along the horizontal axis and look at the gap between the lines.

Amendment activity rises sharply with constitution length, especially for young constitutions. An increase in constitution length from one standard deviation below the mean (14,900 words) to one standard deviation above it (50,000 words) increases by 8.2 the predicted amendments per state-biennium for a young constitution, a large effect.[17] Age also has powerful effects, but only for lengthy constitutions. A 60,000-word constitution has 5.5 more predicted amendments per biennium if it is young rather than old; this difference declines to 1.4 predicted amendments per biennium for a 30,000-word constitution. This analysis strongly favors H1 (lengthier constitutions receive more amendments). It also favors H2 (younger constitutions, especially if lengthy, receive more amendments).

Procedural amendment barriers reduce amendment rates, but less strongly than constitution length increases them. With other variables held at their medians, the regression predicts that states with complex legislative procedures will adopt 2.3 fewer amendments per biennium than states where the legislature can propose an amendment by simple majority. States with amendment limits are also predicted to adopt 2.3 fewer amendments per biennium. As for voter ratification, requiring ratification by simple majority has no effect compared to having no ratification requirement at all. However, increasing the ratification requirement from a simple majority vote to a two-thirds supermajority vote results in 2.7 fewer predicted amendments per state-biennium. The analysis therefore favors H3 (burdensome procedures reduce amendments), though these procedural variables nevertheless have milder effects than constitution length does. The presence of an initiative option to amend the constitution has no relationship with amendment rates.

To aid in interpreting these effects and those described below, Figure 3.2 shows scatterplots for several variables, with plots shown in the order I will discuss them.[18] Within each panel, the independent variable depicted on the horizontal axis generally spans its observed range.[19] The first (upper-left) panel again shows the relationship between amendment rates and constitution length, with one dot for each state-biennium. The dots in this first panel are the same as in Figure 3.1, but the lines are different.

In each panel, the solid baseline plots predictions for states without legislative complexity or amendment limits, with other variables held at their medians. The dashed line plots predictions for states with an amendment

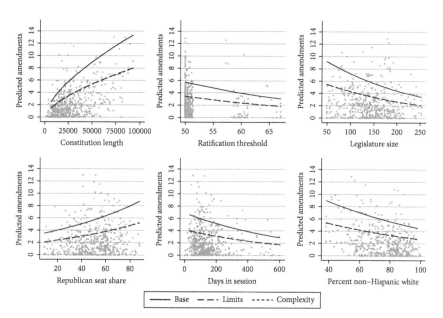

Figure 3.2 Predicted Amendments per State-Biennium.

limit. The dotted line plots predictions for states with legislative complexity. These latter two lines overlap almost perfectly, indicating that legislative complexity and amendment limits have essentially the same effect on amendment rates. The other procedural variable I examine—voter ratification thresholds—appears in the second (upper-middle) panel. Supermajority ratification requirements lower amendment rates significantly.

The next three panels plot variables related to the general legislative environment. Larger legislatures have somewhat lower amendment rates than legislatures with fewer members (upper-right panel), for example, as do legislatures with fewer Republicans (lower-left panel).[20] (Curiously, chapter 6 will show that Republican voters profess greater constitutional veneration, even though Republican legislators apparently produce more amendments.) Legislatures with shorter sessions propose more amendments than those with lengthier sessions (lower-middle panel). Perhaps legislators with shorter sessions are more likely to rush their proposed amendments through, forcing them to enact corrective amendments in the future—an admittedly post-hoc speculation about an atheoretical control variable. Moving from one standard deviation below the mean to one standard deviation above it on these variables (with other variables held at their medians) changes the predicted number of amendments per state-biennium by −3.4 (legislature size), +2.1 (Republican seat share), and −1.6 (session length). These effects are similar in magnitude to those of legislative complexity, amendment limits, and supermajority ratification requirements.[21] Perhaps surprisingly, the number of bills passed per biennium does not have a significant relationship with the number of amendments adopted, so this variable is not included in Figure 3.2. Findings are therefore mixed with respect to H4 (barriers to legislative action will reduce amendment rates), with some legislative variables having significant relationships but the most obvious variable having no effect.

As for controls, the model predicts 2.1 more amendments per state-biennium in southern states than elsewhere; this is the only statistically significant variable that does not appear in Figure 3.1 or Figure 3.2. The controls for socioeconomic stress—population, income, and racial composition—contribute little to the final model, though an increase in a state's non-Hispanic white share from one standard deviation below the mean to one standard deviation above it reduces the prediction by 2.1 amendments per state-biennium; see the lower-right panel of Figure 3.2.

Burdensome amendment procedures—legislative complexity, high ratification thresholds, and amendment limits—slow amendment rates, with effects comparable to those of a larger legislature, a more racially diverse state, or a more Democratic chamber. Still, constitution length has much stronger effects than any of these variables, as Figure 3.2 makes apparent.

Voter Ratification

As an aside, consider how voters evaluate proposed amendments at the ballot box. An important line of inquiry explores how voters learn about and evaluate ballot measures generally (Binder, Boudreau, and Kousser 2011; Boudreau and MacKenzie 2014; Druckman, Peterson, and Slothuus 2013; Lau and Redlawsk 2006; Lupia 1994; Lupia and McCubbins 1998). Outside Delaware, all proposed amendments appear before voters for ratification, whether initiated or referred, yet initiated and referred amendments have different origins. Referred amendments originate in the legislature, where professional staff contribute expertise and where committee hearings, floor debates, and bicameral concurrence provide opportunities to catch errors and build consensus. Initiated amendments, by contrast, originate with interest groups, which can place any language they want before voters if they can get enough signatures (Damore, Bowler, and Nicholson 2012). These different origins imply differences in quality—not in the sense of partisan favorability but of drafting skill, technical expertise, and foreseeing a proposal's implications.

In November 2016, for example, California voters evaluated an initiated amendment to require future infrastructure projects involving $2 billion or more in revenue bonds to appear before voters for advance approval. During the ratification campaign, opponents pounded this seemingly simple amendment for its inattention to the sort of details that legislative committee hearings would have identified and corrected. Opponents emphasized that the amendment would require a statewide vote even on local projects and that it failed to carve out an exception for natural disaster responses. Voters ultimately rejected this amendment.

Generalizing from California's experience, if we observe higher ratification rates for referred than initiated amendments, then we would have evidence that voters can distinguish well-drafted from poorly considered proposals. Initiative processes are not created equal (Bowler and Donovan

2004), of course, and it matters especially how many signatures proponents must gather to qualify for the ballot (Gerber 1996). If we observe that citizens ratify referred amendments at a higher rate than initiated ones—particularly in states with lower signature requirements, where initiated amendments can reach the ballot with less support—then we could draw an optimistic inference about voters' ability to evaluate ballot questions generally. Moreover, we would have even less cause to lament the shift from constitutional revision to piecemeal amendment, since we could have greater confidence in the amendment process's results.

This side analysis calls for separate counts of referred and initiated amendments; I discuss sources and measurement in this chapter's appendix. Table 3.1 confirms that the initiative option may not affect the number of amendments ratified so much as the number defeated. Aggregating over the 11 biennia considered here, there is no statistical difference in the mean number of legislative-referred amendments adopted in noninitiative (24.1) and initiative (22.4) states (p = 0.80), nor is there a statistical difference in the mean number of total amendments adopted (24.1 vs. 29.9, p = 0.44). There is, however, a tremendous difference in the mean number of total amendments defeated at the ballot box: 5.4 in noninitiative states versus 20.9 in initiative states (p < 0.01). Voters in initiative states are more willing to reject any proposed amendment, regardless of its source, but the difference between initiative and noninitiative states is driven mostly by voter rejection of initiated amendments. In initiative states, voters reject 57 percent of initiated amendments but only 33 percent of referred amendments.

Table 3.1 Mean Amendments Ratified, 1994–2015

	Noninitiative states	Initiative states	Difference
Referred amendments adopted	24.1	22.4	−1.7 (p = 0.80)
Referred amendments defeated	5.4	11.2	+5.7 (p = 0.03)
Initiated amendments adopted	—	7.4	—
Initiated amendments defeated	—	9.7	—
Total amendments adopted	24.1	29.9	+5.8 (p = 0.44)
Total amendments defeated	5.4	20.9	+15.5 (p < 0.01)
Observations	30	18	

Notes: Delaware and Alabama omitted. "Referred" includes 1,470 legislative- and 22 commission-referred amendments.

Taking the next step, I replicated the previous section's regression analysis, but this time running one model estimating the number of amendments ratified per state-biennium, and a separate model estimating the number of amendments defeated per state-biennium. Raw results appear as Table 3.4 in this chapter's appendix. This analysis omits Delaware, since the legislature may amend the constitution directly there without voter involvement.

Unsurprisingly, when the dependent variable is the number of amendments ratified per state-biennium, the results are essentially the same as those reported in the previous section. Ratifications rise sharply when the constitution is lengthy, especially if it is also young. Ratifications fall somewhat when the legislature must follow complex procedures to propose an amendment, when there is a limit on how many amendments the legislature may propose, when the legislature is larger, and when Democrats hold more seats.

The results differ profoundly when modeling the number of amendments rejected by voters per state-biennium. There is no relationship at all between constitution length, constitution age, complex legislative procedures, or any of these other variables on the number of amendments rejected per state-biennium. Instead, only two variables attain statistical significance. First, higher ratification thresholds unexpectedly lead to fewer defeated amendments, not more. Perhaps those who would propose amendments take notice of higher thresholds and avoid submitting low-quality amendments that risk an embarrassing loss. Second, and more to the point, the presence of an initiative option increases the number of defeated amendments. (Controlling for the difficulty of qualifying an initiative for the ballot has no effect.) With other variables at their medians, voters in a noninitiative state will reject 0.52 amendments per state-biennium, but this prediction nearly triples to 1.4 rejections per state-biennium in initiative states.

This side analysis suggests that voters distinguish referred amendments from initiated amendments and evaluate them differently. Voters ratify amendments that correct constitutional obsolescence and other defects, as indicated by the strong relationship between ratification and a constitution's length and age. By contrast, those amendments that fail to win voter approval generally arise through the initiative process and have no relationship with constitutional variables. These findings have implications for the broader literature on direct democracy, suggesting that voters can separate high-quality from low-quality proposals. They also provide reassurance that the shift from wholesale revision to piecemeal amendment has not set constitutions on a destructive course.

Summary

From 1994 through 2015, six states adopted a total of 4 or fewer amendments while seven adopted 40 or more. Constitution length drives this difference more than anything else, especially in younger constitutions. Constitutional specificity binds states to the past, accelerating constitutional obsolescence and creating targets for reform. Detailed constitutions bind policymakers, forcing them to resort to extraordinary amendment procedures to respond to changing situations.

In addition to highlighting the role of constitutional specificity, this chapter has also contributed three additional results to the general literature on constitutional amendment. First, it has separately evaluated three barriers to amendment, showing that legislative complexity, amendment limits, and supermajority ratification thresholds can all reduce amendment rates. Second, its longitudinal data frame allows consideration of socioeconomic and legislative variables overlooked in past work, some of which have substantive effects comparable to amendment procedures. Third, the analysis of ratification behavior implies that voters can distinguish between high- and low-quality amendments at the ballot box, suggesting some optimism about the shift from revision to amendment.

Recent scholarship has framed lengthy but flexible constitutions as a viable alternative to short but rigid ones (Versteeg and Zackin 2016). States with detailed constitutions do experience higher amendment rates, but not because they have deliberately chosen to pair detail with procedural flexibility. After all, chapter 2 found no correlation between constitution length and amendment difficulty. Rather, states with detailed constitutions wind up with high amendment rates whether they choose flexible amendment procedures or not. Burdensome procedures do slow amendment rates but not as much as constitutional specificity raises them, bearing witness to the constraints imposed by constitutional specificity. Specificity disrupts a democratic constitution's balance between responsiveness and stability, leading to frequent constitutional amendment whether founders adopt simple amendment procedures or not.

Methodological Appendix

This appendix contains full statistical details of models summarized in this chapter. This chapter's primary dependent variable is the number of constitutional amendments adopted per state-biennium. The primary independent variable is constitution length, interacted with constitution age, with both logged to reduce skew. These variables are measured as described in the appendix to chapter 1, with Alabama omitted. Figure 3.3 plots amendments per biennium (right axis) and constitution length (left axis, in thousands of words) by state, showing abundant cross-sectional and longitudinal variance.

Socioeconomic controls include state population, wealth (as median household income), and racial-ethnic diversity (as the non-Hispanic white share of the population), drawn from the US Census and other official sources and collapsed from annual data to biennial means. I scale all percentages from 0 to 100 rather than 0 to 1.

Legislative complexity, amendment limits, ratification requirements, and initiative procedures are compiled from *Book of the States*. Complexity is coded 0 in the 10 states allowing the legislature to propose an amendment by simple majority and 1 in states with more complex procedures, as described in the appendix to chapter 1. Amendment limits are coded dichotomously to indicate states that have them. Ratification requirements are coded using two variables: a dummy indicating whether voters must ratify amendments (effectively an inverted dummy for Delaware, the only state not to require ratification), and an interacted variable recording the percentage of voters who must support an amendment.[22] The analysis includes a dummy for the 18 states allowing initiated amendments.

Republican seat shares and legislative session lengths are measured as described in the appendix to chapter 1. Seven observations from Nebraska are lost due to missing data on legislator partisanship, reducing the analysis from 539 state-biennium observations to 532. Data about legislative bill enactments and related variables come from *Book of the States*. Bill enactments (logged due to skew) include both regular and special session bills but exclude resolutions. Bill counts are missing for 10 observations, further reducing the analysis to 522 observations.[23] Dropping the bill enactments variable to restore these observations does not meaningfully change the results reported below.

In addition to variables already described, the analysis includes a dummy for the 11 states of the former Confederacy. This regional variable is not

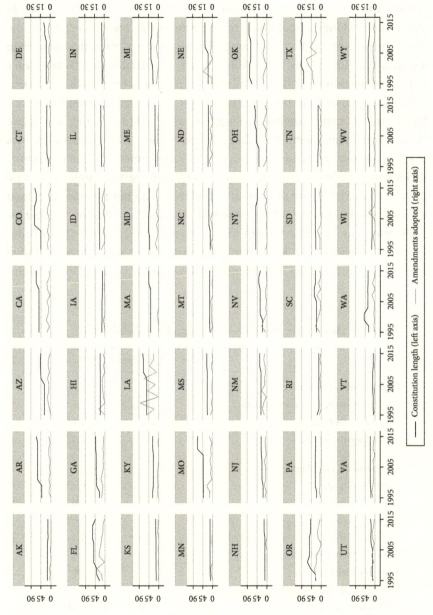

Figure 3.3 Constitution Lengths and Amendment Adoptions, by Biennium.

70 THE DEAD HAND'S GRIP

theoretically motivated, and omitting it does not meaningfully change the results, but I include it to reassure the reader.

Table 3.2 provides descriptive statistics for time-variant indicators, including the mean, the cross-sectional standard deviation between the 49 states, and the longitudinal standard deviation within states over 11 biennia. The "amendments ratified" and "amendments defeated" variables come from a source described elsewhere in this chapter. All variables in this table vary both cross-sectionally and longitudinally. Some important variables are constant over time and are therefore omitted from this table. Even in a much longer series, many ostensibly longitudinal variables, particularly those dealing with amendment procedures, would remain unchanged for decades at a time. (I have provided descriptive statistics for time-invariant regressors, including amendment procedures, in the preceding text and notes.) Because these static variables are of substantive interest, I do not include state fixed effects in the analysis below. State fixed effects—that is, a dummy variable for each state—would prevent the model from estimating coefficients for time-invariant indicators like legislative complexity. Time-series cross-sectional analysis remains valuable, however, as it allows for the effects of time-variant

Table 3.2 Descriptive Statistics for Longitudinal Variables

	Mean	SD between	SD within
Dependent variables			
Amendments per state-biennium	2.3	2.5	2.1
Amendments ratified	2.4	2.5	2.1
Amendments defeated	1.0	1.2	1.4
Independent variables			
Constitution age	106	54	6.3
Constitution length (1,000s)	30	18	5.0
Population (millions)	5.9	6.6	0.69
Median household income ($1,000s)	46	6.6	7.2
Non-Hispanic white (%)	74	15	3.6
Seats in legislature	148	61	2.6
Bills enacted (all session types)	765	446	195
Unilateral majority	0.43	0.39	0.31
Republican seat share (%)	50	14	7.8
Total days in any type of session	150	77	60

regressors to be separated from time-invariant ones better than in cross-sectional analysis. All the same, the following analysis presents reduced cross-sectional specifications for comparison alongside the primary longitudinal specifications.

Table 3.3 presents the results of four statistical models predicting state constitutional amendment rates. The first two are cross-sectional; their dependent variable is the total number of amendments adopted from 1994 to 2015 in each state, estimated with negative binomial regression, with regressors collapsed to medians, sums, or means as appropriate.[24] Because these cross-sectional models have only 49 observations, they omit a few peripheral variables to preserve scarce degrees of freedom. The latter two models are longitudinal; the dependent variable is the number of amendments adopted during each state-biennium, estimated with random effects negative binomial regression using biennial fixed effects. The latter models are of greatest interest, but I include the cross-sectional models to give a sense for how biennial effects aggregate over time. In all four models, similar results obtain when converting the dependent variable to the incremented and natural logged number of amendments and then employing ordinary least squares regression. Nevertheless, negative binomial regression is the most appropriate specification for an overdispersed count variable, so I rely on it here.

All four models produce broadly similar results, especially for the variables of greatest theoretical interest. Model 3.3b reduces model 3.3a using the Akaike information criterion (AIC); model 3.3d does the same for model 3.3c.[25] Interpretations in the text rely on model 3.3d, the final longitudinal specification. Consistent with existing literature, models in Table 3.3 estimate positive coefficients for constitution length and age—but only when ignoring the interaction. As shown graphically in the main text, the interaction predicts that younger constitutions will generally receive more amendments than older ones, with the difference growing larger as the constitution grows in length.

The text observes that requiring ratification by simple majority has no effect compared to no ratification requirement at all. Since the ratification dummy interacts with the ratification threshold variable, drawing this conclusion requires a quick calculation: 1.8 + (−0.037) × 50 = −0.05, which is essentially zero. Only Delaware lacks a ratification requirement, so this calculation tells us only that Delaware's amendment rate does not significantly differ from the rate in states with a simple majority ratification requirement.

Table 3.3 Adoptions of Constitutional Amendments

	(3.3a)	(3.3b)	(3.3c)	(3.3d)
Constitution age (ln)	6.7*	6.2*	3.9*	3.7*
	(2.2)	(2.2)	(1.5)	(1.5)
Constitution length (ln)	3.8*	3.8*	2.5*	2.4*
	(1.0)	(1.0)	(0.69)	(0.67)
× Age (ln)	−0.67*	−0.62*	−0.39*	−0.38*
	(0.22)	(0.22)	(0.15)	(0.15)
Population (millions)	0.018		0.018	0.019
	(0.015)		(0.011)	(0.011)
Household income ($1,000s)	−0.017		0.0064	
	(0.012)		(0.0092)	
Percentage white	−0.0085		−0.011*	−0.011*
	(0.0064)		(0.0050)	(0.0050)
Legislative complexity	−0.45*	−0.38*	−0.55*	−0.52*
	(0.20)	(0.19)	(0.17)	(0.15)
Voter ratification required	1.0		1.9*	1.8
	(1.3)		(0.94)	(0.93)
× Ratification majority	−0.016		−0.038*	−0.037*
	(0.023)		(0.017)	(0.017)
Seats in legislature	−0.0071*	−0.0067*	−0.0048*	−0.0049*
	(0.0018)	(0.0016)	(0.0014)	(0.0015)
Total bills enacted (ln)	0.22	0.30*	0.13	0.15
	(0.15)	(0.15)	(0.10)	(0.10)
Initiative amendments	−0.35	−0.39*	−0.25	−0.25
	(0.19)	(0.18)	(0.14)	(0.14)
Limit on amendments	−0.68*	−0.64*	−0.48*	−0.51*
	(0.30)	(0.31)	(0.24)	(0.23)
Unilateral majority			0.0068	
			(0.11)	
Republican seat share			0.012*	0.012*
			(0.0036)	(0.0036)
Total legislative days			−0.0014*	−0.0015*
			(0.00064)	(0.00064)
Southern state			0.37*	0.32*
			(0.18)	(0.16)
Constant	−35*	−37*	−23*	−22*
	(10)	(10)	(7.1)	(6.9)
Observations	49	49	522	522

Notes: *p ≤ 0.05 (two-tailed). Negative binomial coefficients with standard errors in parentheses, rounded to two significant digits. The dependent variable is the number of amendments adopted within each state from 1994 to 2015 (3.3a and 3.3b) or per state-biennium with biennium dummies (3.3c and 3.3d). Alabama omitted.

Table 3.4 Voter Ratification of Proposed Amendments

	(3.4a)	(3.4b)	(3.4c)	(3.4d)
Dependent variable	Adopted	Adopted	Defeated	Defeated
Constitution age (ln)	3.1*	3.1*	2.4	2.4
	(1.6)	(1.6)	(2.9)	(2.9)
Constitution length (ln)	2.2*	2.2*	2.0	2.1
	(0.70)	(0.70)	(1.3)	(1.3)
× Age (ln)	−0.32*	−0.32*	−0.24	−0.24
	(0.16)	(0.16)	(0.28)	(0.28)
Population (millions)	0.014	0.014	−0.038	−0.037
	(0.011)	(0.012)	(0.020)	(0.020)
Percentage white	−0.013*	−0.013*	−0.013	−0.013
	(0.0052)	(0.0052)	(0.0086)	(0.0086)
Legislative complexity	−0.56*	−0.56*	−0.22	−0.23
	(0.16)	(0.16)	(0.25)	(0.26)
Ratification majority	−0.030	−0.030	−0.066*	−0.067*
	(0.017)	(0.017)	(0.030)	(0.030)
Seats in legislature	−0.0052*	−0.0052*	−0.0020	−0.0018
	(0.0015)	(0.0016)	(0.0021)	(0.0021)
Total bills enacted (ln)	0.15	0.15	0.090	0.090
	(0.10)	(0.10)	(0.18)	(0.18)
Initiative amendments	−0.26	−0.24	1.00*	0.86*
	(0.15)	(0.27)	(0.24)	(0.40)
× Signature requirement		−0.0046		0.028
		(0.044)		(0.060)
Limit on amendments	−0.54*	−0.54*	−0.72	−0.71
	(0.25)	(0.25)	(0.44)	(0.44)
Republican seat share	0.013*	0.013*	0.0048	0.0046
	(0.0037)	(0.0037)	(0.0062)	(0.0062)
Total legislative days	−0.00077	−0.00077	−0.00023	−0.00018
	(0.00063)	(0.00063)	(0.0011)	(0.0011)
Southern state	0.26	0.26	−0.16	−0.16
	(0.17)	(0.17)	(0.31)	(0.31)
Constant	−18*	−18*	−23	−23
	(7.0)	(7.0)	(13)	(13)
Observations	510	510	510	510

Notes: *p ≤ 0.05 (two-tailed). Negative binomial coefficients with standard errors in parentheses, rounded to two significant digits. The dependent variable is the number of amendments adopted or defeated within each state-biennium. Models include year dummies. Alabama and Delaware omitted.

I turn now to the side analysis that considers ratified and rejected amendments separately. Since *Book of the States* does not provide separate counts of referred and initiated amendments, I rely instead on Ballotpedia here.[26] Table 3.4 presents these models. To set a baseline for comparison, model 3.4a replicates the final model from Table 3.3 but using Ballotpedia's count of voter-ratified amendments rather than the *Book of the States* count of total amendments. I omit Delaware from all models in this table, leading to the omission of the ratification dummy, but the ratification threshold variable remains. A few coefficients and standard errors wobble slightly when compared to Table 3.3—partly because of the change in data source, partly because of Delaware's omission—yet the results resemble those reported earlier.

In the second column, model 3.4b adds an additional variable: the percentage of voters who must sign a petition for an initiated amendment to qualify for the ballot, drawn from *Book of the States*.[27] Among initiative states, this variable ranges from 1.26 to 10, with a mean of 4.7. This variable is set to zero in noninitiative states, so it must be read as an interactive variable with the dichotomous initiative indicator. As it happens, this qualification variable does not attain statistical significance, nor does its inclusion change other coefficients.

The latter two models use the same specifications, but replacing the dependent variable with the number of amendments rejected by voters per state-biennium. As can be seen, all variables lose statistical significance except for the ratification (super)majority indicator, and the initiative dummy gains significance.

4
Specificity and Judicial Review

In Federalist 78, Alexander Hamilton imagined judges having no "will but merely judgment" (quoted in Rossiter 1961, 464). Research has found judges to be more complicated than Hamilton expected.[1] Leveraging the institutional variance and large number of judges found in the American states, scholars have found that "state supreme court justices are not the mechanical appliers of law conceptualized by normative legal theory but instead are strategic actors deciding cases within a complicated environment" (M. G. Hall 2014, 337). Beyond conflict between partisan "will" and neutral "judgment," this complicated judicial environment includes interbranch conflicts, judges' personal characteristics and attitudes, diverse judicial selection mechanisms, and the legal substance of the laws and constitutions that judges must interpret.

Though overlooked by previous work, constitutional specificity further complicates this already complicated environment. State constitutions confer plenary power, so adding provisions to a plenary constitution can only reduce state authority, as shown in chapter 2. Each additional provision in a plenary constitution represents one additional Lilliputian cord, binding the state more firmly to a past generation's solutions to past problems. As new problems arise requiring new solutions, states will flail against these cords. This flailing may take the form of increased constitutional amendment activity, as shown in chapter 3. But it can also take the form of statutory or regulatory strategies that press constitutional limits, the subject of this chapter. If state supreme courts fulfill their duty and enforce the state constitution's constraints, then constitutional specificity will result in more frequent judicial invalidations of state actions. The statistical analysis presented in this chapter affirms this expectation, showing that judicial invalidations rise with constitution length.

This chapter also considers whether constitutional amendment or revision can counteract the effects of specificity. Frequent amendments do turn out to reduce invalidations somewhat, ameliorating some of the problems caused by constitutional specificity. On the other hand, recently revised (i.e., younger) constitutions exacerbate these problems. Though perhaps counterintuitive, this latter finding is consistent with the finding in chapter 3 that younger constitutions attract more amendments than older ones. Just as younger constitutions bring tenuous compromises, drafting errors, and other issues that can increase amendment rates, they can also bring uncertain language and judicial uncertainty that increase invalidations. A constitution's age and amendment rate therefore join with specificity to change the jurisprudential environment in ways that directly influence state supreme court behavior, with specificity having the strongest effect.

Literature on judicial review has scrutinized judicial selection mechanisms, judges' personal attitudes, pressure from the legislative and executive branches, and legal substance as influences on judicial decision-making. This chapter contributes to this broader literature by introducing constitutional specificity, amendment rates, and constitution age as additional considerations. Within the narrower context of this book, this chapter strengthens my general argument that constitutional specificity binds states to the past. Constitutional detail would pose no hurdle if officeholders and voters were content with the provisions inherited from a past generation of constitution writers. But when detailed constitutions lead states to more frequently amend their constitutions, as shown in the previous chapter, or to more frequently enact policies that cannot withstand judicial scrutiny, as shown here, then we must conclude that constitutional specificity presents an actual burden. Detailed constitutions must be problematic if policymakers seek so often to escape their constraints.

Four Approaches

State supreme courts exercise judicial review. Like federal judges, state supreme court judges can invalidate state actions for violating the US Constitution; unlike federal judges, state supreme court judges can also invalidate state actions for violating the state constitution. Each of the 50 states has erected a judicial system that broadly resembles the federal judiciary, but with important differences that have fueled a well-developed literature on judicial review in state supreme courts. Briefly reviewing this literature will clarify how my argument about constitutional specificity adds to it.

Existing scholarship views judicial review through four general lenses: the balance-of-powers, neo-institutional, attitudinal, and jurisprudential approaches (Langer 2002; Brown 2018a). The first two approaches lean heavily on the tremendous institutional variance found in the 50 states. The balance-of-powers approach, for example, explores conflict between the judiciary and other government branches. State supreme court judges defer more to the legislative and executive branches when they fear being ignored, punished, or overruled (Eskridge 1991; Epstein and Walker 1995; Epstein and Knight 1998; Brace, Hall, and Langer 2001; Langer 2002). Because state courts lack the authority to enforce their own rulings, their power rests on popular perceptions of legitimacy (Cann and Yates 2016). To protect the court's long-term interest, appellate judges who fear executive nonimplementation (M. E. K. Hall 2014) or court-curbing legislation (Clark 2009) exercise self-restraint.

The neo-institutional approach examines how features of the judicial branch itself change judges' incentives (Canon and Jaros 1970; Hall and Brace 1989; Brace and Hall 1990, 1993; Hall 1992; Leonard and Ross 2014; Bonneau and Hall 2016), with special attention to the varying ways that states select their judges (Bonneau and Hall 2009, 2016; Gill 2013). Some states elect their judges in partisan or nonpartisan elections; a few rely on gubernatorial or legislative appointment; and many use the "merit plan," where special commissions propose nominees and judges stand for occasional retention elections after taking office. Relative to judges selected by other means, elected judges write simpler opinions (Goelzhauser and Cann 2014; Leonard and Ross 2016; Nelson n.d.), favor their campaign donors (Cann 2007), respond differently to amicus curiae briefs and other lobbying efforts (Kane 2017), get reversed more often by the US Supreme Court (Owens et al. 2015), take a harsher stance against crime (Huber and Gordon 2004; Gordon and Huber 2007), issue rulings more in line with constituent preferences (Brace and Hall 1997, 2001; Brace and Boyea 2008; Lewis, Wood, and Jacobsmeier 2014), and change their behavior when mandatory retirement looms (M. G. Hall 2014).

The attitudinal approach asks how personal characteristics and attitudes affect a judge's behavior. This approach sometimes considers judges' sex (Boyd, Epstein, and Martin 2010; Gill, Kagan, and Marouf 2019) or professional background (Jaros and Canon 1971), but more often it examines their ideological or partisan predispositions. At both the state and federal level, conservative and liberal judges behave so differently that scholars can map their rulings onto ideological scales (Segal and Cover 1989; Epstein and Knight 1998; Brace, Langer, and Hall 2000; Grofman and Brazill 2002; Martin and Quinn 2002; Bonica and Woodruff 2015; Windett, Harden, and Hall 2015).

Finally, the jurisprudential approach returns to Hamilton's ideal of "mere judgment," showing how the legal substance of statutes, regulations, precedents, and constitutions constrains judges (Stumpf 1998)—with an assist from amicus briefs (Kane 2017). Putting it "quite simply, judges are constrained by law" (Langer 2002, 22). State judges react to the substance of state law (Fino 1987) and the facts pertaining to a particular case (Emmert 1992). Lengthier, more detailed statutes limit judicial discretion within a specific policy domain (Randazzo, Waterman, and Fix 2011). State constitutions differ in how they frame citizen rights, and these differences influence how state supreme courts rule on the death penalty (M. G. Hall 2014) and abortion (Brace, Hall, and Langer 1999, 2001). Legal scholarship on the substance and development of state constitutions also fits this jurisprudential approach (Gardner 1992; Kahn 1993; Tarr 1998; Tarr and Williams 2006a; Grad and Williams 2006; Williams 2009; Dinan 2006, 2018).

Together, these four approaches have shed great light on judicial behavior. Often, they work together; jurisprudential variables can interact with a judge's personal attitudes (Segal and Spaeth 1993; Kane 2017) and with institutional rules internal to the judiciary (Brace and Hall 1990), for example. Yet nowhere has this rich literature addressed constitutional specificity as a separate concept. Jurisprudential studies come close, but they engage with the legal substance of specific laws, constitutions, and rulings rather than contemplate constitutional specificity as a broader concept.

Constrained Discretion

Constitutional specificity constrains judges. The brief US Constitution provides only a general framework for federal governance. Its silence on congressional procedure, bureaucratic operations, and judicial structure preserves institutional flexibility; its lack of constitutionalized policies preserves policy flexibility. For better or worse, the vagueness of the Necessary and Proper Clause and the breadth of the Commerce Clause create openings for federal expansion into emerging policy areas. The Constitution has its flaws, of course, and a simpler amendment process would help remedy them (Levinson 2006). But its brevity and avoidance of detail preserve enough institutional and policy flexibility that it has endured despite its difficult amendment procedure.

A few state constitutions follow the US Constitution's model, but most are much more specific. For example, the 50 state constitutions contain a cumulative total of 309 different types of provision affecting legislative organization, power, and procedure; from this long menu, the median state constitution contains 26 legislative provisions (Miller, Hamm, and Hedlund 2015). States also elevate diverse policy matters to constitutional stature. The Utah and Arizona constitutions, written for desert environments, contain an article each on water rights. Colorado includes an article on funding and administration of the Great Outdoors Colorado program. California and New York include articles dealing with public housing. Washington includes an article on harbors. Various state constitutions address lotteries, alcohol, recreation, and transportation, as well as environmental rights, labor rights, social rights, and economic rights (Tarr 1998; Dinan 2006; Williams 2009; Zackin 2013).

Earlier chapters have already argued that constitutional specificity binds states to the past both by multiplying framework provisions that increase institutional inflexibility and by incorporating policy provisions that restrict the options available to officeholders. Research has already shown how statutory detail can limit bureaucratic (Huber and Shipan 2002) and judicial discretion (Randazzo, Waterman, and Fix 2011) specifically. Similarly, we should expect constitutional detail to limit state discretion generally. Adding provisions to a plenary constitution can only reduce the state's power, as shown in chapter 2, leaving the state supreme court to enforce narrower limits on legislative and executive actions.

Three examples will illustrate how specificity can lead to invalidations. All come from the mid-1990s, a period examined more closely later in this chapter. These examples come from Missouri, Louisiana, and California, which have some of the nation's lengthiest constitutions, at 69,000 words, 73,000 words, and 67,000 words, respectively.[2] These constitutions contain numerous framework and policy provisions that may seem innocuous when considered individually but, like the Lilliputians' tiny cords, aggregate to a substantial burden on government action.

Missouri's constitution includes provisions on legislative procedure, declaring, among other restrictions, that all bills must have a single subject stated clearly in their title. To give this provision teeth, the Missouri constitution further declares that no bill shall be amended sufficiently that it deviates from its original purpose. That is, the bill's original title must remain relevant and unchanged throughout the legislative process. In *National*

Solid Waste Management Association v. Department of Natural Resources, the Supreme Court of Missouri invalidated a statute for violating these procedural provisions.[3] A Missouri legislator had introduced a bill imposing new regulations on solid waste management. Shortly before the bill passed, legislators amended it so that its new regulations would also restrict hazardous waste management. The court ruled that addressing hazardous waste went beyond the bill's original purpose of regulating solid waste; moreover, because the bill's title referenced solid waste but not hazardous waste, the court ruled that the final bill violated both the "single subject" and "clear title" provisions. The US Constitution, like other brief constitutions, leaves questions of legislative procedure to Congress. Because Missouri elevates certain procedural questions to constitutional stature, these provisions increase institutional inflexibility, opening the door to judicial invalidation.

Louisiana's constitution grants local parishes independent authority to levy and collect taxes, providing further for a tax collection entity within each parish. The state legislature enacted a statute that would have consolidated motor vehicle tax collection into a single statewide office acting as agent for all the parishes. Under this statute, parishes would still levy their own motor vehicle taxes but would no longer collect them directly. A dispute ensued between a parish and the state over this statute, with the parish asserting its right to collect its own taxes free of state interference. In *Caddo-Shreveport Sales and Use Tax Commission v. Office of Motor Vehicles*, the Supreme Court of Louisiana sided with the parish, invalidating the legislature's statute for infringing on local governments' constitutional authority to collect their own revenues.[4] As in Missouri, a seemingly minor provision had the effect of tying the legislature's hands, preventing it from streamlining government administration and opening the door to judicial invalidation.

In California, the legislature once enacted a statute requiring pregnant minors seeking an abortion to obtain either parental consent or judicial authorization. The bill never took effect owing to a series of judicial holds as it worked its way through the state's court system. Eventually, the Supreme Court of California held in *American Academy of Pediatrics v. Lungren* that the state constitution's explicit guarantee of privacy, being "broader and more protective of privacy than the [implied] federal constitutional right of privacy as interpreted by the federal courts," conflicted with the parental consent statute and required its invalidation.[5]

In the Missouri and Louisiana cases, state supreme courts enforced framework provisions. In the California case, the state supreme court enforced a policy provision. In all three cases, detailed constitutional provisions restricted the options available to the state. These cases illustrate how constitutional specificity can lead state courts to invalidate actions that would have survived judicial scrutiny under a briefer, more general constitution. The point is not that each state happened to have one specific constitutional provision that drove up its judicial invalidation rate. Rather, these three constitutions contain many detailed provisions that aggregate into a tremendous burden, and in each of these cases, one of those many provisions became relevant. Constitutional specificity kills not with a single stroke but with a thousand small cuts. We arrive at this chapter's first hypothesis:

> H1: State supreme courts will invalidate more state actions if the constitution is lengthier.

Amendment and Revision

Perhaps frequent amendment rates can negate the burdens of constitutional specificity. After all, Versteeg and Zackin (2016) have argued that a lengthy constitution can be a viable alternative to a brief one if it is also easily amended. The US Constitution receives so few amendments that it reads almost the same today as a century ago. Even if we assume their magnanimity and wisdom, the framers were nevertheless unacquainted with many of the challenges facing modern American society. The Constitution's silence on major issues—privacy, abortion, assault weapons, sexual orientation, gender identity, electronic surveillance, antiterrorism and torture, campaign contributions, corporate personhood—has left Americans to battle over these matters by extraconstitutional means. Rather than amend the US Constitution, Americans argue whether to interpret it through originalist, textualist, purposive, or living approaches (Brennan 2017).

Detailed state constitutions deny citizens the luxury of meeting new challenges through these sorts of extraconstitutional conversations. Rather, constitutional specificity demands a steady stream of new amendments to keep pace with modern concerns, as shown in chapter 3. Most state constitutional amendments originate from state legislatures. As a result, legislatures that update their constitutions regularly ensure that their constitutions accommodate their statutory interests, reducing the risk of judicial invalidation.

State constitutional amendments ratified in November 2016, for example, addressed income taxes, e-cigarettes, election rules, the minimum wage, officeholder qualifications, conservation taxes, gasoline taxes, bail procedures, oil extraction taxes, alcohol, lotteries, technical school management, investment of state funds, victims' rights, hunting and fishing, property tax exemptions, medical marijuana, fireworks taxes, administrative rules, transportation spending, legislative salary commissions, campaign finance, and energy development. This "endless process of amendment is for state constitutions what judicial review has been for the federal charter" in ensuring they keep the constitution current (Keller 1981, 69). Without constitutional amendments as a safety valve, "the more likely it is that calls for change will be channeled into legal action."[6] This logic motivates this chapter's second hypothesis:

H2: State supreme courts will invalidate more actions if the constitution has a lower amendment rate.

Incidentally, the only analysis to focus specifically on the link between amendments and invalidations confirmed that judicial invalidations decline as amendments increase, but only to a point. Five states went against the trend, combining high amendment rates with high invalidation rates: California, Georgia, Hawaii, Louisiana, and Texas (Marshfield 2018, 118). However, this otherwise excellent study did not consider constitutional specificity; as it happens, four of these five "outlying" states have exceptionally lengthy constitutions.

Constitutional revision has murkier theoretical effects on judicial review than constitutional amendment. Thirty-one states have replaced their constitutions at one time or another, with Louisiana's 11 constitutions marking the extreme. On the one hand, we might expect old constitutions to have similar effects as low amendment rates, compelling courts to enforce antiquated boundaries on modern policy. By this logic, judicial invalidations should rise with a constitution's age. On the other hand, important differences between piecemeal amendments and wholesale revision suggest the opposite hypothesis, since "frequent change is not the same as fundamental change" (Tarr 2006a, 3). First, an entirely new constitution will lack judicial precedents guiding legislators and judges in their application of critical clauses, increasing invalidations as policymakers muddle through the new constitution's applied meaning. Second, an entirely new constitution covers so much ground that convention staff working through draft after draft may miss errors, infelicitous phrasing, or inadvertent conflicts with existing policy, any of which can provoke litigation leading to judicial review. Similar flaws are less likely to escape notice in piecemeal amendments as they work their way through legislative committee hearings, floor debates, and voter ratification, drawing scrutiny at each stage. In their guidebook for constitutional revision Grad and Williams (2006, 57) warn specifically about this problem:

> Inevitably, too, the drafter will have made certain minor, interstitial decisions to fill the gaps in policy instructions that, in all likelihood, emerged quite late in the drafting process.... And finally, there is always the possibility, particularly in a lengthy and complex draft, that the policy maker failed to convey his intentions accurately or that the drafter failed to comprehend them entirely.

Moreover, wholesale replacement invites logrolling in a way piecemeal amending does not. Just as an omnibus statute can bring together logrolled compromises on diverse policy matters that would not be enacted if considered separately (Brown 2012; Townsend 1985), an "omnibus" constitutional revision can bring together logrolled constitutional compromises that would not have survived consideration as separate amendments. Kogan (2010) reminds us that the logrolled compromises that lead to a successful revision convention can just as easily be spun as "poison pills" by those critical of what was given up. Though Kogan's purpose was to show how these poison pills can prevent a new constitution from being ratified in the first place, we can extend his argument to consider how these poison pills may influence constitutional politics even after a successful ratification. As circumstances change in the years after a new constitution's adoption, policymakers may seek opportunities to push the limits of these delicate compromises, prompting litigation leading to judicial review.

For these three reasons—lack of judicial precedents, drafting errors, and tenuous compromises—wholesale constitutional replacement may well have the opposite effect on invalidations as piecemeal amending, so that younger constitutions provoke more invalidations than older ones. This argument parallels the argument from chapter 3 about younger constitutions attracting more amendments. We arrive at this chapter's third hypothesis:

84 THE DEAD HAND'S GRIP

H3: State supreme courts will invalidate more actions if the constitution was adopted more recently.

Complications

These hypotheses about constitution length, age, and amendment rates derive from jurisprudential logic, yet other approaches can produce similar hypotheses, albeit with different causal logic. Most notably, Langer (2002) linked invalidations to amendment rates using balance-of-power logic, whereas I have linked invalidations to amendment rates using a different causal approach. Langer was interested only in a relationship between amendments and invalidations; she did not consider a relationship between constitutional specificity and invalidations, the primary focus of this chapter. Still, careful consideration of her logic will lead to refinements in the statistical analysis below that can disentangle her argument from mine.

Langer reasoned that an activist court could provoke the legislature into enacting retaliatory constitutional amendments, especially in states with low procedural barriers to amending the constitution; in turn, fear of retaliatory amendments could deter judges in those states from invalidating state actions. With a positive relationship in one direction (invalidations increase amendments by provoking legislative retaliation) but a negative one in the other (frequent amendments reduce invalidations by deterring judges), Langer's balance-of-power logic has complicated implications that her empirical analysis did not fully address.[7] Her statistical analysis looked only for the negative effect of amendments on invalidations, finding mixed results— perhaps because of interference from an overlooked positive effect running in the opposite causal direction. To avoid this difficulty, the analysis below will use instrumental techniques to isolate the causal relationship flowing from amendments to invalidations without interference from any relationship flowing in the opposite direction.

Still, because Langer's balance-of-power logic concurs with this chapter's jurisprudential logic in expecting amendments to decrease invalidations, the findings below must be interpreted carefully, with empirical results for amendment rates contrasted with results for constitution length and age. Strong evidence for H2 (amendments) but not for H1 (length) would be suggestive of Langer's balance-of-power logic, which makes a prediction only for amendments; strong evidence for H2 (amendments) alongside strong evidence for H1 (length) would be more suggestive of jurisprudential logic, which makes a prediction for both variables.

Separately, attitudinal logic could also imply an indirect correlation between constitutional features and invalidations. As ideological distance between the legislature and the court grows, judges' personal ideological preferences may motivate them to invalidate more legislative actions. Anticipating these invalidations, legislators who perceive ideological distance from the court may amend the constitution more frequently to give their statutory preferences greater weight. They may also seek to inoculate their actions against judicial review by moving their policy preferences from statute to the constitution, inflating its length. Failure to account for the ideological distance between the legislative and judicial branches could therefore bias the estimated effects of constitution length and amendment rates on invalidations. As a precaution, the analysis below will include a measure of interbranch ideological distance.

Research on judicial review draws on many other attitudinal, institutional, and jurisprudential variables. Unfortunately, the data source used in this chapter is available only as a single cross-section, precluding longitudinal analysis. When conducting a cross-sectional study of only 49 states, one must carefully choose which variables to include and which to omit. Omitting a variable will not bias a statistical model's results unless the omitted variable plausibly relates to both the dependent variable and a critical independent variable. Although past literature gives reason to believe that, for example, the method of selecting judges, a court's total caseload, judges' professional background, and legislative professionalism may correlate with judicial invalidations, these variables have little theoretical connection to constitution length, amendment rate, and constitution age, making it unnecessary to control for these variables in the analysis below. As a precaution, however, this chapter's analysis will include as a robustness check models that include some of the most plausible confounding variables, none of which winds up changing the results.

To summarize, a state constitution's length (H1), amendment rate (H2), and age (H3) can influence the jurisprudential environment sufficiently to change the rate at which state supreme courts strike down state actions. Lengthy constitutions limit institutional and policy options; rarely updated constitutions may insufficiently address modern policy concerns; and young constitutions may bring fragile compromises, drafting errors, and interpretive ambiguity. Any of these circumstances makes it likely that the state supreme court will find itself invalidating policy actions more often.

Analysis and Results

This chapter's primary dependent variable is the number of state supreme court invalidations per state, counting only invalidations that cite the state constitution for justification—including those that cite both the state constitution and the US Constitution. I rely on coding from the State Supreme Court Data Project (Brace and Hall 1999). Since this source spans only 1995 through 1998, I conduct cross-sectional analysis of 49 states, omitting Alabama. The primary independent variable is each constitution's length, supplemented by its amendment rate and age, measured toward the beginning of this 1995–98 period.

Some models add four control variables: a measure of the ideological distance between the legislature and the court, ranging continuously from 0 (no distance) to 2 (extreme distance); a dichotomous indicator coded 1 where state supreme court judges are chosen in partisan elections and 0 otherwise; a measure of the state supreme court's total caseload from 1995 through 1998; and legislative session length as an indicator of legislative professionalism. This chapter's appendix provides measurement details and descriptive statistics for all variables, as well as justification for choosing these specific controls.

I use Poisson regression to estimate the effect of each variable on invalidations while holding others constant. Because amendment rates may have a reciprocal relationship with invalidations, as discussed above, I use first-stage instruments derived from the previous chapter's analysis of amendment rates to isolate the effect of amendments on invalidations without interference in the other direction. Complete methodological details appear in this chapter's appendix, including examination of the instruments' properties. The appendix shows that the results are robust to a variety of alternative estimation strategies. Here, I focus only on interpretation of two final models: one with control variables, and one without. These models appear in the last columns of Table 4.2 and Table 4.3 (respectively) in the appendix.

To briefly summarize the statistical results: Whether with or without controls, the analysis finds a strong, positive, statistically significant relationship between constitution length and invalidations, as well as a

SPECIFICITY AND JUDICIAL REVIEW   87

moderate (but still significant) negative relationship between amendments and invalidations. Including the four controls mildly strengthens these estimated effects. Constitution age has a marginal but significant negative effect, but significance fades after adding controls. Of the four controls, only ideological distance has a statistically significant relationship with invalidations.

Using these statistical models, Figure 4.1 plots predicted judicial invalidations against constitution length, total amendments, constitution age, and interbranch ideological distance. The solid lines plot predictions without controls; the dashed lines plot predictions with them. (The ideological distance variable was treated as a control, so there is no solid line in the lower-right panel.) All four panels constrain the vertical axis to the same range to simplify visual comparisons.[8] Each chart plots its respective independent variable from its 10th to its 90th percentile, with other variables held at their medians.

Constitution length strongly influences judicial invalidations across its observed range. Looking at the upper-left panel's solid line, increasing (logged) constitution length from one standard deviation below the mean to one standard deviation above it—from 12,778 to 39,270 words—is associated

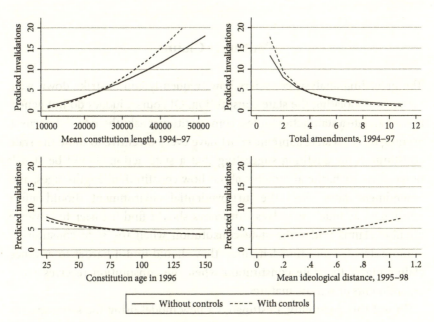

Figure 4.1 Predicted Invalidations in the Median State.

with an increase from 1.2 to 14 predicted invalidations.[9] This effect grows somewhat stronger as constitutions grow lengthier.

By contrast, amendment rates have sharply diminishing effects on invalidations. Increasing logged amendment rates from one standard deviation below the mean to one standard deviation above it—from 1.4 to 3.4 amendments—is associated with a decrease from 13 to 1.2 invalidations. However, this effect rapidly attenuates once a state exceeds roughly 4 amendments total from 1994 through 1997—that is, once a state exceeds an average rate of one amendment per year. Moving from 4 amendments to 5 is associated with a much smaller decrease (from 4.2 to 3.2 predicted invalidations) than moving from 1 to 2 amendments (from 18 to 9.4 predicted invalidations).[10]

Constitution age and ideological distance have weaker effects by comparison. Increasing logged age from one standard deviation below the mean to one standard deviation above it—from 36 to 166 years—is associated with a decline from 6.3 to 3.6 invalidations. The corresponding change in ideological distance (from 0.23 to 0.93) is associated with an increase from 3.2 to 6.4 invalidations. These are meaningful effects. Still, it is striking that constitutional specificity has a much stronger relationship with predicted invalidations than ideological distance does.

Petitioner Claims

The preceding analysis considers how frequently courts strike down state actions for violating the state constitution. Of course, judges do not generally invalidate a state action unless some petitioner asks them to.[11] Attorneys arguing before a state supreme court have every incentive to mine the state constitution for anything suggesting that a state action should be struck down.[12] As such, the arguments about how constitution lengths, ages, and amendment rates affect the jurisprudential environment should affect petitioners as much as judges. Attorneys should find it easier to advance credible claims under the state constitution when the state constitution is more detailed and thus lengthier; they should find it harder to advance claims under the state constitution when the constitution receives more amendments or is more mature.

To test this possibility, I estimated a new model using the same specification as the model discussed above, but with a new dependent variable.

Rather than predict invalidations, this model predicts the number of cases wherein petitioners claimed that a state action violates the state constitution. Obviously, claims that an action violates the constitution arise more frequently than actual invalidations. This variable ranges from 3 to 62, with a mean (21.5) nearly 5 times larger than the original dependent variable's mean and a standard deviation (12.6) more than 3 times larger. Methodological details and full regression results appear in this chapter's appendix.

Figure 4.2 plots predicted values from this new model, which included all control variables discussed above. Once again, I plot each independent variable from its 10th to 90th percentile, with other variables held at their respective medians. It turns out that Figure 4.2 is nearly identical to Figure 4.1 other than the expanded range of its vertical axis. Petitioners are much more likely to claim that a state action violates the state constitution when the constitution is lengthy. Constitutional claims decline sharply after the first few amendments, with a rapidly attenuating effect thereafter. Constitution age has a weaker but still significant relationship with constitutional claims. Petitioner claims rise somewhat as the ideological distance between the legislature and the court grows, but the effect is less robust than when modeling invalidations, fading in and out of significance with different specifications.

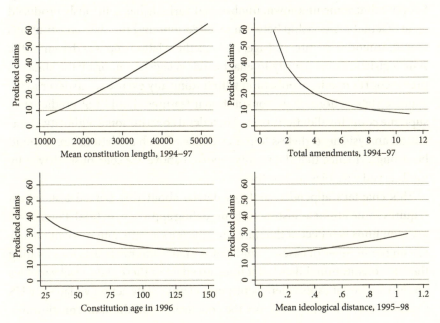

Figure 4.2 Predicted Constitutional Claims in the Median State.

A Critical Test

The preceding analysis has demonstrated a strong relationship between constitution length and judicial invalidations. As detailed in this chapter's appendix, this relationship persists through several modeling approaches. This relationship also persists whether examining actual invalidations or the petitioner claims that precede them. These results favor the conclusion that judicial invalidations vary meaningfully in response to the length, amendment rate, and age of the state constitution.

For readers who remain skeptical, I present here one additional robustness check, showing that this finding disappears when it ought to. The preceding section used as its dependent variable the number of state supreme court invalidations citing a violating of the state constitution. State supreme courts need not cite state constitutional authority when invalidating a state action, of course; they may also cite federal constitutional authority. There is, however, no reason to expect the state constitution's length, amendment rate, or age to influence the state supreme court's interpretation of the federal Constitution. To the contrary, all state supreme courts apply the same federal Constitution and the same federal precedents.

Suppose for a moment that the findings reported above are wrong. Suppose that some unknown, unobserved variable has spuriously produced an artifactual relationship between invalidations and the state constitution's length, amendment rate, and age. Perhaps the relationship was driven by the state legislature's propensity to enact careless legislation, or by the state supreme court's maniacal obsession with finding any excuse whatsoever to invalidate state actions. State constitutional features should not predict state supreme court invalidations rooted in federal constitutional authority. If statistical analysis nevertheless found evidence of such a relationship, it would be strong evidence that the results reported above are spuriously driven by unobserved variables such as these.

This chapter's appendix contains details about this critical test, which requires some minor adjustments in modeling approach. In brief, Poisson regression finds no effect of the state constitution's length, amendment rate, or age on the number of cases invalidated in state supreme courts for violating the US Constitution. Likewise, it finds no effect of these state-level variables on the number of cases where petitioners claim a state action violates the US Constitution. The analysis favors the conclusion that the state constitution's length, amendment rate, and age predict invalidations and claims under the state constitution but not under the federal Constitution.

Summary

Hamilton expected federal judges to have no "will but merely judgment." The extensive literature on state supreme courts shows that judges are more complicated than Hamilton's dichotomy allows. Judges have personal preferences; they react to credible legislative or executive pressures; they adapt to the judiciary's structure; yet they also take careful account of the relevant case facts, laws, and precedents. They are indeed "strategic actors deciding cases within a complicated environment" (M. G. Hall 2014, 337).

This chapter has added one additional dimension to that complicated environment, demonstrating how constitutional specificity can provoke judicial invalidations. The most detailed state constitutions are an order of magnitude longer than the shortest constitutions, containing hundreds of additional framework and policy provisions. Each additional provision may raise the risk of judicial invalidation only slightly, yet these hundreds of provisions aggregate into a genuine burden on the state's policy discretion. The lengthiest state constitutions witness more invalidations than the shortest as policymakers struggle against their countless Lilliputian bonds.

States can reduce the threat of invalidation by amending their constitutions regularly. Amendment rates have a substantive effect almost equal to (but opposite) that of constitutional specificity, and it does not take many amendments to achieve this effect. Over the four-year period examined here, the first two or three amendments adopted by the median state dramatically reduced invalidations; after that, additional amendments brought rapidly diminishing marginal returns. Because these predictions come from the median state, however, states that are far from the median on other variables—particularly states with the lengthiest constitutions—would need to adopt more amendments before encountering similarly diminishing returns. Though amendments reduce invalidations, revisions do not. To the contrary, older constitutions are associated with fewer invalidations than younger constitutions, though the effect is modest. Ideological distance between the legislative and judicial branches has a similarly modest effect.

These results derive from an analysis that employed instrumental estimation techniques to isolate the effect of amendments on invalidations without interference in the other causal direction. The findings reported here persist through diverse statistical specifications and after controlling for the most plausible confounding variables. Moreover, the results wane when they ought to wane: state constitutional specificity predicts state supreme court invalidations based on state constitutional authority but not based on federal constitutional authority. The analysis therefore favors this chapter's central claim.

The previous chapter showed that states adopt more constitutional amendments where the constitution is lengthier. This chapter has shown that state courts invalidate more state actions for violating the state constitution where the constitution is lengthier. If constitutional specificity causes policymakers to rely more frequently on burdensome amendment procedures rather than simpler statutory or regulatory procedures, and if constitutional specificity also causes statutory and regulatory policies to attract more frequent judicial scrutiny, then we must conclude that constitutional specificity imposes genuine, painful constraints. In the next chapter, I will show the implications of those constraints for state policy performance.

Methodological Appendix

This chapter's dependent variable is the number of state supreme court invalidations per state. I draw this variable from the State Supreme Court Data Project, which codes every state supreme court case heard from 1995 through 1998 on dozens of dimensions (Brace and Hall 1999; M. G. Hall 2014). I include all invalidations, whether from civil, criminal, or other cases, and whether targeting a legislative or executive action. The State Supreme Court Data Project coded whether written opinions explained each invalidation in terms of the state constitution, the US Constitution, or both. I count all invalidations that cited the state constitution for justification, regardless of whether they also cite the US Constitution. This data spans too few years to sustain longitudinal analysis, so I collapse to the total number of invalidations per state. All independent variables are measured at the state level, so nothing is lost by collapsing the Brace and Hall data from cases to states. The effective degrees of freedom for state-level independent variables would still be only as high as the number of states, even in a multilevel model including all 28,345 court cases (cf. Snijders 2005).

Constitution length, amendment rates, and age are measured as described in the appendix to chapter 1, with Alabama omitted and each variable logged to account for skew. To overlap but slightly precede the State Supreme Court Data Project's 1995–98 window, I use each constitution's mean length and total amendments from 1994 to 1997 and its age in 1996.

I calculate the ideological distance between the legislature and the state supreme court by subtracting the median justice's ideology score from the median legislator's ideology score, then take the absolute value. Judicial ideology scores are the collapsed four-year (1995–98) mean of Bonica and Woodruff's (2015) annual common-space estimate of each state court's median justice. Legislature ideology scores are the collapsed four-year (1995–98) mean of Shor and McCarty's (2015) annual common-space estimate of each legislature's median member; outside Nebraska, which has a unicameral legislature, the annual lower and upper chamber medians are first averaged together. Since judicial and legislative ideology scores both range from −1 (liberal) to +1 (conservative), my ideological distance scores have a hypothetical range from 0 (no distance) to 2 (extreme distance). Observed values range from 0.08 to 1.63, with a median of 0.52 and modest rightward skew.

Figure 4.3 contains descriptive scatterplots of judicial invalidations against the three constitutional variables, all plotted on log scales, with ideological distance included for comparison. Each plot includes a basic linear trendline, omitting any controls. There are no apparent outliers except Illinois, which has an unusually high invalidation rate for such a short constitution. Whatever influence Illinois has will bias the estimated effect of constitution length on invalidations toward zero rather than inflating it. Thus, omitting Illinois can only strengthen the results reported here.

Collapsing to cross-sectional analysis means I have only 49 observations. Various rules of thumb recommend including no more than one independent variable for every 10 to 20 observations, suggesting a maximum of 3 to 5 variables for this sample size. The literature on judicial review has identified many correlates of invalidations, but most can be safely excluded from this chapter's analysis. After all, an omitted variable cannot produce omitted variable bias unless it correlates with both the dependent variable and an independent variable of interest—and few variables are likely to correlate with both invalidations and constitution length.

To err on the safe side, some models control for three variables that have the most plausible hypothetical arguments for inclusion. First, judicial selection is coded dichotomously from *Book of the States* to indicate states that

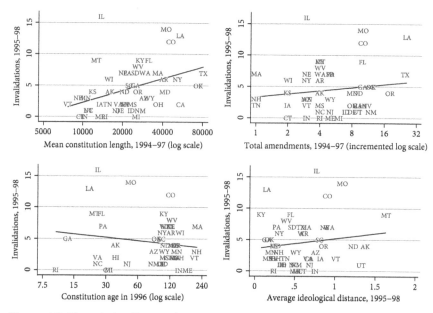

Figure 4.3 Descriptive Scatterplots.

choose state supreme court judges in partisan elections rather than by other means. The neo-institutional research cited above has paid special attention to these judges. Elected judges may have different incentives than appointed judges when it comes to invalidating state actions. This variable correlates modestly with the dependent variable (r = 0.33, p = 0.02) but not with constitution length, age, or amendment rate.[13] Table 4.1 presents a correlation matrix for all variables used in the analysis, with probabilities in parentheses.

The second control variable is total caseloads. States vary in how many cases reach the state supreme court, whether due to judicial structure (i.e., the presence or absence of an intermediate court of appeals) or due to provisions granting the state supreme court control over its docket. Based on the State Supreme Court Data Project, total caseloads range from 219 to 863 for rulings from 1995 to 1998, with a nearly normal distribution around the mean (562).[14] Caseloads turn out not to correlate with constitution length, age, and amendment rate, nor do they even correlate with the number of invalidations, which may come as a surprise. After all, we might expect the number of invalidations to rise with the number of rulings. On reflection, however, it becomes clear why these two variables do not correlate. Docket control and intermediate courts of appeal shield state supreme courts

Table 4.1 Pairwise Correlations

	Invalidations (ln)	Constitution length (ln)	Amendments adopted (ln)	Constitution age (ln)
Invalidations (ln)	—			
Constitution length (ln)	0.40 (0.00)	—		
Amendments adopted (ln)	0.14 (0.32)	0.54 (0.00)	—	
Constitution age (ln)	–0.16 (0.28)	0.05 (0.71)	–0.25 (0.09)	—
Ideological distance	0.15 (0.31)	–0.22 (0.14)	–0.01 (0.93)	0.01 (0.95)
Partisan judicial elections	0.33 (0.02)	0.19 (0.20)	0.20 (0.17)	–0.22 (0.12)
Total caseload	0.16 (0.26)	0.07 (0.63)	–0.08 (0.60)	0.02 (0.89)
Session length	–0.06 (0.66)	0.08 (0.60)	–0.12 (0.41)	–0.06 (0.68)

Note: Pairwise correlation coefficients shown with probabilities in parentheses.

from minor cases so they can focus on major ones. Major cases—and cases raising credible constitutional claims are major cases—generally reach the state supreme court regardless. Much of the variance in state supreme court caseloads reflects variance in how many minor cases make it to the highest court, not in how many major cases do. As such, state supreme courts that hear more total cases do not strike down more actions than state supreme courts that hear fewer ($r = 0.16$, $p = 0.26$).

The third control variable is legislative professionalism, particularly session length. Some legislatures may be more prone to enacting careless legislation that attracts constitutional scrutiny. There is no direct measure of legislative carelessness, but one variable that may proxy for carelessness is the length of the legislative session. State legislatures that meet for only a month or two each year have less time to vet bills and catch errors than states with year-round sessions. The analysis therefore includes the mean number of days per year spent in any kind of session by each state legislature from 1994 through 1997, measured as described in chapter 3.

Primary analysis. Table 4.2 presents results from four models, omitting any controls. The dependent variable is the total number of invalidations per

Table 4.2 Invalidations in State Supreme Courts under the State Constitution, 1995–98

	(4.2a)	(4.2b)	(4.2c)	(4.2d)
Specification	OLS	2SLS	LIML	Poisson
Constitution length (ln)	3.5*	7.0*	7.9*	1.7*
	(1.1)	(2.4)	(2.8)	(0.42)
Amendments (ln)	−0.98	−5.6*	−6.7*	−1.2*
	(0.84)	(2.7)	(3.3)	(0.39)
Constitution age (ln)	−1.1	−2.5*	−2.8*	−0.44*
	(0.71)	(1.1)	(1.3)	(0.19)
Constant	−24*	−46*	−51*	−12*
	(10)	(17)	(20)	(3.7)
Observations	49	49	49	49

Notes: *p ≤ 0.05 (two-tailed). The dependent variable is the total number of state actions struck down by each state supreme court for violating the state constitution from 1995 through 1998. Rounding to two significant digits. Instrumental specifications include legislative complexity, legislature size, and amendment limits in the first stage, in addition to other variables shown here. Standard errors in parentheses. Alabama omitted.

state. All models find a substantively strong, statistically significant relationship between constitution length and invalidations.

The first model ignores any potential for a reciprocal relationship between invalidations and amendments, using an ordinary least squares (OLS) specification without instruments. If, following Langer's (2002) logic, amendment rates have a negative causal effect on invalidations but invalidations have a positive causal effect on amendment rates, then we would expect these effects to cancel out in OLS regression. Indeed, that is what we see in model 4.2a: a null estimate for the amendment rate.

Though this book's primary interest is in constitution length, we can draw out better insights from a specification that appropriately models the relationship between invalidations and amendments. When good instruments are available, instrumental regression can disentangle reciprocal relationships, allowing a clean estimate of the effect of amendments on invalidations without interference from any reverse effect of invalidations on amendments. Good instruments must strongly predict the problematic independent variable (amendment rates) without being causally influenced by the dependent variable (invalidations).

Fortunately, this is a case where good instruments may exist. In its final cross-sectional model, the previous chapter identified seven variables that predict amendment rates, all of which are potential instruments here. Two of these variables, constitution length and constitution age, will enter the present analysis both as first-stage instruments and as second-stage independent variables.[15] Three other variables are used only as first-stage instruments. They are (1) whether amending the constitution by legislative referral requires legislative procedures more complex than a simple majority, such as a supermajority vote or concurrent votes in consecutive legislative sessions, with complex procedures reducing amendment rates; (2) the total membership of the legislature, with larger legislatures proposing fewer amendments; and (3) whether the state constitution limits the number of amendments the legislature may propose for voter ratification at each election.[16] I do not report first-stage regression results here, since they are similar to the models reported in the previous chapter.

All models in Table 4.2 other than the first employ these instruments. Model 4.2b presents results from two-stage least squares (2SLS) instrumental regression, providing strong support for all hypotheses. For these instrumental specifications to be appropriate, we must observe three conditions: that an independent variable is potentially endogenous, that available instruments are exogenous (the "exclusion restriction"), and that instruments explain a substantial amount of the endogenous variable's variance. Diagnostic tests suggest that model 4.2b clearly meets the first two conditions.[17] The third condition is less clearly defined, as it involves judging whether the first-stage regression has "good enough" fit. Readers familiar with debates over the value of R-squared and related measures will understand why this last condition is difficult to apply in practice. A soft rule of thumb suggests that instruments are unquestionably "strong" when the first stage regression has an F statistic of roughly 10 or greater (Staiger and Stock 1997). Regressing the (incremented and natural logged) number of amendments on all five first-stage regressors produces an F statistic approaching but not quite meeting this standard ($F = 7.4$, $p < 0.01$, $R^2 = 0.46$, adj $R^2 = 0.40$).[18]

When, as here, the instruments are valid but perhaps weak, limited information maximum likelihood (LIML) estimation has better properties than 2SLS (Staiger and Stock 1997). As it happens, the LIML estimates presented in model 4.2c yield the same substantive conclusions as the 2SLS estimates in model 4.2b. In fact, LIML produces stronger estimated coefficients. Other instrumental specifications not shown here, including instrumental tobit, produce similar results.[19]

OLS, 2SLS, and LIML all assume a continuous dependent variable, and all produce coefficients with the same straightforward interpretation. Strictly speaking, the dependent variable—judicial invalidations per state—is not continuous, but a count variable. Model 4.2d therefore reports results from an instrumental Poisson regression.[20] This is the final and most appropriate specification from Table 4.2, and the one interpreted in the main text.

Table 4.3 demonstrates further robustness by replicating all four models but with controls for partisan judicial elections, total supreme court caseload, interbranch ideological distance, and legislative session length. Inserting these controls mildly strengthens the estimated effect of constitution length and amendment rates in all specifications.

Petitioner claims. Table 4.4 replicates the models from Table 4.3, but changing the dependent variable from invalidations to petitioner claims—that is, the number of cases in each state (from 1995 through 1998) in which petitioners urged the court to invalidate a state action for violating the state action. Other than this change to the dependent variable, Table 4.4 replicates Table 4.3 exactly, with the same controls and specifications. For the most part, the same patterns arise here as in Table 4.3. In all specifications, constitutional specificity has a strong relationship with constitutional claims. In all but the naïve OLS specification, higher amendment rates are associated with fewer constitutional claims. Older constitutions are also associated with fewer constitutional claims. As before, the control variables contribute only minimally to these models.

A critical test. I show here that state constitutional specificity predicts invalidations based on state constitutional authority but not invalidations based on federal constitutional authority. Table 4.5 presents the results for the first part of this test. Model 4.5a predicts the number of state actions struck down in the state supreme court for violating the federal Constitution. Model 4.5b predicts the number of state supreme court cases in which petitioners claimed that a state action violates the federal Constitution. These two models are otherwise similar to the final models from Table 4.3 and Table 4.4, respectively, employing the same Poisson specification, the same first-stage instruments, and the same controls.

Surprisingly, models 4.5a and 4.5b do find a relationship between a state constitution's length, age, and amendment rate and the number of state supreme court invalidations under the federal Constitution. These estimated coefficients are generally smaller than in previous tables, and the standard errors are generally larger. Still, these unexpectedly significant results

Table 4.3 Invalidations in State Supreme Courts under the State Constitution, 1995–98

	(4.3a)	(4.3b)	(4.3c)	(4.3d)
Specification	OLS	2SLS	LIML	Poisson
Constitution length (ln)	4.0*	8.6*	9.0*	2.2*
	(1.1)	(2.7)	(2.9)	(0.40)
Amendments (ln)	−1.4	−6.9*	−7.4*	−1.6*
	(0.84)	(3.0)	(3.2)	(0.40)
Constitution age (ln)	−1.1	−2.7*	−2.8*	−0.37
	(0.70)	(1.2)	(1.2)	(0.20)
Partisan judicial elections	2.6	2.8	2.8	0.40
	(1.4)	(1.8)	(1.8)	(0.34)
Total caseload	0.0016	−0.0025	−0.0028	−0.00074
	(0.0029)	(0.0043)	(0.0045)	(0.00084)
Ideological distance	3.3*	4.8*	4.9*	0.99*
	(1.4)	(2.0)	(2.1)	(0.32)
Session length	−0.0040	−0.014	−0.014	−0.0033
	(0.0052)	(0.0084)	(0.0089)	(0.0017)
Constant	−31*	−58*	−61*	−16*
	(10)	(19)	(20)	(4.5)
Observations	49	49	49	49

Notes: *$p \leq 0.05$ (two-tailed). The dependent variable is the total number of state actions struck down by each state supreme court for violating the state constitution from 1995 through 1998. Rounding to two significant digits. Instrumental specifications include legislative complexity, legislature size, and amendment limits in the first stage, in addition to all variables shown here. Standard errors in parentheses. Alabama omitted.

demand some reflection, since there is no reason to expect a direct relationship between state constitutional features and the state supreme court's interpretation of the federal Constitution.

As it happens, these unlikely results reflect spillover effects of state constitutional features on state judicial behavior. Nationwide, Brace and Hall count 1,074 total cases from 1995 to 1998 in which state actions were challenged in a state supreme court under a state constitution. In 35 percent of these cases, plaintiffs simultaneously raised a challenge under the federal constitution. There is an exceptionally high correlation between the number of petitioner claims per state rooted in the state constitution and the number of claims rooted in the federal Constitution ($r = 0.74$, $p < 0.01$). Similarly, there is a strong correlation between the number of invalidations citing state constitutional authority and the number of invalidations citing federal Constitutional

100 THE DEAD HAND'S GRIP

Table 4.4 State Actions Provoking State Constitutional Claims, 1995–98

	(4.4a)	(4.4b)	(4.4c)	(4.4d)
Specification	OLS	2SLS	LIML	Poisson
Constitution length (ln)	11*	27*	30*	1.4*
	(3.7)	(9.5)	(11)	(0.36)
Amendments (ln)	−4.2	−24*	−27*	−1.2*
	(2.7)	(10)	(12)	(0.30)
Constitution age (ln)	−6.1*	−12*	−13*	−0.48*
	(2.3)	(4.2)	(4.6)	(0.12)
Partisan judicial elections	6.6	7.2	7.3	0.24
	(4.5)	(6.2)	(6.7)	(0.29)
Total caseload	0.016	−0.00092	−0.00092	0.00015
	(0.0093)	(0.015)	(0.016)	(0.00054)
Ideological distance	6.1	11	12	0.62*
	(4.6)	(6.8)	(7.4)	(0.29)
Session length	−0.010	−0.045	−0.049	−0.0022*
	(0.017)	(0.029)	(0.032)	(0.0011)
Constant	−65	−164*	−176*	−6.9*
	(33)	(66)	(73)	(3.0)
Observations	49	49	49	49

Notes: *p ≤ 0.05 (two-tailed). The dependent variable is the total number of cases heard in state supreme courts from 1995 through 1998 wherein petitioners raised claims that the state constitution had been infringed. Rounding to two significant digits. Instrumental specifications include legislative complexity, legislature size, and amendment limits in the first stage, in addition to all variables shown here. Standard errors in parentheses. Alabama omitted.

authority (r = 0.52, p < 0.01)—bearing in mind that a single ruling can cite both types of authority.

When a case features petitioner claims rooted in both the state constitution and the federal Constitution, the State Supreme Court Data Project codes it positively on both variables. The same applies to invalidations that cite both state constitutional authority and federal constitutional authority. Thus, the surprising results in models 4.5a and 4.5b may reflect mere overlap between these two variables caused by attorneys attempting to beef up their state constitutional claims with federal claims and judges following suit by citing both types of constitutional authority to defend their invalidations.

The latter two models in Table 4.5 control directly for this overlap between state and federal authority. Like model 4.5a, model 4.5c predicts the number of state supreme court invalidations that cite federal constitutional authority—but controlling this time for the number of invalidations within

Table 4.5 Invalidations and Claims in State Supreme Court under the US Constitution, 1995–98

	(4.5a)	(4.5b)	(4.5c)	(4.5d)
Specification	Poisson	Poisson	Poisson	Poisson
Dependent variable	Invalidations	Claims	Invalidations	Claims
Constitution length (ln)	0.97*	1.0*	−0.21	−0.13
	(0.49)	(0.33)	(0.54)	(0.27)
Amendments (ln)	−0.87*	−0.82*	0.0064	0.12
	(0.41)	(0.30)	(0.46)	(0.23)
Constitution age (ln)	−0.43	−0.41*	−0.048	−0.018
	(0.23)	(0.11)	(0.28)	(0.12)
Partisan judicial elections	−0.070	0.23	−0.54	−0.12
	(0.45)	(0.25)	(0.43)	(0.11)
Total caseload	−0.00036	0.00038	0.00098	0.00060
	(0.0012)	(0.00048)	(0.0011)	(0.00040)
Ideological distance	−0.025	0.24	−0.79	−0.13
	(0.36)	(0.27)	(0.48)	(0.19)
Session length	0.00016	−0.00063	0.0019	0.0012*
	(0.0017)	(0.00092)	(0.0015)	(0.00057)
State invalidations			0.17*	
			(0.050)	
State claims				0.032*
				(0.0037)
Constant	−5.6	−4.5	1.7	2.6
	(3.5)	(2.6)	(3.5)	(1.8)
Observations	49	49	49	49

Notes: *$p \leq 0.05$ (two-tailed). The dependent variable "invalidations" is the total number of invalidations by the state supreme court based on federal constitutional authority from 1995 through 1998. The dependent variable "claims" is the number of state supreme court cases wherein petitioners raised claims that the federal Constitution had been infringed during the same years. Rounding to two significant digits. First-stage variables include legislative complexity, legislature size, and amendment limits, in addition to all variables shown here. Standard errors in parentheses. Alabama omitted.

each state that cite state constitutional authority. This new control has a strong relationship with the dependent variable. More to the point, inserting this control causes the state constitution's length, amendment rate, and age to lose any relationship with the dependent variable. All three coefficients drop nearly to zero, and two see their signs reverse. Likewise, model 4.5d replicates model 4.5b, predicting the number of state supreme court cases featuring petitioner claims rooted in the federal Constitution—but controlling this time for the number of cases featuring petitioner claims rooted in

Table 4.6 Invalidations and Claims under State Constitutions, 1995–98

	(4.6a)	(4.6b)
Specification	Poisson	Poisson
Dependent variable	Invalidations	Claims
Constitution length (ln)	1.7*	1.0*
	(0.43)	(0.30)
Amendments (ln)	−0.88*	−0.82*
	(0.44)	(0.28)
Constitution age (ln)	0.025	−0.32*
	(0.28)	(0.12)
Partisan judicial elections	0.34	0.024
	(0.30)	(0.24)
Total caseload	−0.00058	0.00016
	(0.00076)	(0.00043)
Ideological distance	1.1*	0.46*
	(0.26)	(0.22)
Session length	−0.0050*	−0.0017*
	(0.0018)	(0.00084)
Federal invalidations	0.31*	
	(0.10)	
Federal claims		0.028*
		(0.011)
Constant	−15*	−4.7*
	(3.2)	(2.2)
Observations	49	49

Notes: *p ≤ 0.05 (two-tailed). The dependent variable "invalidations" is the total number of invalidations by the state supreme court based on state constitutional authority from 1995 through 1998. The dependent variable "claims" is the number of state supreme court cases wherein petitioners raised claims that the state constitution had been infringed during the same years. Rounding to two significant digits. First-stage variables include legislative complexity, legislature size, and amendment limits, in addition to all variables shown here. Standard errors in parentheses. Alabama omitted.

the state constitution. Again, this new control has a strong relationship with the dependent variable. And again, inserting this control causes the state constitution's length, amendment rate, and age to lose their estimated effects.

Taking this one step further, Table 4.6 presents models showing that the inverse is not true. That is, adding federal constitutional controls to the preceding section's analysis does not wipe out the effects of state constitutional variables on invalidations rooted in state constitutional authority. Model

4.6a replicates the final model from Table 4.3. The dependent variable is the number of state supreme court invalidations based on violations of the state constitution. Unlike the earlier model, however, model 4.6a controls for the number of invalidations citing federal authority. Including this control attenuates the estimated effects of the state constitution's length and amendment rate. Nevertheless, these effects remain strong. (The state constitution's age ceases to have a significant estimated effect, but constitution age is of secondary interest.)

Similarly, model 4.6b replicates the final model from Table 4.4, with a dependent variable counting the number of cases wherein petitions claimed a state action violated the state constitution—but inserting a control for the number of petitioners claiming violations of the federal Constitution. Again, including this control attenuates the estimated effects of the state constitution's length, amendment rate, and age, but does not eliminate them. Comparing Table 4.5 to Table 4.6 favors the conclusion that the state constitution's length, amendment rate, and age predict invalidations and claims under the state constitution but not under the federal Constitution.

5
Specificity and Prosperity

If constitutional specificity binds states to the past, hindering efforts to adapt to modern circumstances, then states with detailed constitutions should experience worse outcomes than other states. Otherwise, constitutional specificity would be a matter of mere academic concern. This chapter examines the relationship between specificity and lived experience directly, showing that constitutional specificity harms common citizens who may not even be aware that their state has a constitution at all.

The book's argument therefore climaxes with this chapter. Chapter 2 showed that constitution writers during certain historical eras increased constitutional specificity with the explicit goal of limiting state discretion. Chapter 3 demonstrated that constitutional specificity causes states to more often resort to extraordinary amendment procedures rather than rely on routine statutory or regulatory processes, suggesting that policymakers feel so constrained by constitutional specificity that they seek to escape it. Chapter 4 showed that state supreme courts enforce the narrow constraints imposed by detailed constitutions, striking down more state actions where the state constitution is lengthier. Combined, these chapters demonstrate that policymakers working under the most detailed constitutions feel sufficiently bound by the past that they actively seek to escape those bonds, whether by amending the constitution or by enacting policies that test the limits of their circumscribed authority. Taking the next step, this chapter demonstrates that binding states to the past has measurable impacts on state performance, resulting in reduced policy innovativeness, lower income per capita, higher unemployment, and increased income inequality—not only cross-sectionally when comparing states, but longitudinally within states.

An emerging literature has raised the possibility of a negative relationship between constitution length and economic performance. This chapter makes both an empirical and a theoretical contribution to this work. First, it uses a harder empirical test to demonstrate more conclusively the connection between constitution length and economic performance. Existing studies have shown only a cross-sectional correlation between constitution length and reduced income per capita. Not only does cross-sectional analysis struggle with temporal causality, but it is also sensitive to omitted sociocultural or institutional variables that may lead to spurious results—and such variation is great among the nations included in existing studies. This chapter instead employs time-series cross-sectional data from 49 US states. Because these states are relatively minor parts of the highly centralized American political and economic system (Chhibber and Kollman 2004; Hopkins 2018), studying them presents something of a "least likely" case selection. That is, it seems unlikely that the length of the Tennessee, Connecticut, or Washington state constitutions should have much effect on state economic performance when so much economic policy comes out of Washington, DC. States, after all, do not have central banks, nor do states tax as much per capita as the federal government. Moreover, controlling for state and year fixed effects swallows up potentially confounding sociocultural and institutional differences—which, in any event, are far less pronounced than the cross-national differences that threaten other studies. All these considerations make it much less likely that a relationship between constitution length and economic performance will emerge in this analysis when compared to previous cross-national studies, biasing this chapter toward null effects. That this analysis nevertheless finds such a relationship breathes new confidence into past work.

This chapter's contribution is not merely empirical, though. It also adds to the literature by proposing a new theoretical explanation for the relationship between constitutional specificity and economic performance. Explanations offered in existing work cannot explain the relationship between constitutional specificity and economic underperformance found here, since the analysis below is able to account for mechanisms proposed in the past. As a result, the analysis strongly favors this book's argument that constitutional specificity harms lived outcomes by impairing the state's ability to adapt to changing conditions.

Cross-National Research

Very little work has examined the direct effects of constitutions on governance outcomes, and even less has considered the effects of constitutional specificity. To be sure, a great deal has been written about how specific institutional arrangements may influence economic performance, with attention to the economic effects of presidentialism, majoritarianism, democracy, and so on (Stevens 1993; Przeworski et al. 2000; Haggard and McCubbins 2001), but this research examines the institutions erected by constitutions rather than the effects of constitutions themselves. A typical example is *The Economic Effects of Constitutions* (Persson and Tabellini 2003), an important volume to be sure, but one that focuses not on constitutions so much as on the resulting institutions: presidential versus parliamentary governance, majoritarian versus proportional electoral systems, and so on. Persson and Tabellini's book could more accurately have been titled *The Economic Effects of Institutions*.

By contrast, a constitution's specificity is distinct from whatever institutions it may establish. Constitutional specificity reflects something broader about the delegation of authority from people to state, with detailed constitutions conferring less authority. Only a handful of studies, all cross-sectional, have contemplated a relationship between constitutional specificity and economic performance. Using constitution length as an arm's-length proxy for societal distrust rather than as a theory-driven variable in its own right, for example, Montenegro (1995) found a negative correlation with gross domestic product per capita. And employing gross national product only as a right-hand control variable when modeling constitution length cross-sectionally, Ginsburg (2010) likewise found a negative correlation—though his modeling approach assumed that the relationship ran from economic performance to constitution length rather than the other way around, a proposition I test and reject later in this chapter.

Most relevant, Tsebelis and Nardi (2016, 459) demonstrated a negative cross-sectional relationship between constitution length and income per capita among 32 OECD countries—that is, among "constitutional systems in which the text of the [constitution] does in fact regulate political practice." Seeking a causal mechanism, they explain the relationship between constitution length and reduced income through two premises. First, they observe that lengthy constitutions are more difficult to amend, at least among their OECD sample, than shorter constitutions; second, they observe that lengthy constitutions are in practice more frequently amended despite these higher barriers. Connecting the second observation to the first leads to "a fundamental point of [their] argument: Frequent revisions [despite higher barriers] indicate that a constitution is not simply garrulous, but also imposes significant negative costs on society" (467). When amendment barriers are high, "the very attempt to amend the constitution indicates that . . . overwhelming majorities understood and suffered from [their constitution's] shortcomings" (467). All this leads to a damning inference: pairing specificity with high amendment barriers reflects "at least in part . . . a deliberate choice by the drafters" (467) to lock in key provisions, apparently to protect their own corrupt interests. Tsebelis and Nardi therefore conclude that lengthier constitutions are necessarily poorer governing documents, or, as they memorably write, "A long constitution is a (positively) bad constitution."

Their argument and analysis are compelling, leaving little doubt that Tsebelis and Nardi (2016) uncovered genuine relationships within their OECD sample. Tsebelis (2017) later replicated these findings with a broader sample of national constitutions, concluding again that "long constitutions are restrictive." However, the foundational premises in Tsebelis and Nardi are apparently not universal, as they do not arise among the US state constitutions examined here. While it is true that lengthier US state constitutions receive more amendments regardless of amendment rules, as shown in chapter 3, it is not true that lengthier US state constitutions also have higher amendment barriers. To the contrary, there is no correlation whatsoever between constitution length and amendment procedures. If anything, the correlations run in the opposite direction: state constitutions are marginally shorter in states with complex amendment procedures than elsewhere (30,648 versus 41,397 words, $p = 0.14$); they are also shorter in states with amendment limits than elsewhere (30,858 versus 33,017 words, $p = 0.84$), though neither of these differences attains statistical significance.[1] More to the point, Tsebelis and Nardi's argument requires that corruption correlate with constitution length—but, as shown in chapter 2, there is no such correlation in the states.

Again, Tsebelis and Nardi (2016) argue that long (national) constitutions arise when corrupt, rent-seeking elites collude to write their own economic interests into the constitution and then protect these rents by imposing high amendment barriers, leading to a correlation between constitution length and economic underperformance. The preconditions assumed by Tsebelis and Nardi do not occur in the states; state constitutions are not lengthier where there is more corruption or where amendment is more difficult. As such, their theory would not predict any relationship between constitution length and economic performance in that context. If a statistical relationship between constitution length and economic performance nevertheless emerges within the states, then some other causal mechanism must be at work.

Specificity in the States

This book proposes an alternative causal mechanism linking constitutional specificity to economic underperformance that can apply to the states as much as to nations. Like most national constitutions, US state constitutions confer plenary power. That is, state constitutions are presumed to confer power to do anything not explicitly prohibited in the constitution itself. It takes few words to confer plenary power. Louis XIV needed only these: *L'état, c'est moi*. It takes more words to place institutional or policy limits on that power. Even among the US states, where the Fourteenth Amendment to the US Constitution has nationalized many civil rights and placed a floor on states' bad behavior, state constitutions vary in how many additional restrictions they place on state authority. As shown in chapter 1, adding specificity to a constitution or other legal document is costly, so differences in specificity imply meaningful differences in scope or detail (Ehrlich and Posner 1974; Elkins, Ginsburg, and Melton 2009; Ginsburg 2010). As shown in chapter 2, constitution writers have been most willing to bear these costs during periods of heightened distrust of political elites and of centralized authority, with constitutions adopted between 1870 and 1900 remaining much lengthier today than constitutions adopted earlier or later in the nation's history. These constitutions were expanded not to secure rents for corrupt elites but to restrict the people's grant of authority to the state, barring legislative majorities from working against popular majorities.

Constitutional specificity restricts state authority either by increasing the state's institutional complexity or by reducing the amount of policy discretion conferred on policymakers. However, states must continually adapt to small economic, demographic, and social shifts, and occasionally they must adapt rapidly in the face of recession, natural disaster, or pandemic. Detailed constitutions bind a state to a particular moment in time, limiting the state's ability to adapt to new situations and strengthening the dead hand of the past.

Some constitutional constraints target fiscal and economic flexibility specifically. Half the states have stringent balanced budget requirements, for example.[2] Some state constitutions contain tax and expenditure limits (Kousser, McCubbins, and Moule 2008). Others prevent the state from infringing labor rights, commercial rights, social rights, economic rights, or environmental rights (Dinan 2006; Zackin 2013).

California provides an apt illustration. Its constitution limits state use of property tax and sales tax, restricts budget growth, earmarks much of the budget to public education and other purposes, requires voter approval to take on state debt, demands a two-thirds legislative vote to impose new taxes or fees, and, despite all these restrictions, still mandates a balanced budget.[3] Until 2010, it also required a two-thirds supermajority to adopt a new state budget. As Levinson (2012, 5) writes, "There is a connection between the perceived deficiencies of contemporary government and formal constitutions.... To take the easiest case, almost no one believes that one can discuss California's problems without paying attention to the particularities of its state constitution." When the Great Recession struck, California's severe restrictions plunged it into fiscal chaos. The legislature found itself unable to muster a two-thirds supermajority to cut the budget, much of which was earmarked within the constitution anyway, nor could it raise taxes or take on debt, making it impossible to meet the balanced budget requirement.

Meanwhile in Utah, as General Fund and Education Fund revenues declined 19 percent in the Great Recession's first two years, legislators made corresponding spending cuts in a series of special sessions. These cuts enabled the state to stay ahead of declining revenues, preventing a deficit without raising taxes. For this feat, *Forbes* declared Utah the nation's "best managed state." Elected officials were quick to claim credit, but few recognized the constitution's role. The relatively lean Utah constitution was only one-third the length of the California constitution, preserving Utah's flexibility when fiscal disaster loomed. We cannot understand "the travails of many of our states, including the shutdown of the government of Minnesota or the chaotic government of California," without "knowledge of state constitutions" (Levinson 2012, 16).

Whether constitutional specificity reflects framework provisions that increase institutional inflexibility or policy provisions that reduce the range of options available to policymakers, a detailed constitution limits the state's ability to adapt. To be sure, there have been in the past and are today many poorly governed societies that would benefit from a more restricted government. However, my analysis, similar to that of Tsebelis and Nardi (2016), focuses on developed democracies that take their written constitutions seriously. As such, the concern in these systems is not with inadequate institutions but rather with ossified ones. Stated differently, the concern here is not with too few restrictions on government authority but too many. An analysis that looked at every polity, including autocracies, would obviously need to develop a different theoretical approach at the lower end of the political development spectrum. But at least among stable constitutional democracies, the foregoing discussion has a straightforward observable implication: detailed constitutions can go too far in restricting state performance.

The primary state performance indicators examined in this chapter are economic. Though states also address a variety of other policy concerns, including public education, healthcare, land use, professional licensing, pollution abatement, and criminal justice, economic performance receives the most consistent attention from both policymakers and the public. Moreover, economic performance has close ties to these other policy concerns, directly influencing the state's ability to raise sufficient revenues to meet its other obligations. The analysis will therefore examine each state's real GDP per capita, unemployment rate, and Gini coefficient of inequality.[4] We arrive at this chapter's primary hypothesis:

H1. Lengthy constitutions hinder economic performance.

Looking beyond economic indicators, the analysis will also consider each state's policy innovativeness. Walker (1969) once supposed that some states might be inherently more innovative than others, and he sought to identify the factors helping some states innovate while others stagnate. Gray's (1973) critique shifted this emerging line of inquiry from examining innovation within states to examining diffusion between them, inspiring a continuing series of studies exploring the conditions under which policies spread from one state to the next (e.g., Berry and Berry 1990; Shipan and Volden 2006; Nicholson-Crotty 2009; Boushey 2010). Recent work has revived Walker's original interest in innovativeness as a general trait of American states (Boehmke and Skinner 2012; Nicholson-Crotty et al. 2014; Karch et al. 2016). An innovative state is one that regularly adopts "a program or policy which is new to the [state] adopting it, no matter . . . how many other states may have adopted it" previously (Walker 1969, 881). On average, an innovative state "adopt[s] new policies sooner than less innovative states" (Boehmke and Skinner 2012, 304). If, as argued here, constitutional specificity limits the state's ability to adapt to new circumstances, then detailed constitutions should lead to reduced policy innovativeness. We arrive at this chapter's secondary hypothesis:

H2. Lengthy constitutions reduce policy innovativeness.

Though the theoretical focus here is on constitutional specificity, states could presumably compensate for an overly constraining constitution through regular amendments. After all, the previous chapter showed that regular amendments can reduce judicial invalidations almost as much as constitutional specificity provokes them. The analysis below will therefore control for each constitution's amendment rate, with the presumption that frequent amendments will, if anything, improve economic performance.

It is less clear what role a constitution's age may play as a control variable. In their analysis of constitutional survival, Elkins, Ginsburg, and Melton (2009) show in passing that older national constitutions appear to have higher incomes per capita than younger ones, in addition to other favorable outcomes. They write, "On average, countries are richer, more democratic, more politically stable, and experience fewer crises as their constitution ages" (32). On its face, their finding is consistent with arguments raised in the previous two chapters suggesting that younger constitutions may be more likely to suffer from delicate compromises or outright drafting errors, while older constitutions will have had such flaws corrected by amendment.

However, the link between constitution age and economic performance gets murkier with closer scrutiny. While it is clear why a young constitution's delicate logrolls might trigger corrective amendments or judicial invalidations, it is less clear why these logrolls would have economic effects. Moreover, Elkins, Ginsburg, and Melton (2009) do not demonstrate that older constitutions *cause* economic prosperity; to the contrary, they could just as easily be observing a survival effect wherein prosperous societies retain their constitutions rather than replacing them, or where the only constitutions that endure to a ripe age are those that avoided critical flaws from the start. For these reasons, I make no specific prediction about any causal effects of constitution age on economic performance, though I do include constitution age as a control variable. Other political and economic controls are addressed in the next section.

Analysis and Results

This chapter examines four dependent variables across states and over time—that is, at the state-biennium level of analysis. The first three outcomes are economic: each state-biennium's real GDP per capita, unemployment rate, and Gini coefficient of income inequality. The fourth independent variable, state policy innovativeness, comes from Boehmke et al. (2018). As described in Boehmke and Skinner (2012), this variable examines dozens of policies adopted over more than a century, tracking when each state adopts each policy. Once the first state adopts a novel policy, such as a lottery or indoor smoking ban, Boehmke and colleagues view it as a policy now available for adoption elsewhere and track its adoption in other states. States are coded as more innovative in a particular year if they have adopted more of the available policies than other states have. Policies range across the ideological spectrum, ensuring that this measure does not proxy for partisanship or ideology. Still, because these scores are new and relatively untested, I analyze them only as a secondary outcome, prioritizing the three economic dependent variables. Descriptive statistics and measurement details for these variables and others discussed below appear in this chapter's appendix.

This chapter's primary independent variables are each state-biennium's constitution length, age, and amendment rate, each logged to account for skew, with Alabama omitted. I lag these constitutional variables one biennium behind the various dependent variables to ensure that past constitutional features are compared to future economic performance and not the other way around. State constitutions are dynamic, creating an opportunity to see how changes in a state constitution might correlate with changes in state economic performance over a 20-year span. Among the 490 state-biennia considered here, constitutions grew longer in 106 and shrank in 48. Aggregating up to the entire 10-biennium span, 23 states lengthened their constitutions by at least as many words (4,500) as the US Constitution contained in 1787, and another 3 states reduced their constitutions by at least the same amount, a tremendous amount of ongoing constitutional development. During this time, the median state adopted a total of 18 new constitutional amendments, with a range spanning from 2 to 127 adoptions. Constitutions therefore have enough cross-sectional and longitudinal variance in their length and amendment rate to sustain longitudinal analysis. The series used here is even long enough to produce meaningful longitudinal variance in constitution age.

Time-series cross-sectional data sets present many advantages but also demand careful analysis. Careless model selection can change estimates profoundly, producing misleading results (Wilson and Butler 2007). Fixed effects estimation is more consistent than random effects when differences between units (i.e., states) correlate with variables of interest. I will use fixed effects estimation (i.e., a dummy variable for each state) since there is reason to expect such correlation.[5]

Among other advantages, these state fixed effects rule out competing causal mechanisms proposed by previous literature. Tsebelis and Nardi (2016) built their argument largely on a link between constitution length and the procedural difficulty of amending the constitution, with secondary attention to each state's tendency toward corruption. Because each state's amendment procedures and other core institutions are constant in nearly every state from 1994 through 2015, they are swallowed up in the state fixed effects.[6] Separately, Montenegro (1995) argued that stable, cultural differences in social trust might explain the (cross-sectional) relationship between constitution length and economic performance that he observed. State fixed effects would also capture these cultural differences. With state fixed effects included in my models, any relationship that emerges between constitution length and economic performance necessarily reflects causal mechanisms beyond those identified by Montenegro and by Tsebelis and Nardi.

More generally, state fixed effects will also control for any other cross-sectional differences that might drive a spurious relationship, as long as those features are mostly constant within each state. Thus, fixed effects control for state-to-state differences in legislative professionalism (cf. Squire 2007), constitutional culture (cf. Bridges 2015; Ginsburg and Melton 2015; Herron 2017), political culture (Elazar 1966), and any other regional differences. Some previous chapters have used regional controls, such as for the South. Those are unnecessary here, since there is no added value in including a regional dummy when I have already included separate dummies for each individual state. Including state fixed effects causes statistical models to isolate the "within" effect—that is, the average effect of changes in lagged constitution length on changes in economic outcomes within each state.

As for other possible controls, an omitted variable does not cause omitted variable bias in fixed effects analysis unless it correlates (longitudinally within states) with both the dependent variable and the independent variable of interest. That is, an omitted variable would need to correlate over time with both a state's changing constitution length and, for example, its changing unemployment rate. I include biennium fixed effects—that is, a dummy for each time period—to control for any national trends that might fit this description. I also include a few control variables that may plausibly meet this narrow condition. First, I control for the percentage of legislative seats held by Democrats in each state-biennium, scaled between 0 and 100.

Second, I control for the percentage of state GDP derived from natural resources, from trade, and from manufacturing, all scaled between 0 and 100. Third, I control for corruption rates in each state-biennium, following Tsebelis and Nardi (2016). Finally, the analysis controls for the percentage of each state's population who are Hispanic (of any race) or (non-Hispanic) Black in each biennium, scaled between 0 and 100, to account for possible impacts of immigration or racial discrimination. When the dependent variable shifts from economic outcomes to policy innovativeness, I include a few legislative variables also. Additional details appear in this chapter's appendix.

I estimate a separate ordinary least squares regression for each dependent variable, always including state and biennium fixed effects, with the additional precaution of clustering standard errors by state. Each model finds a negative, statistically significant relationship between (lagged and logged) constitution length and current economic performance. A lengthier constitution leads to lower GDP per capita ($p < 0.01$), higher unemployment ($p = 0.04$ one-tailed), and higher income inequality ($p = 0.02$ one-tailed). Complete regression results appear in Table 5.2 of this chapter's appendix. Here, I focus only on substantive interpretation. Figure 5.1 illustrates these relationships by plotting predicted values for each economic variable over

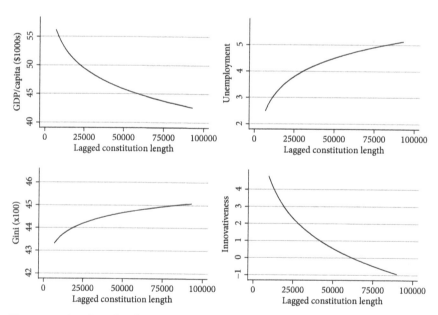

Figure 5.1 Predicted Policy Performance by Constitution Length.

the observed range of constitution length, with other variables held at their median values.[7] (This figure also includes predicted values from the model of policy innovativeness presented below; I discuss that portion of the figure shortly.) To standardize visual comparisons, each vertical axis has a range equal to two standard deviations of its respective outcome, coming out to $17,518 for GDP per capita, 3.8 points for unemployment, and 4.4 units on the Gini index of income inequality.[8]

Substantively, increasing the constitution's (logged and lagged) length from one standard deviation below the mean to one standard deviation above it (from 14,009 words to 46,630 words) leads to a large predicted drop in real GDP per capita: a 0.7 standard deviation fall from $52,480 to $46,222 when other variables are held at their medians. The same change in lagged length leads to a large predicted rise in the unemployment rate, a 0.6 standard deviation increase from 3.2 to 4.4 percent. As for the Gini coefficient of inequality, the prediction rises by 0.4 standard deviations, from 43.8 to 44.6. Real GDP per capita and unemployment have strong relationships with constitution length; the effect is modest but still meaningful for income inequality.[9] That these relationships arise within US states, even though so much economic policy comes from Washington, DC, makes them all the more remarkable—especially since fixed effects specifications have such strong internal validity.

Other constitutional features do not have meaningful relationships with these economic indicators. Lagged amendment counts have no significant relationship with GDP per capita or unemployment. Amendment rates do have a marginally significant estimated relationship with the Gini coefficient, but it is substantively weak and is not robust to alternative specifications, as detailed in this chapter's appendix. The appendix also tests a different approach to modeling amendment rates to account for longer-term trends, but this, too, finds no relationship. When it comes to GDP per capita, unemployment rates, and income inequality, frequent amendment activity does not counteract the damage done by constitutional specificity.

Likewise, there is no evidence that a constitution's age affects income or inequality, though older constitutions may have a weak link with higher unemployment. Interestingly, this weak relationship with unemployment runs in the opposite direction from that reported by Elkins, Ginsburg, and Melton (2009). Given that this relationship emerges with respect to only one of these three economic indicators, however, and weakly at that, it may be a false positive.

To be sure, constitution length is not the only variable contributing to these models, which include a variety of economic and demographic controls that have unsurprising relationships with economic outcomes. Economic reliance on natural resources has a greater impact on GDP per capita and unemployment than constitution length, as does the Hispanic share of the population.[10] All the same, it is remarkable that constitution length can have economic effects in the same league as these more obvious candidates. Moreover, it bears emphasizing that constitution length has a relationship with inequality even though the economic controls do not.

Results are similar when modeling the fourth dependent variable, policy innovativeness. As with economic outcomes, there is a strong relationship between innovativeness and constitution length. Increasing (logged and lagged) constitution length from one standard deviation below the mean to one standard deviation above it is associated with a decrease from 3.7 to 0.65 in the innovativeness score, a whopping 1.1 standard deviation decline.[11] This powerful relationship is apparent in the lower-right panel of Figure 5.1, which draws on Table 5.5 from this chapter's appendix. This innovativeness measure is still new to the literature, yet it seems plausible that constitutional specificity reduces economic performance at least partly because it first reduces policy innovativeness.

Granger Causality

My modeling strategy isolates the over-time "within" effect, showing that within the average state, changes in lagged constitution length are associated with changes in current economic performance. These specifications are conservative but do not necessarily demonstrate causality. Granger (1969) argues that we may take an additional step toward inferring causality by controlling for the lagged value of the dependent variable in each model. As it happens, lagged constitution length continues to predict current economic outcomes and innovativeness even after controlling for lagged economic outcomes. Importantly, the opposite is not true. That is, lagged economic performance and innovativeness do not predict current constitution length when controlling for lagged constitution length. Details appear in Tables 5.3, 5.4, and 5.5 of this chapter's appendix.

We may therefore say that constitution length Granger-causes economic and policy performance, but economic and policy performance do not

Granger-cause constitution length—and this is true for all four outcomes considered here. Granger's approach cannot provide a perfect test of causality, of course, since no observational analysis can conclusively demonstrate causality. Fully establishing causality would require randomly manipulating the length of actual state constitutions, a field experiment beyond this author's means. Taken together, however, the specifications presented here accumulate to provide compelling evidence of a causal relationship, with constitution length causing poor performance rather than the other way around.

Summary

Constitutional specificity brings, first, a more rigid and complicated institutional structure and, second, a narrower range of policy options available to officeholders working within those institutions. Detailed constitutions bind states to the dead hand of past, erecting governments less able to react quickly or completely to changing circumstances. Though this logic could apply to many government functions, this analysis has focused on economic performance specifically, finding that lengthier constitutions lead to lower real GDP per capita, higher unemployment rates, and higher income inequality. Constitutional specificity also leads to lower state policy innovativeness. High amendment rates do not counteract these effects. Detailed constitutions harm states no matter how frequently they are amended.

The state and year fixed effects employed in the longitudinal analysis make it unlikely that omitted social, cultural, or institutional variables drive these results. Moreover, Granger (1969) tests strongly suggest temporal causation: lagged constitutional specificity is associated with current performance measures, but lagged performance measures are not associated with current constitutional specificity. Remarkably, these findings arise within the US states, where so much economic policy comes out of Washington, DC. Collectively, all these considerations boost confidence in the internal validity of these findings; meanwhile, existing cross-sectional findings based on national constitutions boost confidence in their external validity (Montenegro 1995; Ginsburg 2010; Tsebelis and Nardi 2016; Tsebelis 2017). Together with this previous research, this chapter contributes toward an increasingly confident claim. Both in US states and among independent nations, both in cross-national and in time-series analysis, lengthier constitutions hurt economic performance, apparently by restricting policy innovativeness.

Causal mechanisms proposed in previous work cannot explain these results. Montenegro (1995) based his theory on cross-sectional differences in social trust, while Tsebelis and Nardi (2016) based theirs on variations in amendment difficulty driven ultimately by rent-seeking and corruption. While this chapter's analysis neither tests nor disproves these theories, it does control for them by including state fixed effects and other variables. Constitution length may well reduce economic performance through the mechanisms these scholars identified, but the findings presented here show that there must also be other mechanisms at play.

Constitutional specificity restricts the government's general ability to react quickly and completely to new situations, hurting the state's innovativeness and economic performance. If detailed constitutions impose such costs, we do well to reflect on who benefits. If constitutions grow only because of rent-seeking and corruption, then these diffuse economic costs benefit only a few elite interests, and lengthy constitutions are necessarily bad under all circumstances. But if, as argued in chapter 2, constitutions can also grow because of efforts to limit state authority—whether to protect citizen rights or to ensure political elites do not stray from citizens' preferences (Marshfield 2022)—then these diffuse economic costs may possibly have diffuse and defensible benefits. To put the most positive gloss on these results, we might see in them the difficult tension between democratic equality and economic efficiency—what Okun (1975, 120) once called "the big tradeoff," where "the conflict between equality and economic efficiency is inescapable." Such a trade-off would mean that lengthy constitutions are not inherently bad, but rather that polities should reflect carefully on how they wish to balance equality and efficiency.

On the other hand, chapter 2 shows that most of the modern variance in constitution length endures today as a historical accident with roots far in the past. If so, then constitutional specificity may have no upside at all, reflecting no more than a state bound by the same inertia that keeps inoperative provisions about poll taxes and school segregation in Alabama's constitution to this day. This inertia preserves countless other antiquated provisions in other state constitutions, simply because the costs of each individual antiquated provision are not sufficient to motivate an amendment campaign. Yet the low costs of those individual provisions aggregate like countless Lilliputian cords into substantial total costs. Constitutional specificity causes unambiguous harm, and, to borrow a phrase from Tsebelis and Nardi (2016), a long constitution really is a bad constitution. Lengthy constitutions strengthen the grip of the dead hand of the past.

To be clear, this chapter's analysis includes only politically stable, economically developed states. It does not speak to old questions about whether economic or political development should come first in economically and politically impoverished places. But within the developed and democratized world, these findings do suggest there can be such a thing as an overly constrained government. Moreover, this chapter does not imply that randomly removing constitutional provisions in the name of constitutional brevity will necessarily improve governance. As Grad and Williams (2006, 15, emphasis in original) write, "the best state constitutions are usually brief—but they are not the best *because* they are brief, but because they best meet the needs of state government."

Methodological Appendix

Real GDP per capita comes from the Bureau of Economic Analysis, unemployment rates from the Bureau of Labor Statistics, and Gini coefficients of income inequality from the Census Bureau's American Community Survey. Each of these sources provides an annual figure for each state, which I collapse to biennial means. I have rescaled Gini coefficients from 0 to 100 rather than 0 to 1 to improve readability of data tables, with higher values indicating more inequality. Policy innovativeness scores come from Boehmke et al. (2018). I multiply these innovativeness scores by 100, so they range from 0 to 22. State unemployment rates and Gini coefficients were unavailable for the earlier part of the data series, reducing the number of observations in models using those dependent variables. Figure 5.2 plots real GDP per capita (in thousands of dollars) and state unemployment rates by state and biennium, revealing plenty of cross-sectional and longitudinal variance.

I measure constitution length, age, and amendment rates as defined in the appendix to chapter 1. Lagging these variables reduces the analysis from 11 to 10 biennia, for a total of 490 potential state-biennium observations. I measure partisan control of the legislature as described in the appendix to chapter 1. Including this variable causes observations from Nebraska prior to 2009 to drop out of the model due to missing data. Measures of the percentage of state-biennium GDP derived from natural resources, from trade,

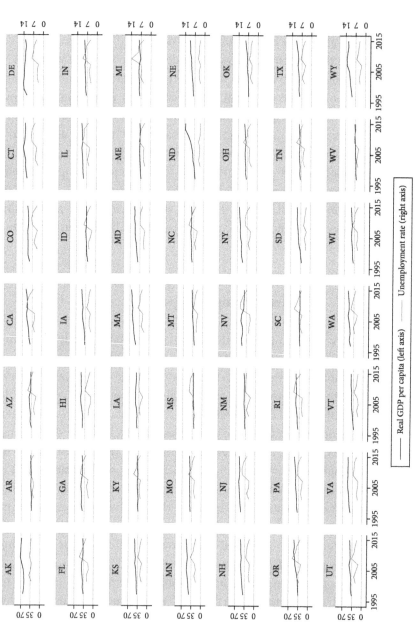

Figure 5.2 Biennial Income per Capita and Unemployment Rates.

Table 5.1 Descriptive Statistics

	Mean	SD between	SD within
Dependent variables			
Real GDP per capita ($1,000s)	45	8.0	3.6
Unemployment rate	5.9	1.1	1.6
Gini coefficient (×100)	45	1.9	1.1
Innovativeness	5.0	1.0	2.5
Independent variables			
Constitution length (1,000s)	31	19	4.7
Adopted amendments	2.3	2.4	2.1
Constitution age	107	54	5.8
Democratic seat share	49	15	7.0
Natural resources (% GDP)	4.5	6.3	1.4
Trade (% GDP)	12	1.7	0.62
Manufacturing (% GDP)	12	5.4	1.7
Corruption per million	4.1	2.3	2.8
Hispanic (% population)	9.5	9.5	1.9
Black (% population)	9.8	9.3	0.46

and from manufacturing were obtained from the US Bureau of Economic Analysis. Corruption is measured as described in chapter 2. Racial and ethnic variables drawn from the US Census Bureau. Descriptive statistics appear in Table 5.1, which provides the mean, cross-sectional ("between") standard deviation, and longitudinal ("within") standard deviation for each variable. All these measures exhibit ample variance both between and within states, supporting their inclusion in this analysis.

Results: Economic outcomes. Table 5.2 presents results for each economic outcome using ordinary least squares regression with state and biennium fixed effects, clustering standard errors by state. All three models show a negative relationship between constitution length and economic performance. The effect is more substantively modest for income inequality. Similar results arise when estimating these models using random effects analysis omitting state and biennium fixed effects, at least for the primary variable of interest: constitution length. Where differences do arise, fixed effects coefficients are more consistent; as such, only these results are presented here. Moreover, the Hausman test does not support random effects

Table 5.2 Economic Outcomes and Constitutional Specificity

	(5.2a)	(5.2b)	(5.2c)
Dependent variable	GDP/capita ($1,000s)	Unemployment	Gini (×100)
Constitution length (ln), lagged	−5.2* (1.3)	1.0† (0.55)	0.68* (0.32)
Amendments adopted (ln), lagged	0.096 (0.14)	−0.0069 (0.082)	0.12* (0.062)
Constitution age (ln), lagged	2.0 (2.7)	1.9† (0.98)	0.76 (0.75)
Democratic share of legislature	−0.0026 (0.027)	0.0017 (0.010)	0.0042 (0.0080)
Natural resources (% GDP)	0.92* (0.33)	−0.15* (0.046)	−0.036 (0.033)
Trade (% GDP)	−1.5* (0.48)	−0.22† (0.12)	0.057 (0.081)
Manufacturing (% GDP)	0.34* (0.11)	−0.078* (0.029)	−0.0033 (0.024)
Corruption	−0.0081 (0.064)	−0.012 (0.018)	−0.048* (0.018)
Hispanic (% population)	−0.56* (0.26)	0.32* (0.10)	−0.085 (0.066)
Black (% population)	−0.48 (0.43)	0.27† (0.16)	0.20† (0.10)
Constant	112* (24)	−15† (8.4)	32* (5.5)
Observations	484	388	388

Notes: *p ≤ 0.05 (two-tailed), †p ≤ 0.05 (one-tailed). Ordinary least squares coefficients with standard errors (clustered by state) in parentheses, rounded to two significant digits. Models include state and biennium fixed effects. Alabama omitted.

analysis, at least when estimating GDP per capita (p < 0.01). As an interesting sidelight, one feature of random effects analysis is that the models estimate the cross-sectional and longitudinal fit independently, with separate estimates of the "within R-squared" and "between R-squared." These values are 0.45 (within R^2) and 0.02 (between R^2) when estimating GDP per capita, 0.22 (within R^2) and 0.21 (between R^2) when estimating unemployment, and 0.60 (within R^2) and 0.25 (between R^2) when estimating income inequality, suggesting that these findings are driven primarily by longitudinal variance within states rather than cross-sectional differences between them.

Table 5.3 Replication with Lagged Dependent Variables

	(5.3a)	(5.3b)	(5.3c)
Dependent variable	GDP/capita ($1,000s)	Unemployment	Gini (×100)
Dependent variable, lagged	0.62* (0.053)	0.20* (0.061)	−0.00095 (0.12)
Constitution length (ln), lagged	−2.2* (0.78)	0.82† (0.49)	0.54† (0.31)
Amendments adopted (ln), lagged	0.0040 (0.13)	−0.013 (0.094)	0.16* (0.060)
Constitution age (ln), lagged	2.5 (1.7)	2.2* (0.81)	1.1 (0.93)
Democratic share of legislature	−0.020 (0.015)	−0.0032 (0.0083)	0.0091 (0.0081)
Natural resources (% GDP)	0.63* (0.17)	−0.16* (0.048)	−0.040 (0.050)
Trade (% GDP)	−0.63* (0.30)	−0.26* (0.13)	0.044 (0.086)
Manufacturing (% GDP)	0.26* (0.067)	−0.074† (0.041)	−0.022 (0.026)
Corruption	0.013 (0.038)	−0.029 (0.026)	−0.041 (0.028)
Hispanic (% population)	−0.47* (0.14)	0.39* (0.11)	−0.094 (0.076)
Black (% population)	−0.60* (0.21)	0.25 (0.16)	0.15 (0.11)
Constant	41 (14)	−16 (6.8)	33 (6.6)
Observations	436	340	340

Notes: *p ≤ 0.05 (two-tailed), †p ≤ 0.05 (one-tailed). Ordinary least squares coefficients with standard errors (clustered by state) in parentheses, rounded to two significant digits. Models include state and biennium fixed effects. Alabama omitted.

Other constitutional features do not have significant estimated effects. Lagged amendment counts are entirely insignificant in models 5.2a and 5.2b. Though there is a significant relationship in model 5.2c, the effect is substantively inconsequential besides being in the wrong direction, with amendments worsening rather than reducing inequality. Moreover, the Bayesian information criterion (Raftery 1995) supports dropping the amendment rate variable from all models, including model 5.2c. Granted, the amendment variable counts only amendments adopted during a single

Table 5.4 Reverse Granger Causality Checks

	(5.4a)	(5.4b)	(5.4c)	(5.4d)
Dependent variable	Constitution length (ln)	Constitution length (ln)	Constitution length (ln)	Constitution length (ln)
Dependent variable, lagged	0.52* (0.058)	0.53 (0.075)	0.51* (0.072)	0.49* (0.070)
GDP per capita ($1,000s), lagged	−0.0044 (0.0028)	—	—	−0.0044 (0.0031)
Unemployment rate, lagged	—	−0.0033 (0.0073)	—	−0.0097 (0.0087)
Gini coefficient (×100), lagged	—	—	0.0071 (0.0087)	0.0052 (0.0083)
Amendments adopted (ln), lagged	−0.0022 (0.0079)	−0.0061 (0.0085)	−0.0065 (0.0087)	−0.0065 (0.0086)
Constitution age (ln), lagged	−0.20* (0.10)	−0.19 (0.12)	−0.20 (0.13)	−0.18 (0.13)
Democratic share of legislature	−0.0013 (0.00098)	−0.0014 (0.0012)	−0.0015 (0.0012)	−0.0014 (0.0011)
Natural resources (% GDP)	−0.0054 (0.0045)	−0.0072 (0.0054)	−0.0015 (0.0012)	−0.0043 (0.0061)
Trade (% GDP)	−0.013 (0.015)	−0.027* (0.013)	−0.026 (0.014)	−0.031* (0.014)
Manufacturing (% GDP)	−0.010* (0.0037)	−0.010* (0.0039)	−0.010* (0.0041)	−0.010* (0.0042)
Corruption	−0.0021 (0.0.0017)	−0.0020 (0.0021)	−0.0023 (0.0022)	−0.0028 (0.0023)
Hispanic (% population)	0.0033 (0.0070)	0.016 (0.014)	0.016 (0.014)	0.017 (0.014)
Black (% population)	−0.0084 (0.014)	0.014 (0.019)	0.012 (0.019)	0.012 (0.018)
Constant	7.0* (0.94)	6.5* (1.1)	6.4* (1.2)	6.9* (1.2)
Observations	436	340	340	340

Notes: *p ≤ 0.05 (two-tailed). Ordinary least squares coefficients with standard errors (clustered by state) in parentheses, rounded to two significant digits. Models include state and biennium dummies. Alabama omitted.

biennium, making this variable somewhat erratic. However, I also attempted these models using a smoother version of this variable that, for any given biennium, added in the number of amendments adopted for the preceding two biennia, producing a moving six-year total. This approach, too, found no meaningful relationship between lagged amendment activity and economic

SPECIFICITY AND PROSPERITY   125

Table 5.5 Policy Innovativeness and Constitutional Specificity

	(5.5a)	(5.5b)	(5.5c)
Dependent variable	Innovativeness	Innovativeness	Constitution length (ln)
Innovativeness, lagged	—	−0.035 (0.12)	−0.0011 (0.0019)
Constitution length (ln), lagged	−2.5† (1.5)	−2.5† (1.5)	0.57* (0.0077)
Amendments adopted (ln), lagged	0.11 (0.26)	0.23 (0.26)	0.00017 (0.0077)
Constitution age (ln), lagged	0.66 (4.0)	0.64 (4.1)	−0.081 (0.11)
Democratic share of legislature	0.058* (0.028)	0.058* (0.029)	−0.011 (0.00098)
Session length	−0.0036 (0.0024)	−0.0035 (0.0024)	<0.00001 (0.00006)
Total bills enacted (ln)	−0.032 (0.62)	−0.011 (0.66)	−0.0024 (0.018)
Seats in legislature	−0.30* (0.13)	−0.31* (0.14)	0.0087† (0.0046)
Unemployment rate	0.059 (0.21)	0.051 (0.21)	0.0068 (0.0085)
Hispanic (% population)	−0.39 (0.31)	−0.39 (0.32)	−0.010 (0.014)
Black (% population)	−0.026 (0.54)	−0.012 (0.53)	−0.0022 (0.018)
Constant	69* (30)	70* (31)	3.5* (0.91)
Observations	382	382	382

Notes: *p ≤ 0.05 (two-tailed), †p ≤ 0.05 (one-tailed). Ordinary least squares coefficients with standard errors (clustered by state) in parentheses, rounded to two significant digits. Models include state and biennium dummies. Alabama omitted.

performance. In fact, the amendment coefficient reported in model 5.2c lost its statistical significance in this alternative specification.

I also considered models that interacted constitution length with amendment counts or with constitution age, as well as a model containing the triple interaction between constitution length, amendment rate, and age. These interactions were not statistically significant. It is constitution length alone that has a persistent relationship with these economic indicators.

Granger causality. Table 5.3 presents specifications that control for lagged values on each dependent variable. In each model, the lagged dependent variable combines with the state and year dummies to eat up so much variance that little remains for the remaining independent variables to explain. The unsurprising result is that all coefficients decline in magnitude and some lose statistical significance. Despite all these considerations working against a significant result, lagged constitution length continues to predict current income per capita (p < 0.01), unemployment (p = 0.05, one-tailed), and income inequality (p = 0.04, one-tailed).

Table 5.4 demonstrates that the opposite is not true. Lagged economic performance does not predict current constitution length when controlling for lagged constitution length. GDP per capita, unemployment, and income inequality predict constitutional specificity neither individually (models 5.4a, 5.4b, and 5.4c) nor jointly (model 5.4d).

Results: Innovativeness. Table 5.5 presents models using policy innovativeness as a dependent variable. Because policy innovativeness depends heavily on legislative action, four controls deal with the legislature: the Democratic share of legislative seats, the number of days per biennium spent in any type of session, the logged number of bills enacted per biennium, and the total number of seats in the legislature. Previous chapters have discussed measurement of these variables and provided descriptive statistics. I also control for the unemployment rate and the Hispanic and Black shares of the population. Because Tennessee in 2015 falls near the median on policy innovativeness, state and year dummies leave this observation as the omitted category.

The first model in Table 5.5 finds a substantively strong relationship between innovativeness and constitution length. The next two models conduct the same Granger causality test as above. Model 5.5b replicates model 5.5a but includes the lagged value of the dependent variable (innovativeness) as an independent variable. Even with this change, constitution length retains its relationship with innovativeness. Model 5.5c flips the relationship, testing whether lagged innovativeness predicts current constitution length after controlling for lagged constitution length; it does not. As with the economic variables, then, it appears that constitutional specificity Granger-causes reduced innovativeness.

6
Evaluating State Constitutions

Previous chapters have shown that constitutional specificity harms states.[1] Detailed constitutions hinder economic performance and reduce policy innovativeness. Flailing against these constraints, policymakers working under detailed constitutions resort more often to burdensome amendment procedures. They also test the limits of their authority more often, leading to more frequent judicial invalidations. If constitutional specificity brings such harm, an obvious remedy would be for states to revise their constitutions, carefully revisiting past decisions about what to include and what to omit. This chapter departs from the book's broader focus on specificity to consider the willingness of American voters to support such reform.

At the federal level, conversations about revising the US Constitution are all but doomed from the start. Many Americans venerate it so highly that they "find the notion of seriously criticizing it almost sacrilegious" (Levinson 2006, 17; cf. Levinson 1988). Nearly all Americans (85 percent) call the US Constitution "a major reason ... America has been so successful," and the same percentage believe other countries should imitate it (Farkas, Johnson, and Duffett 2002). Three-quarters call it "an enduring document that remains relevant today."[2] Many label its drafters "inspired" (40 percent), while few call it "outdated" (20 percent) or "flawed" (19 percent).[3] The median American rates the US Constitution at 9 on a 10-point scale (Stephanopoulos and Versteeg 2016).

This chapter reports results from a survey experiment showing that Americans view their state constitutions more flexibly. In contrast to the "amendmentphobia" that prevails at the federal level (Mazzone 2017), this experiment finds that Americans favor frequent amendment and revision when it comes to state constitutions. Respondents prefer a more democratic approach to state constitutions than to the US Constitution.

More generally, this survey experiment also sheds light on the unique role the US Constitution plays in the American mind. Respondents know nearly as little about the US Constitution as about their state constitutions, yet they evaluate the two documents by different standards. Americans venerate the

US Constitution not for its substance but for its role in the nation's founding story, valuing it more as a patriotic symbol than as a practical governing document. State constitutions enjoy no such association with a vaunted past, freeing Americans to evaluate them based on their democratic attributes, particularly their age and amendment rate.

Founding Feuds

The US Constitution had scarcely taken effect before Jefferson and Madison began arguing about its future and the proper role of a constitution in a democratic society. A democratic constitution is something of an oxymoron, as argued in chapter 3, pitting constitutional stability against democratic responsiveness. Madison argued for stability, Jefferson for democracy. Despite taking opposing stances, both can claim some victory over the modern American mind, but in different ways. Americans today tend to view the US Constitution through the Madisonian lens but state constitutions through a Jeffersonian one. I will first review their dispute.

Only a few months after Washington began his service as the nation's first president, Jefferson wrote to Madison with the still provocative claim that laws and constitutions should die with those who wrote them:

> [N]o society can make a perpetual constitution, or even a perpetual law. The earth belongs always to the living generation. They may manage it then, and what proceeds from it, as they please. . . . They are masters too of their own persons, and consequently may govern them as they please. . . . The constitution and the laws of their predecessors [expire] with those who gave them being. . . . Every constitution then, and every law, naturally expires at the end of 19 years. If it be enforced longer, it is an act of force, and not of right. . . . [A] law of limited duration is much more manageable than one which needs a repeal.[4]

Jefferson pursued this argument with various interlocuters for decades. Writing to a British reformer in 1824, he recounted the "successive improvements" states had made to their constitutions over the preceding half century, several holding conventions to replace their initial attempts. Jefferson observed, "[W]e have not yet so far perfected our constitutions as to venture to make them unchangeable."[5] Writing to a Greek scholar in

1824, he advocated flexible amendment processes in addition to these periodic conventions: "A greater facility of amendment is certainly requisite to maintain [a constitution] in a course of action accommodated to the times and changes thro' which we are ever passing."[6] On another occasion, he condemned those who "look at constitutions with sanctimonious reverence, and deem them like the ark of the covenant, too sacred to be touched."[7]

This last criticism addressed, most directly, Jefferson's friend Madison. Writing in Federalist 49, Madison feared that frequent change "would carry an implication of some defect in the government," thereby "[depriving] the government of that veneration which time bestows on every thing, and without which perhaps the wisest and freest governments would not possess the requisite stability."[8] Though Madison endorsed the stringent Article V amendment process as a "constitutional road" for change under "certain great and extraordinary occasions," he remained skeptical about broader reform.[9] When it comes to writing a constitution, "it must be confessed that the experiments are of too ticklish a nature to be unnecessarily multiplied." It is hard not to see a criticism of modern state constitutional amendment practices in Madison's 1790 letter to Jefferson: "Would not a Government so often revised become too mutable to retain those prejudices in its favor which antiquity inspires, and which are perhaps a salutary aid to the most rational Government in the most enlightened age?"[10]

For all their disagreement about constitutional change, Jefferson and Madison had less to say about constitutional specificity—perhaps because neither lived to see state constitutions grow to exorbitant lengths.[11] However, others have applied their logic to support claims for or against constitutional specificity. Invoking Madison, John Marshall wrote that a venerable constitution should not reach beyond the "great outlines" and "important objects" of governance lest it take on "the prolixity of a legal code" that "could scarcely be embraced by the human mind."[12] Madisonian stability "works against constitutional specificity [because] it is generally easier for diverse groups to agree on broad standards than on specific policies" (Versteeg and Zackin 2016, 659; cf. Lerner 2011). Only "a frivolous people who are unable to distinguish between things that are truly important and things that are not" would burden their constitutions with detail (Gardner 1992, 820). Madisonian stability demands constitutional brevity.

Meanwhile, the "prolixity" that Marshall condemned seems at least acceptable (if not preferable) within a Jeffersonian paradigm. As discussed in chapter 2, state constitutions grew more detailed as 19th-century constitution writers sought to protect popular from legislative majorities. Indeed, Jefferson might see the higher amendment rate of lengthier constitutions as evidence of their more democratic nature. Short, rigid constitutions "endow constitutional interpreters with significant room to make, and potentially change, constitutional meanings," posing "significant problems for democratic self-governance" (Versteeg and Zackin 2016, 659).

Different Frames for Different Constitutions

Madison's view prevailed at the federal level, where the Constitution has become "a central feature of American 'civil religion'" (Levinson 1988, 90; see also Breslin 2009; Sink 2004; Lind 2011; Levinson and Blake 2016; Zink and Dawes 2016; Dawes and Zink 2021). Rather than "an outdated document that needs to be modernized," Americans see in their 18th-century charter "an enduring document that remains relevant today" (National Constitution Center 2012). Americans reflexively resist amending the US Constitution (Zink and Dawes 2016; Dawes and Zink 2021), impeding essential reforms (Levinson 1988, 2006, 2012, 2016; see also Dahl 2003).

Yet Madison's view failed to take hold at the state level—though not for lack of trying. As states have endlessly rewritten and amended their constitutions over the years, occasional dissenters have invoked language that Madison might confuse for his own. William Meredith, a delegate to the 1837–38 Pennsylvania convention, argued that amendments "ought not to be made on trivial or light grounds," and the process "ought not to be rendered too easy" (quoted in Dinan 2006, 40). A few years later, Delaware delegate Andrew Gray opined that a constitution "is not to be put on and put off as we would our coats" (quoted in Dinan 2006, 40). Volney Dorsey, a delegate to the 1873–74 Ohio convention, hoped his state's new constitution would "provide for something like stability," claiming that the state needs a constitution "which the people should become used to; which they may learn to like; which they may regard with a certain degree of reverence" (quoted in Dinan 2006, 40–41).

Ultimately, these dissenters lost. As recounted in chapter 2, states adopted increasingly streamlined amendment procedures. Eventually, all states made it easier to amend their constitutions than to amend the US Constitution, and partly as a result, all states now have higher amendment rates. Theodore Roosevelt endorsed this flexible approach in a speech to the 1912 Ohio convention, calling it "false constitutionalism" and "perverted ingenuity" to pretend "to give to the people full power and at the same time trick them out of it" through rigid constitutions (quoted in Dinan 2006, 51). State constitutions "have kept the Jeffersonian tradition alive, generally privileging the idea of progress and the desire to meet current needs over a commitment to constitutional stability" (Versteeg and Zackin 2014, 1670).

The vast difference in amendment rates at the state and federal levels serves as straightforward evidence for this claim, but we need not stop there; this claim that Americans view the US Constitution through Madison's frame and state constitutions through Jefferson's has additional observational implications tested later in this chapter. Before getting there, though, it is worth considering for a moment longer why Americans might view their different constitutions through different frames.

Optimistically, perhaps Americans base these different judgments on the different substance of their state and national constitutions. As it happens, though, there is little cause to suppose that Americans have come to the informed conclusion that the US Constitution deserves veneration while their state constitutions deserve flexibility, for the simple reason that few Americans know enough about either constitution to draw an informed judgment.[13] Only a bare majority of Americans even realize that their state has its own separate constitution.[14] Matters are not much better at the federal level. Even in self-reports, which are ripe for inflation, only 16 percent claim a "detailed" knowledge of the US Constitution; the next 66 percent—perhaps generously—claim only a "general familiarity" (Farkas, Johnson, and Duffett 2002). Nor do Americans seem to notice the lack of amendments to the US Constitution or the relative frequency of state amendments. In a representative survey administered in 2015, respondents guessed (on average) that the US Constitution had received 8.8 amendments over the preceding 30 years, exceeding the average guess for their respective state constitutions (7.5).[15] The correct answer was one: the Twenty-seventh Amendment, ratified in 1992. And all respondents, from all states, ought to have guessed that their state constitution receives more amendments than the US Constitution. These patterns make it hard to suppose that Americans have come to a reasoned decision to venerate the stable US Constitution while regularly updating their more democratic state constitutions.

If not informed judgment, then perhaps status quo bias explains why Americans would venerate the US Constitution but not their state constitutions. Psychological research has shown that people hesitate more to change an older status quo than a recent one (Samuelson and Zeckhauser 1988; Kahneman, Knetsch, and Thaler 1991). The US Constitution is a much older status quo than almost every state constitution. It is also older than every written national constitution—much older, since 94 percent of national constitutions were adopted within the past 100 years.[16] In part, status quo bias reflects risk aversion (Tversky and Kahneman 1991; Kam and Simas 2010, 2012; Kam 2012; Eckles et al. 2014), but it also reflects a tendency to attach normative value to things that endure (Eidelman, Pattershall, and Crandall 2010). However, clever experiments show that veneration for the US Constitution has deeper roots than status quo bias alone. Randomized experiments that account for status quo bias find that respondents show greater reluctance to adopt a policy when doing so requires amending the US Constitution than when it requires only passing a statute or even amending a state constitution (Zink and Dawes 2016; Dawes and Zink 2021). Apparently "there is something about [the US Constitution] per se that biases individuals against proposals that would result in [federal] constitutional change" (Zink and Dawes 2016, 537).

Rather than look to informed judgment or status quo bias, we should look to popular conceptualizations of the American founding story to understand why Americans apply a different standard to the US Constitution than to their state constitutions. The American education system enculturates students to the norms and traditions of American society. Critical to this enculturation is a founding story that starts with the Pilgrims, accelerates with the war for independence, and reaches its climax with near-demigods meeting in Philadelphia to craft an enduring Constitution. Societies around the world have been unified by national myths involving varying amounts of fact and fiction (Anderson 2006; Bouchard 2013). While other nations might look to a Bastille, a Great Pyramid, a Colosseum, a royal family, a Long March, or Abraham's foundation stone for tangible validation of their founding myth, Americans look to their Constitution as a political Shroud of Turin. Abstract support for the US Constitution rises with education (Hibbing and Theiss-Morse 1996)—not because Americans are especially informed about civics (Pew Research Center 2015) but because of increasing exposure to this enculturation.

Americans see the US Constitution more as a relic of the founding than as a practical governing document, leading them to project their patriotism onto their evaluations of it. State constitutions benefit from no such mythos, nor do most national constitutions. Even in states with lively founding myths of their own, like Texas and Utah, the state constitution plays only a minor role in the story. Americans therefore feel free to evaluate their state constitutions based on their attributes alone.

This argument that Americans apply a different standard to the US Constitution than to their state constitutions generates testable hypotheses. A Jeffersonian lens would favor a constitution that receives frequent amendments or has been replaced more recently; it may also favor a lengthier constitution. As shown above and confirmed below, Americans are generally ignorant about the amendment rate, age, and length of their state and national constitutions. Exploiting this ignorance, the survey experiment reported below randomly selects some respondents to receive information about the amendment rate, age, or length of the US Constitution and of the respondent's state constitution. All state constitutions are lengthier and more frequently amended than the US Constitution, and nearly all are younger. We may therefore expect that respondents would evaluate their state constitution more favorably when they receive this information about the state constitution's amendment rate (H1), age (H2), or length (H3). Moreover, the effect should be strongest in states with the highest amendment rates, most recent adoptions, or lengthiest constitutions—that is, where state constitutions are most different from the US Constitution. On the other hand, if Americans venerate the US Constitution for its link to the founding rather than for its attributes, then providing this information should have no effect on how respondents evaluate that document (H4).

Experiment and Results

I collaborated with my colleague Jeremy C. Pope to recruit a national sample of US adults through Amazon's Mechanical Turk service (MTurk). Additional results from this experiment appear in Brown and Pope (2018). Methodological details appear in this chapter's appendix. I present here an abbreviated discussion of the design and analysis, focusing on substantive results.

The questionnaire began by asking participants for their state and whether they happened to know whether their state has a written constitution. Half (52 percent) answered affirmatively.[17] On the next screen, those in the control group (30 percent) encountered this prompt: "We would like to learn more about how you view the United States Constitution. Here are several different things that people might say about the US Constitution. Please mark whether you agree or disagree with each statement." Other respondents saw additional information inserted after the first sentence of the prompt. Those assigned to the full treatment (30 percent) received this information: "As you may know, the US Constitution was written in 1787. It has been amended 27 times since 1787, with no amendments in the past 20 years. It now totals around 8,000 words, which means it can be printed onto about 15 pages."[18] Remaining respondents were assigned to one of three partial treatments (13 percent each) that received only the length (in words and pages), only the adoption year, or only the amendment rate (total and past 20 years). After reading their randomly assigned prompt, all respondents then answered seven evaluative questions about the US Constitution; question wording appears in this chapter's appendix. We used factor analysis to extract first dimension loadings from this seven-item battery. Higher factor scores indicate a respondent with a more favorable evaluation of the US Constitution.

On the next screen, respondents encountered the same prompt and the same battery of questions, but with each reference to the US Constitution replaced with a reference to the respondent's state constitution. For example, a respondent from Oklahoma assigned to the full treatment would have seen this prompt: "As you may know, the current Oklahoma State Constitution was written in 1907. It has been amended 165 times since 1907, with 42 amendments in the past 20 years. It now totals around 77,000 words, which means it can be printed onto about 139 pages." The study employed no deception; respondents received accurate information about their state's particular constitution.

The next few screens contained unrelated questions that are not discussed here. Following advice from Mutz (2011), the questionnaire then included two manipulation checks assessing whether participants who received information about the state and national constitutions understood and remembered it. The first asked respondents whether their state constitution is longer or shorter than the US Constitution. (All state constitutions are lengthier than the US Constitution.) Most (58 percent) of those who received this information answered correctly, compared to only 14 percent of other respondents.[19] The second asked whether the state or national constitution had received more amendments in the preceding 20 years. (All state constitutions received more amendments.) Again, most (62 percent) of those who received this information answered correctly, compared to only 19 percent of other respondents.[20] Low accuracy among those who did not

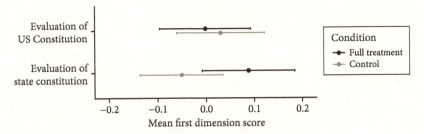

Figure 6.1 Effects of Full Treatment on Constitutional Evaluations.

receive this information demonstrates just how little the typical American knows about their state and national constitutions. High scores among those who did receive the information—even though they had answered several questions spread over multiple screens in the meantime—boost confidence that the findings reported below arise as a result of the randomization.

Figure 6.1 presents results from this experiment, comparing constitutional evaluations among respondents assigned to the full treatment or to the full control. Participants provided similar evaluations of the US Constitution regardless of experimental condition, as shown in the upper portion of the figure. (Dots show the mean evaluation from respondents assigned to a particular condition; bars indicate a 90 percent confidence interval. For evaluations of the US Constitution, the difference between respondents in the control and respondents who received the full treatment is statistically insignificant.) However, participants who received information about their state constitution's age, amendment rate, and length rated their state constitution more favorably than those who received none of this information (p = 0.04).[21]

Taking the next step, Figure 6.2 compares respondents who received only one piece of information—only the constitution's length, only its adoption year, or only its amendment rate—to respondents who did not receive that piece of information.[22] As shown in the upper panel, none of the partial treatments affected evaluations of the US Constitution, consistent with H4. However, the lower panel finds different results for evaluations of state constitutions. Consistent with H1, state constitutional evaluations rise significantly (p = 0.04) among those informed of their state's amendment rate.[23] Consistent with H2, evaluations also rise (p = 0.06) among those informed of their state constitution's age. As for H3, evaluations rise only insignificantly (p = 0.16) among those informed of their state constitution's length.

136   THE DEAD HAND'S GRIP

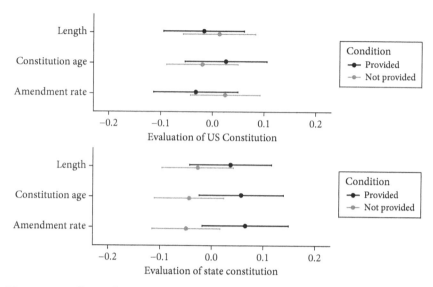

Figure 6.2 Effects of Partial Treatments on Constitutional Evaluations.

These effects are strongest among participants living in states with the lengthiest, most frequently amended, or youngest constitutions, as shown in Figure 6.3. Participants from states with constitutions longer than the median (24,000 words) reacted more strongly to information about their state constitution's length (p = 0.13) than participants from other states (p = 0.44), though neither effect meets the traditional threshold for statistical significance. Participants from states with amendment rates above the median (16.5 amendments in the past 20 years) reacted more strongly to information about their state's amendment rate (p = 0.02) than participants from other states (p = 0.34). And participants from states with constitutions younger than the median (adopted after 1890) reacted more strongly to information about their constitution's age (p = 0.06) than participants from other states (p = 0.26). These patterns support the conclusion that respondents evaluate their state constitutions through a Jeffersonian lens.

Summary

This book argues that lengthy constitutions harm states, resulting in higher amendment rates, more judicial invalidations, and reduced policy

EVALUATING STATE CONSTITUTIONS   137

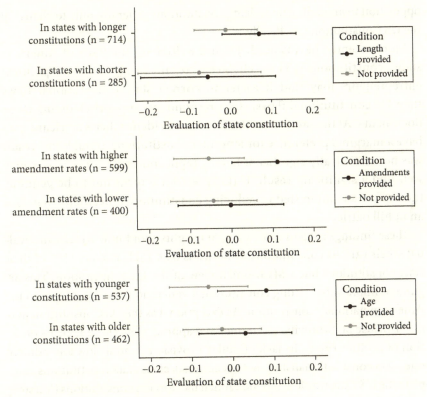

Figure 6.3 Heterogeneous Effects of Partial Treatments.

performance. This chapter contributes by gauging public knowledge of and opinions about state constitutions to estimate the prospects for reform. This is a challenging endeavor; only half of Americans even know their state constitution exists, and far fewer know anything about it. Accordingly, interpreting this chapter's results requires some caution.

That said, it appears that respondents react favorably to high amendment rates and recent replacement. Respondents randomly assigned to learn that their state constitution receives frequent amendments or was adopted recently evaluated their state constitution more favorably than respondents in the control group—and the difference is strongest among respondents with the youngest and most frequently amended constitutions. Levinson (1988, 2006) has long argued that popular veneration for the US Constitution prevents Americans from seriously considering essential reforms. Consistent with his view, these findings suggest that Americans do not have any opposition to amending or revising constitutions generally, only to changing the US Constitution specifically.

More recently, Levinson (2012) has written on the flaws of America's state constitutions. This chapter's results suggest that political entrepreneurs may find it easier to correct state constitutional flaws than US constitutional flaws, since respondents support changing these documents. At the same time, there is some evidence that Americans may have a marginal preference for lengthier constitutions; though this result was not statistically significant here, a replication with more power may well find a significant result. If this preference turns out to be genuine, then reformers interested in reducing constitutional specificity may face an uphill battle.

These findings suggest more general insights about how Americans evaluate their various constitutions. Americans take a Jeffersonian view of their state constitutions but a Madisonian view of the US Constitution. This argument implies that strong constitutional veneration may be unique to the American national Constitution. As exceptional as the US Constitution may be—because of its brevity, its enumerated approach, its endurance, its omission of positive rights, its lack of policy provisions, and its low amendment rate—US constitutionalism is not exceptional, since state constitutions complete the US Constitution and look much like foreign constitutions (Versteeg and Zackin 2014). Extending this insight, citizen evaluations of American constitutionalism may be less exceptional than citizen evaluations of the US Constitution specifically. In every state and in most countries, people have little reason to view their constitution as anything other than a practical governing document. Madison may have prevailed with respect to American views of the US Constitution, but Jefferson's approach may well prevail everywhere else.

Methodological Appendix

We recruited participants through Amazon's Mechanical Turk (MTurk) in June 2016, restricting participation to people in the United States with an MTurk rating of 90 percent or higher. Each participant received $0.40. MTurk is a nonrepresentative sample (Huff and Tingley 2015), but randomized experiments generally produce the same estimated treatment effects on MTurk as on other platforms (Berinsky, Huber, and Lenz 2012). Random assignment renders demographic controls unnecessary; as a precaution, Table 6.1 shows that groups are demographically balanced, especially the full control group and full treatment group, which contain a larger number of participants. Probit analysis of each treatment group against the control reveals no significant ($p < 0.05$, two-tailed) relationships for participant sex, education, ethnicity/race, ideology, age, partisanship, or length of residence in state, nor does treatment correlate with state-level constitutional variables.

We developed our seven-item constitutional evaluation battery by drawing on two existing sources. Five items came from polls reported by the National Constitution Center (2012). For these items, respondents "strongly agree," "agree," "neither agree nor disagree," "disagree," or "strongly disagree" with five statements: "The US Constitution is an enduring document that deserves our respect" (abbreviated below as *enduring*); "The people who wrote the US Constitution were only looking out for themselves" (*selfish*); "We should amend the US Constitution more frequently so that it addresses modern concerns" (*amend more*); "The US Constitution is an outdated document that needs to be modernized" (*outdated*); and "The people who wrote the US Constitution were wise and visionary" (*visionary*). The final two items in our battery come from Cann and Yates (2016). First, we presented respondents with two statements anchoring either end of a sliding scale: "Judges should base their rulings on what they believe the US Constitution means in today's world" and "Judges should base their rulings on what they believe the US

Table 6.1 Group Demographics

	All	Control	Full treatment	Length only	Amend only	Age only
N	999	304	301	131	130	133
Percent in group	100	30	30	13	13	13
Median age	32	32	34	31	31	31
Female (%)	51	53	48	48	57	51
Democrat (%)	52	53	53	56	49	50
College degree (%)	49	49	52	47	41	53
White (%)	75	74	78	76	77	74
11+ years in state (%)	77	79	76	77	73	79

Constitution meant when it was originally written" (*originalism*) The battery's final question asked, "Would you say the US Constitution is amended too much, not enough, or about the right amount?" (*too amended*).

Within both the state constitution battery and the US Constitution battery, correlations among the seven items are high (p < 0.01 in every pairwise comparison). Summary statistics for each item in each battery, along with demographic breakdowns by item, appear in Brown and Pope (2018). In short, Republicans, conservatives, men, and respondents over 55 give higher evaluations of the US Constitution across every indicator shown, with mixed effects for respondent education. Patterns are similar but somewhat more modest for evaluations of state constitutions.

Table 6.2 gives the factor loadings for the US Constitution battery, while Table 6.3 gives the loadings for the state constitution battery. In each case,

Table 6.2 US Constitution Battery Factor Loadings

	Factor 1	Factor 2
The US Constitution is enduring	0.57	0.54
Authors were looking out for themselves	−0.61	−0.46
Amend to address modern concerns	−0.81	0.32
The US Constitution is outdated	−0.85	0.10
Authors were visionary	0.65	0.51
Living versus originalist interpretation	0.71	−0.36
The US Constitution is amended too much	0.76	−0.41
Proportion of variance	0.51	0.17

Table 6.3 State Constitution Battery Factor Loadings

	Factor 1	Factor 2
The [state] constitution is enduring	0.60	0.59
Authors were looking out for themselves	−0.64	−0.45
Amend to address modern concerns	−0.78	0.41
The [state] constitution is outdated	−0.81	0.15
Authors were visionary	0.58	0.62
Living versus originalist interpretation	0.63	−0.41
The [state] constitution is amended too much	0.63	−0.49
Proportion of variance	0.45	0.22

items load heavily onto the first dimension, with predictable negative and positive signs. For both batteries, the second dimension appears largely residual. For both the US Constitution and state constitutions, regressing first dimension scores on respondent partisanship, ideology, sex, and age reveals strong relationships.[24]

7

Conclusion

States have revised and amended their constitutions endlessly since the nation's founding. This ceaseless churn has created "a mine of instruction for the natural history of democratic communities" where one may read "the annals of legislation and political sentiment . . . more easily and succinctly than in any similar series of laws in any other country" (Bryce 1888, 434). Legal scholarship has long worked this rich vein, but political science has more to do. For all the discipline's concern about legislative procedure, bureaucratic discretion, judicial structures, and public policies, political science takes less interest in whether those matters have constitutional rather than extraconstitutional stature.

This book steps back to consider what happens when states choose to expand their constitutions with institutional or policy details that might otherwise have been left to democratic discretion. Each additional provision added to a constitution may have little individual effect, but hundreds of provisions can aggregate like Lilliputian cords to bind a state. Detailed constitutions tie states to a former day's compromises, limiting their ability to adapt to changing circumstances. A certain amount of clarity is essential for any constitution to survive, of course. A constitution that fails to allocate government power among well-defined institutions would serve little purpose. In the states, though, we observe no cases of inadequate constitutional clarity—but we do observe cases at the other extreme, where the dead hand of the past keeps a stranglehold on the present.

In this book I have operationalized constitutional specificity as constitution length. Even excluding outlying Alabama, the lengthiest state constitution is an order of magnitude longer than the shortest. These differences did not arise by accident but "from a deliberate choice on the part of constitution-makers to employ specificity as a means of controlling their governments" (Versteeg and Zackin 2016, 664). State constitutions adopted in the late 19th century reached exorbitant lengths, resembling "a mass of codelike specifications" as popular distrust of legislatures and other political elites peaked (Keller 1981, 70). Popular majorities revised constitutions to constrain legislative majorities, seeking "to constrain the powers of the government and the legislature in particular" (Fritz 1994, 965). Even after a century of amendment activity, these historical differences endure today. State constitutions adopted between 1870 and 1900 remain lengthier on average than state constitutions adopted at other times, to the point that a constitution's age predicts its length better than any modern variable. This happy accident has allowed this book to treat modern variations in constitutional specificity as essentially exogenous.

The results are alarming. Chapter 3 found that constitution length affects amendment rates more powerfully than anything else. Burdensome amendment procedures do reduce amendment rates somewhat, but even the strictest procedural barriers cannot dam the immense reform pressures caused by constitutional specificity. Similarly, chapter 4 found that lengthy constitutions drive up judicial invalidation rates in state supreme courts. Together, these results show that constitutional specificity affects states not by a single blow but with countless Lilliputian cords. The more detailed the constitution, the more policymakers flail against these bonds, desperately resorting to burdensome amendment procedures and to policies that test constitutional limits.

Chapter 5 demonstrates that policymakers working under detailed constitutions are correct to feel so constrained. States with lengthier constitutions experience lower incomes per capita, higher unemployment rates, greater economic inequality, and less policy innovativeness generally. These findings arise even after accounting for state and year fixed effects, suggesting a longitudinal link within individual states between constitutional specificity and poor outcomes. Moreover, Granger analysis produces strong evidence that the relationship is causal: past constitution length predicts future economic performance, but past economic performance does not predict future constitution length. This important finding should give pause to citizens and policymakers in states with the most detailed constitutions, and also to reformers anywhere hoping to add new material to their state constitutions.

These results have relevance beyond the American states. State constitutions resemble typical national constitutions more than the US Constitution does. Unlike the federal Constitution, state constitutions "include a broad range of topics (including socioeconomic rights), describe those topics in elaborate detail, and [are] frequently revise[d]" (Versteeg and Zackin 2014, 1705), making them "exceptional in neither scope nor detail" on the global stage (1654–55). It is "[t]hrough the states" that "Americans secure popular sovereignty" (Woodward-Burns 2021, 193). This book may rely on American states for data, but there is every reason to expect its findings to apply elsewhere.

Political science excels at comparing presidentialism to parliamentarism, unicameralism to bicameralism, package to item vetoes, proportional to majoritarian electoral systems, direct to representative democracy, and plural to unitary executives, but the discipline often struggles to say how all these trees aggregate into a forest. Constitution length stands as a compelling variable worthy of additional scholarly attention. Though a constitution's length alone does not reveal specifics of its content, it provides a new way to step back from these specific institutions and consider how they aggregate into an overall institutional environment. Excessive constitutional specificity binds states.

What Is Not Shown

To be clear, this book neither supports nor refutes partisan claims about the appropriate size of the government or the scope of its authority. Neither my theory nor my empirics address whether ski trails, bingo, mines, golf courses, automated teller machines, fishing, tobacco, wages, oil extraction, alcohol, firearms, marijuana, water rights, marriage, education, fireworks, hunting, or campaign finance are appropriate arenas for government regulation. Rather, this book contemplates only the implications of addressing these matters in the constitutional text rather than by statutory, regulatory, or other extraconstitutional means; after all, each of these matters appears in at least one state's constitution.

Likewise, this book takes no stance on specific institutional arrangements. Some arrangements will inevitably lengthen the constitution, of course. After all, it takes more words to establish two legislative chambers rather than one or to describe multiple separately elected members of the executive branch rather than a unitary governor. That said, two constitutions that erect similar institutions can nevertheless vary widely in detail. For example, Utah and Missouri use similar systems to select and retain state judges, but Missouri devotes almost four times more constitutional language to this topic than Utah does.[1] Similarly, the Missouri constitution devotes almost 11 times more words than the Utah constitution to the duties of the lieutenant governor, state auditor, and treasurer. In each case the duties are similar, but Utah provides details by statute that Missouri includes in its constitution.

More generally, governments may adopt diverse policies, procedures, and institutions without granting these matters constitutional stature. Congress, for example, has enacted intricate legislative procedures through internal rule-making processes, contrasting with the many states that dictate specific legislative procedures in their constitutions. Likewise, the federal government has established district and circuit courts and created a vast executive bureaucracy by statute, matters that many states address in their constitutions.

Even far-reaching reforms do not necessarily require tremendous constitutional expansion. Gersen (2013) has advocated "unbundled" government, where authority is divided by policy area rather than by legislative, executive, or judicial function. He points to examples like federal regulatory agencies that blend functions but within only one policy domain; he also speaks approvingly of the plural executives found in many states, where voters directly elect the heads of various executive departments. As the preceding examples from the Missouri, Utah, and US constitutions show, these goals could be pursued through a variety of constitutional or extraconstitutional means. This book's arguments about constitutional specificity are not arguments about institutional form, only about how much detail to constitutionalize.

Institutional and policy choices matter, but they are not the focus of this book. Rather, this book examines the choice to address those questions in the constitution itself rather than by statute or other extraconstitutional means. The more detailed the constitution, the more it binds states to the past, tightening the dead hand's grip.

I now address two challenges to my argument from the existing literature. First, I address arguments in favor of lengthy constitutions as benign alternatives to briefer ones (e.g., Hammons 1999; Versteeg and Zackin 2016). Second, I address evidence that lengthy constitutions endure longer than shorter ones, implying performance advantages (Elkins, Ginsburg, and Melton 2009).

A Benign Alternative?

Scholars have long observed the exceptional length of many state constitutions, often with derision but sometimes with praise. One defender of detailed constitutions urged a "rethinking [of] the American preference for short, framework-oriented constitutions," pointedly asking, "Was James Madison wrong?" (Hammons 1999).

More recently, Versteeg and Zackin (2014, 1646) argue that "constitutional specificity and flexibility can serve as a perfectly rational mechanism for constraining those in power" when "people aiming to bind their governments ... attempt to limit legislative, executive, and judicial discretion alike by giving very specific guidance." They emphasize, however, that lengthy constitutions can serve this role only if they are "unentrenched," or easy to amend:

> While specific provisions might seem attractive at the time of founding, they can quickly grow outdated. Thus, highly specific constitutions typically require frequent updating. ... Perhaps more fundamentally, some degree of flexibility is a central part of a constitutional strategy that envisions continuous control over constitutional agents, since flexibility is required for contemporary majorities to correct governmental policies through textual constitutional instructions. ... [S]pecificity and flexibility are highly correlated with one another and appeared to have increased together in democratic constitutions. ... [T]heir flexibility allows them to avoid the "dead-hand" problem, since the living generation clearly acts as the principal in its frequent revision of the constitutional text. (660)

In other words, a lengthy constitution is a benign alternative to a short one if (and only if) it is flexible. No matter whether this logic works in the abstract, its necessary condition—flexibility—is not fully met in practice among state constitutions. While it is true that amendment *rates* are higher among states with lengthier constitutions (chapter 3), it is not true that amendment *procedures* are less burdensome in these states (chapter 5); constitutional detail increases amendment rates in spite of, not because of, the state's particular amendment procedures. Nor is this necessary flexibility found among national constitutions; Tsebelis and Nardi (2016) show that lengthier constitutions tend to have more rather than less burdensome amendment provisions, despite having higher amendment rates.

It is therefore constitutional specificity itself that drives up amendment rates, not an intentional choice by constitution writers to pair specificity with flexibility. Moreover, the high amendment rates seen in states with the lengthiest constitutions are not high enough: even after controlling for amendment rates, states with lengthier constitutions continue to experience more judicial invalidations and worse economic performance than states with shorter constitutions. Detailed constitutions cover too much ground for formal amendments to keep up. Constitutional specificity gives life to the dead hand of the past. Perhaps it is possible for a state to amend its constitution frequently enough to mitigate the harms of the lengthiest constitutions, but this book's analysis suggests we have yet to observe such a state.

Endurance and Performance

Elkins, Ginsburg, and Melton (2009) find that national constitutions endure longer before replacement if they are inclusive, flexible, and specific. They use "specificity" to refer to the same features I have in mind: "detailed, and infused with self-interest." Constitutions, they argue, must not be "too vague to provide meaningful guidance to subjects, and too high-falutin to induce costly investment by powerful actors in enforcing the terms of the bargain" (211). Though these authors examined national constitutions, Hammons (1999, 2001) has found that lengthier state constitutions, too, endure longer than short ones.

This book has given only passing attention to constitutional endurance, mostly in chapter 2. Still, my argument that constitutional specificity harms states would seem to clash with this finding that specificity promotes survival. Further reflection resolves the puzzle, though. Consider the three mechanisms that Elkins, Ginsburg, and Melton (2009, 86–87) propose to link constitutional specificity and endurance:

> First . . . [specificity] may be particularly helpful with regard to solving problems of hidden information among the bargainers. . . . Second, specificity facilitates endurance precisely because it is costly. . . . The greater the investment in a particular constitutional bargain, the less willing parties will be to deviate from it by switching to a new bargain. . . . Third, specificity provides an incentive for parties to invest resources in keeping the constitutional text current.

In short, these authors argue that specificity promotes survival because negotiating a long constitution is costlier than negotiating a short one. Renegotiating a constitution is indeed costly—and these costs are not only high but uncertain. This uncertainty has long made American reformers fear that invoking Article V's revision mechanism could produce a runaway convention.[2] As Madison put it in Federalist 49, these "experiments are of too ticklish a nature to be unnecessarily multiplied" (quoted in Rossiter 1961, 312).

When the costs and uncertainty of renegotiating the constitution rise, powerful interests gain a shared incentive to protect their investment in the existing constitution. First, they protect their investment by defending the status quo. Second, they protect it by incurring the relatively low costs of amending the constitution regularly rather than renegotiating it in its entirety.

These behaviors have an unfortunate corollary, though. If powerful actors have incentives to protect the constitutional status quo, then those same incentives will lead those same actors to tolerate governmental underperformance. Even if a constitutional status quo is so imperfect that it hinders economic performance and inhibits policy innovation, policymakers and the powerful interests that back them will rationally choose to bear these day-to-day governance costs as long as they do not exceed the very high and uncertain costs of renegotiating the constitution.

Paradoxical though it may seem, constitutional specificity hurts day-to-day governance *because* it promotes long-term survival. Policymakers working under detailed constitutions have reason to tolerate lower incomes, higher unemployment, greater inequality, and reduced innovativeness rather than face the higher costs of renegotiating the constitution. Constitutional specificity promotes endurance at the cost of performance.

To be sure, Elkins, Ginsburg, and Melton (2009, 208) acknowledge that constitutional specificity may have its limits: "Some of these effects have what we might call a Goldilocks quality. Specificity is helpful, but not if the constitution becomes a complete code governing every contingency." The same might be said for brevity: brevity is helpful, but not if the constitution fails to establish sufficient government authority. An implication of this Goldilocks principle is that the findings presented here may not travel well to out-of-sample extrapolations.

Indeed, Elkins, Ginsburg, and Melton may have found different results had they included state constitutions in their analysis. State constitutions average nearly twice the length of national constitutions, as discussed in chapter 1, and the lengthiest state constitution is three times longer than the lengthiest national constitution. Moreover, Friedman (2014, 30) has observed that states' frequent reliance on judicial interpretation may affect their endurance in ways that Elkins, Ginsburg, and Melton do not consider. Perhaps, then, there are enough differences between state and national constitutions for specificity to cause underperformance among states while causing endurance among nations—but this seems unlikely in light of the many similarities between state and national constitutions emphasized by Versteeg and Zackin (2014).

In any event, we may at least conclude that there is no logical reason that specificity cannot impede state performance even while promoting constitutional endurance. After all, "[t]he desire to actually achieve a constitutional settlement . . . may require a willingness to compromise one's basic convictions, including what may be described . . . as 'selling out' the (legitimate) interests of one group in order to achieve the greater goal of establishing a constitutional order" (Levinson 2012, 34).

The Burden of Constitutional Specificity

In their practical guide to constitution drafting and revision, Grad and Williams (2006) caution constitution writers to err on the side of brevity. "Unless there is a reason to believe that the legislature will give active encouragement to the perpetration of crimes," they argue, "there is no reason to specify crimes or fix their punishment by way of the constitution, because ordinary legislation provides an entirely satisfactory alternative. So, too, the regulation of corporations, of banks and banking practices, of railroads, and of canal companies" (20). Their abstract reasoning anticipates this book's empirical findings:

> Because of the enduring quality of constitutional provisions, and because of the considerably greater difficulty in amending a constitution than in changing other law, constitutional regulation of a subject is less flexible, and the greater the specificity of the regulation, the more inflexible it becomes. . . . The consequence . . . is obsolescence . . . [which] will diminish the power and the freedom of the government to deal with new situations. (23–24)

As a result, "the burden of proof concerning the need for inclusion should be squarely on the proponent, and any doubts on the issue should be resolved *against* inclusion and in favor of the freedom of government to respond to emerging problems without constitutional limitations, express or implied" (30, emphasis in original). They based this advice on the best legal scholarship. Little empirical research was then available testing whether lengthier constitutions would produce meaningful, measurable impacts on governance. This book has filled that void, validating Grad and Williams's fears.

Constitutional detail reduces state adaptability, binding states to obsolete provisions. Constitutional specificity leads to more amendments and more judicial invalidations as policymakers struggle against the dead hand's grip. Lengthy constitutions result in lower income per capita, higher unemployment, greater inequality, and reduced policy innovativeness. Those who benefit from the status quo accept this underperformance rather than bear the costs and risks of constitutional change. Long constitutions harm states.

Notes

Chapter 1

1. Coan (2020) provides a brief review of this literature. See also McConnell (1997).
2. These are extrapolations from Ginsburg (2010), who associated constitution length with POLITY scores, and Nardi (2013), who found that democratic constitutions devote more text than authoritarian ones to the legislative branch and to articulating negative rights, such as property rights and rights of the accused. National constitutions are also lengthier in nations with British legal origins (Berkowitz and Clay 2005; Voigt 2009).
3. Only three states have a unitary governor that follows the federal model, whereby voters elect only a single member of the executive branch. The rest vary widely in how many statewide officials they elect (Beyle and Ferguson 2008).
4. Though most legal scholars roughly follow Hammons's delineation, some slice constitutional provisions other ways. Tarr (1998, 65), for example, sees three rather than two types of provision: "the intrastate distribution of political power [via the franchise and reapportionment], the scope of state governmental power, and the relation of the state to economic activity."
5. Knox delivered these remarks on the convention's second day, after his selection as president. The Alabama state legislature preserves transcripts of the 1901 convention's proceedings at http://www.legislature.state.al.us/aliswww/history/constitutions/1901/proceedings/1901_proceedings_vol1/day2.html, accessed July 3, 2018.
6. Hammons counted the provisions in each constitution adopted by each state prior to any amendments. As discussed in later chapters, my state-biennium data go back to 1994–95, omitting Alabama. For the closest temporal overlap with Hammons, I compare his last provision count for each state to my earliest word count.
7. Regressing word counts on the number of framework provisions and the number of policy provisions, separately measured, yields a model with near-perfect fit ($R^2 = 0.85$). Ordinary least squares coefficients are 43.9 (s.e. 4.95) for policy provisions and 31.2 (s.e. 5.71) for framework provisions. F testing fails to reject the null of equal coefficients (p = 0.19).
8. Statistics about national constitutions calculated from data compiled by the Comparative Constitutions Project (see Elkins, Ginsburg, and Melton 2009). Statistics about state constitutions calculated from variables described in this chapter's appendix.
9. In the data introduced in chapter 4, the average state supreme court invalidated 2.7 times as many state actions for violating the state constitution as for violating the

federal constitution. (Many rulings struck down state actions for violating both, deflating this statistic.)

10. The 50 states could differ more in their institutions. Williams and Tarr (2004) argue that the US Constitution leaves more room for constitutional innovation than the states have chosen to exploit, an argument that Hershkoff and Loffredo (2011) term the "underutilization thesis."
11. The actual recorded drop was by 18, from 54 to 36 cumulative amendments, but since two amendments were adopted that year the error is 20.
12. I draw from the Wikipedia entry https://en.wikipedia.org/wiki/Political_party_strength_in_Nebraska, accessed June 28, 2018. Brown (2011) evaluates this source favorably.
13. When the lower and upper chambers reported different numbers of days I took the shorter of the two, since the longer session usually indicated days spent by the upper chamber on executive confirmations or other nonstatutory matters. Some states report session lengths in calendar days (i.e., elapsed days between the start and end dates, including weekends); others report in legislative days (i.e., actual workdays). Session lengths reported in calendar days were multiplied by 5/7 to omit weekends and make them consistent with sessions reported in legislative days. Occasionally *Book of the States* would not contain a session length estimate despite listing the legislature's start and end dates; in these cases, I calculated session lengths. *Book of the States* lacked data for a few years in New Jersey; I estimated session length by counting dates when votes were reported on the legislature's website.

Chapter 2

1. For the source of this quote, and for elaboration of the specific state constitutional experience enjoyed by delegates to the convention, see Williams (1988).
2. From Dr. Thomas Young's April 11, 1777, open letter "To the Inhabitants of Vermont," quoted in Jones (1939, 380). The "very little alteration" Thomas proposed was a veto, so that "all the Bills intended to be passed into Laws should be laid before the Executive Board for their perusal."
3. Some would add "super-statutes" like the Civil Rights Act (Eskridge and Ferejohn 2001, 2010) and the Clean Water Act (Young 2007) to the country's small-c constitution.
4. Though incorporation through the Fourteenth Amendment was unambiguously underway with *Gitlow v. New York* (268 US 652, 1925), others trace incorporation's origins to *Chicago, Burlington and Quincy Railroad v. City of Chicago* (166 US 226, 1897).
5. Even the League expressed some ambivalence about its product. The introduction to its final edition declares, "Strictly speaking there can be no such thing as a 'Model State Constitution' because there is no model state.... Admitting the nonexistence of

a 'model' or even a 'typical' state, the architects of the sixth edition are not interested in a blueprint for Utopia" (National Municipal League 1963, vii).

6. The quoted phrase comes from Jefferson's August 30, 1787, letter to John Adams, found in Boyd (1955, 66–69).

7. Not all concur, of course. Kahn (1993, 1162) emphasized, "My argument that constitutional interpretation by the different state courts has a common object . . . is very similar to the views of Thomas Cooley . . . [who] believed that state constitutionalism could be explained in a single treatise, organized by substantive topics. It did not require a separate handbook covering each state's text and history." Of course, this scholarly approach can also allow room for meaningful differences among state constitutions. In a volume that takes a unified approach to state constitutional interpretation, Williams (2009, 309) nevertheless declares emphatically that there is no "ideal" state constitution.

8. Brandeis dissent in *Burnet v Coronado Oil & Gas Co.*, 285 US 393, p. 409, n. 5, 1932. Brandeis could have added the Thirteenth and Fourteenth Amendments (abrogating *Dred Scott v. Sandford*, 60 US 393, 1857), the Nineteenth Amendment (superseding *Minor v. Happersett*, 88 US 162, 1875), and, aided by a crystal ball, the Twenty-sixth Amendment (reversing *Oregon v. Mitchell*, 400 US 112, 1970).

9. Bridges (2008, 36) writes, "Although [western] delegates were wary of state legislatures, and denied them many powers, [Gilded Age] delegates affirmed and expanded the prerogatives . . . of state government" by "creating positive rights, which mandated activity by state government." Later she added this critique: "Hall argued that state constitutions were 'diffuse, overly long, negative documents that generally prevented the positive exercise of public authority.' . . . Hall's conclusions might well have been different, had he paid more attention to western state constitutions" (Bridges 2015, 16–17). Incidentally, the statistical analyses reported in this book do not change when southern or western regional controls are included.

10. Taking a dimmer view, one critic derided these lengthy state constitutions as suffering from "unclear thinking and bungling workmanship" (National Municipal League 1963, viii).

11. Some sources include the Connecticut and Rhode Island colonial charters in their count of state constitutions, bringing the total to 146 rather than 144.

12. The Dinan-Sturm data includes several pre-statehood conventions, such as Montana's in 1866 and 1884; Montana's 1889 convention produced the state's first adopted constitution. It also includes revision conventions that either failed to agree on a proposal or proposed a constitution that went unratified. Just as some conventions did not produce constitutions, some early constitutions were not preceded by conventions, with the legislature or another entity proposing the constitution (see Dinan 2006, 12). Thus, convention and adoption data are not perfectly comparable.

13. Three initial constitutions (those of Maryland, Delaware, and South Carolina) provided amendment procedures; five provided formal mechanisms for calling revision conventions; and four provided no formal amendment or revision procedure, though the state retained implicit authority to call a new convention, just as the 1787 federal convention gathered without clear authority under the Articles of Confederation

(Dinan 2006, 305). The 12 constitutions tallied here include Vermont but exclude Connecticut and Rhode Island, which operated under their colonial charters into the 18th century.
14. Benjamin (2006, 147) lists the outcome of all mandatory convention referendums since 1970. Blake and Anson (2020) find that voter support for these referendums is complicated. Economic conditions affect voter support for these referendums, but in a quadratic way best understood through prospect theory. Voters interested in correcting problems support a convention when economic and political conditions are bad; voters interested in improving on good times support a convention when economic and political conditions are good.
15. Initiated amendments do not share these deliberative opportunities, but chapter 3 will show that initiated amendments are not only less common than referred amendments but also attract greater skepticism from voters prior to ratification.
16. These are predictions from a survival model that includes many variables, not simple medians like those I present for state constitutions, so my comparison should be understood cautiously.
17. Relatedly, national constitutions are also lengthier in distrustful and fractionalized societies (Bjørnskov and Voigt 2014; Ginsburg 2010). There is a parallel here to historians' findings that constitutions grew lengthier in the late 19th century as distrust of elites rose. Though Tsebelis and Nardi (2016) and Tsebelis (2017) argue that corrupt elites lengthen constitutions to lock in favorable rents, they acknowledge that their analysis cannot separate this mechanism from other possibilities. As Tsebelis writes, "On the one hand, it could be that founders are captured by special interests who are asking for additional detailed provisions to be locked so that their privileges would be guaranteed. Alternatively, it may be that virtuous founders tried to include detailed provisions in order to prevent or reduce the influence of organised interests" (834). Scholars favor the latter mechanism in the American states, as discussed above.
18. The curved lines in the figure represent predicted values from ordinary least squares regressions (a separate regression for each panel) with dichotomous controls for southern and initiative states. For framework provisions, the prediction reaches its maximum in 1885; for policy provisions, the prediction reaches its maximum in 1912. Miller, Hamm, and Hedlund (2015) find that provisions restricting the legislature specifically also peaked around this time.
19. The correlation rises to 0.70 ($p < 0.01$) when both variables are logged.
20. The quote is from Tarr (1996, 4), summarizing what he calls the "historical-movement model," an approach he implies sympathy for but does not fully embrace.

Chapter 3

1. Ginsburg and Melton (2015) are an important exception that uses a longitudinal rather than cross-sectional approach, though they examine national rather than state constitutions.

NOTES 155

2. Letter from Madison to George Washington, October 18, 1787 (Hunt 1904, 5:14).
3. Quoted in Kurland and Lerner (1987, 37).
4. From Marshall's opinion in *McCulloch v. Maryland*, 17 US 319 (1819).
5. From Jefferson's September 6, 1789, letter to Madison (Boyd 1958, 392–98).
6. From Jefferson's July 12, 1816, letter to Samuel Kercheval (Ford 1905, 3).
7. From Jefferson's February 14, 1824, letter to Robert J. Garnett (Washington 1859, 336–37).
8. As Jackson (2015) reminds us, widespread belief that the US Constitution is effectively unamendable—even if this belief is mistaken—can threaten its democratic legitimacy.
9. From 1994 to 2015, the seven states adopted an average of 35.9 total amendments, compared to an average of 19.5 in New Hampshire and South Carolina.
10. Levinson (1988, 2006) would counter that the US Constitution is riddled with anachronistic provisions and flaws, contending that its burdensome amendment procedure and unwarranted popular veneration impede reform, leaving the Supreme Court to "amend" it by judicial fiat.
11. Socioeconomic conditions are more uniform across the American states than across independent nations, so these variables may yield weaker effects here than they would if included in cross-national analysis. For example, an analysis of constitutional change in postcommunist societies finds much stronger effects for these sorts of social factors than are found in the analysis below (Roberts 2009).
12. Arkansas hit its limit in 6 of 11 biennia from 1994 to 2015; Illinois hit it once. Colorado does not limit amendments, but it does prohibit amendments proposed during a single legislative session from cumulatively affecting more than 6 constitutional articles.
13. Reutter and Lorenz (2016) do explore some partisan considerations in their analysis of subnational constitutions in the German Länder, though the German context leads them to focus on majoritarian versus consensus democracy. Separately, Damore, Bowler, and Nicholson (2012) have shown that partisan considerations influence legislators' use of discretionary referendums.
14. Separate from legislative and initiative amendments are commission-referred amendments, which are too rare to warrant separate analysis. From 1994 to 2015, only 12 of 1,285 adopted amendments were referred by commission. These commission-referred amendments explain why the percentages of legislative and initiated amendments given in the text do not quite add to 100.
15. These scatterplots employ minor jittering to separate overlapping points.
16. Constitution age was logged in the regression analysis to reduce skew, so these are the lengths of a constitution one standard deviation above or below the mean logged constitution age, which is 88 years. Constitution length has a similar distribution for both young and old constitutions. If we split the 49 observations from the first two models in Table 3.3 at the median constitution age (115 years), the young constitutions have a mean length of 28,883 words, compared to 30,502 for old ones; the difference is statistically zero (p = 0.76). The two groups also have similar standard deviations (16,976 vs. 20,176), 10th percentiles (13,145 vs. 10,379), and 90th percentiles (51,700

vs. 59,500). The interaction between length and age is not an artifact of an underlying relationship.
17. Constitution length was logged in the regression analysis to reduce skew, so these are the lengths of a constitution one standard deviation above or below the mean logged constitution length.
18. Dots are jittered to separate overlapping points.
19. For legislature size, the plotted range excludes New Hampshire; for percentage non-Hispanic white, the range excludes Hawaii; and for ratification threshold, the range excludes Delaware.
20. New Hampshire has an unusually large legislature. Excluding it does not change the result for legislature size.
21. Gelman (2008) reminds us that a prediction based on a two standard deviation movement around the mean in a continuous variable is comparable to a prediction based on flipping a balanced dichotomous variable.
22. Some states denominate the threshold as a percentage of votes cast on the question, while others denominate it as a percentage of total ballots cast. To account for rolloff (cf. Wattenberg, McAllister, and Salvanto 2000), I bump in-the-election thresholds by 10 points, so that 50 percent in-the-election becomes 60 percent on-the-question. If states specify both an in-the-election threshold and an on-the-question threshold, I use the latter. Other than Florida, this coding places Delaware at 0, 43 states at 50, 4 states at 60, and 1 state at 67. Florida is 50 before 1997, 58 through 2006, and 64 thereafter. A 2006 Florida amendment requires two-thirds in-the-election for amendments involving new taxes or fees, while retaining a simple majority on-the-question otherwise, later raised to 60 percent effective 2007. The 58 percent (pre-2007) and 64 percent (2007+) entered here average these two thresholds.
23. Where *Book of the States* was missing data on bill enactments I counted bills on legislative websites. Data remains missing in CT-01, MA-01, ME-01, NJ-95, NY-95, NY-01, RI-01, SC-95, WV-01, WY-99.
24. Constitution length, age, population, income, and percentage white were collapsed to their medians; amendments and bills were collapsed to their sums; other variables were generally static but collapsed to means when necessary.
25. The Akaike information criterion (AIC) seeks the model that is most adequately descriptive; the Bayesian information criterion (BIC) seeks the model that is closest to the "true" model (Akaike 1974; Burnham and Anderson 2004; Raftery 1995). AIC and BIC are similar, except BIC punishes model complexity more heavily. Put differently, AIC errs on the side of retaining too many predictors, while BIC errs on the side of retaining too few (Dziak et al. 2012).
26. Despite the name, Ballotpedia has no relationship to Wikipedia and is professionally curated. When Ballotpedia lacked data for a particular state-biennium, I turned to the National Conference of State Legislatures ballot measure database. *Book of the States* and Ballotpedia/NCSL occasionally disagree on the total number of amendments for a state-biennium but nevertheless correlate strongly (r = 0.96, p < 0.001).
27. States variously denominate these thresholds as a percentage of votes cast for governor, for secretary of state, for president, or in the last general election, or as a

percentage of registered voters, of eligible voters, or of the population. I converted to a common denominator, percentage of voting-eligible population (VEP), using multipliers derived from McDonald's (2017) voter turnout data. For 2008–16, mean highest-office turnout was 58 percent of VEP in presidential years, 42 percent in gubernatorial years, and 51 percent in the average general election. State population averages 139 percent of VEP. Secretary of state turnout is unavailable but assumed to match gubernatorial turnout. Voter registration numbers were not available, so for states using registration as the denominator, calculations were conducted assuming that half of those who miss presidential elections are registered, resulting in a multiplier of 79 percent of VEP. These adjusted signature requirements correlate with the raw ones at r = 0.52.

Chapter 4

1. Parts of this chapter appeared previously in Adam R. Brown, "The Role of Constitutional Features in Judicial Review," *State Politics and Policy Quarterly* 18 (4): 351–70 (2018). Reprinted with permission.
2. Length as of the end of 2015. All states have shorter constitutions than these three except Texas (87,000 words), Oklahoma (82,000 words), Colorado (73,000 words), and outlying Alabama (389,000 words).
3. *National Solid Waste Management Association v. Director of the Department of Natural Resources*, No. 79737 (Supreme Court of Missouri, February 24, 1998).
4. *Caddo-Shreveport Sales and Use Tax Commission v. Office of Motor Vehicles Department of Public Safety and Corrections of the State*, No. 97-CA-2233 (Supreme Court of Louisiana, April 14, 1998).
5. *American Academy of Pediatrics v. Lungren*, No. S041459 (Supreme Court of California, August 5, 1997).
6. From the European Commission for Democracy through Law's (i.e., Venice Commission's) Report on Constitutional Amendment, published January 19, 2010, Study 469/2008, http://www.venice.coe.int/webforms/documents/default.aspx?pdffile=CDL-AD(2010)001-e.
7. To be clear, her hypothesis linking amendments to invalidations had a relatively low priority among the 15 hypotheses about judicial review addressed in her book. Moreover, Langer operationalized her argument using procedural amendment difficulty rather than amendment rates.
8. Because this approach produces some unobserved combinations of constitutional features, some predictions fall outside the dependent variable's observed range, particularly for the lengthiest constitutions.
9. The regression used logged constitution length, so this calculation uses one standard deviation above and below the logged length. The same is true for subsequent statements about amendment counts and constitution age.

10. To be clear, constitutional specificity still has strong effects even for constitutions that received a larger number of amendments. After all, the plot for constitution length in Figure 4.1 holds other variables at their medians, and the median state adopted four amendments.
11. Petitioners need not argue explicitly that a particular action violates the constitution; judges hearing a case can independently identify constitutional violations, as in the canonical case establishing federal judicial review, *Marbury v. Madison*. Such action is rare, though. Of the 228 state supreme court cases in which justices struck down a state action for violating the state constitution, only 2 did not feature prior constitutional claims by petitioners. Thus, the dependent variable used above (invalidations rooted in the state constitution) correlates strongly with the number of petitioner claims rooted in the state constitution ($r = 0.77$, $p < 0.01$). On the flip side, there were hundreds of cases in which petitioners raised state constitutional claims that courts did not sustain; only 21 percent of cases wherein petitioners raised constitutional claims ended with invalidations. Petitioner claims are almost necessary but far from sufficient for invalidation.
12. Sometimes petitioners fail to do so, of course, with disastrous results for their clients (Sutton 2018, 191–92).
13. Other judicial selection variables, including dummies for gubernatorial appointment, merit selection, and nonpartisan elections, have no correlation with any of these variables.
14. For perspective, the US Supreme Court issued 427 rulings during this period, placing it exactly at the 25th percentile when compared to state supreme courts (calculated from data in Spaeth et al. 2016).
15. Even if the previous chapter had not shown that constitution length and age predict amendment rates, it is standard practice to include all second-stage independent variables as first-stage instruments. The previous chapter reported that interacting the constitution's age and length improved prediction of constitutional amendment rates. Thus, it is no surprise that including an interaction term as a first-stage instrument in the models here does improve the first-stage model's fit. However, adding the interaction term as an instrument causes the model to fail the Sargan (1958) and Basmann (1960) tests for correlation between instruments and second-stage residuals, indicating that it is not a valid instrument.
16. I set aside two other variables from the previous chapter, total bill enactments and the citizen initiative option, owing to their weak substantive relationship with amendment rates. I developed the previous chapter's final model by eliminating variables that did not survive AIC model selection, while observing that AIC model selection is more generous than BIC model selection. These two variables survived AIC model selection by the smallest of margins, so I kept them in the final model even though BIC model selection would have called for removing them. As it happens, neither of these variables has a particularly strong relationship with amendment rates despite surviving AIC model selection, so I omit them here.
17. First, the Durbin (1954) and Wu-Hausman (Wu 1974; Hausman 1978) statistics indicate that the variable we suspect of endogeneity—the total number of amendments

adopted—is indeed endogenous; we reject exogeneity with p < 0.02 under both tests. Second, the Sargan (1958) and Basmann (1960) tests find no evidence that the instrumental variables correlate with the second-stage residuals (p > 0.45 for both tests), suggesting that the instruments are indeed exogenous and the exclusion restriction is satisfied.
18. The partial F statistic for the three "pure" instruments alone (complex procedures, legislature size, and amendment limits) is lower (F = 2.4, p = 0.08), since, as the previous chapter shows, constitution length and age do much of the first stage's heavy lifting.
19. An instrumental tobit model would account for the five observations that are left-censored at zero on the dependent variable. Whether employing conditional maximum-likelihood tobit estimates or Newey's (1987) minimum chi-squared (two-step) estimator, however, the results are essentially the same as those presented here and are therefore not shown.
20. I employ the two-step generalized method of moments estimator and robust multiplicative standard errors.

Chapter 5

1. As of 2015, cross-sectional pairwise correlations reveal no relationship between constitution length and legislative complexity (r = −0.18, p = 0.23), amendment limits (r = −0.04, p = 0.80), or ratification thresholds (r = −0.11, p = 0.44). (Chapter 3 contains details about these procedural amendment barriers.) Not only does each correlation fail to attain statistical significance, but all three correlation coefficients run in the wrong direction: lengthier constitutions are (insignificantly) less likely to require complex amendment procedures, to limit amendments per biennium, or to have higher ratification thresholds.
2. Though nearly all states have some form of balanced budget requirement, the nonpartisan National Conference of State Legislatures (2010) sees only 26 of these as "stringent."
3. Most of these provisions were enacted by initiated amendment, which, under the California constitution, means they can be removed only by a future initiative. For example, Prop 13 (1978) limits growth in property tax revenues; Prop 4 (1979) limits growth in state and local budgets; Prop 98 (1988) established the public education earmark; Prop 1A (2004) reserves property tax and sales tax revenues to local governments unless the governor and two-thirds of the legislature declare a fiscal emergency; and Prop 26 (2010) requires a two-thirds vote to impose new charges and levies, adding to an existing two-thirds requirement for new taxes. Until Prop 25 (2010), the constitution also required a two-thirds majority to approve a new budget.
4. Though predictions for income and unemployment are straightforward, inequality is more fraught. On the one hand, a longer constitution may imply a state less able to address inequality or, as Tsebelis and Nardi (2016) imply, a state more wedded

to past elites' rent-seeking behaviors, either of which would cause inequality to rise with length. On the other hand, a longer constitution may imply a more fully developed welfare state or a state guaranteeing more social and economic rights, reflecting intentions to reduce inequality. Because most US welfare effort comes from the federal government and not from the states, the first mechanism should predominate in the present analysis. In a cross-national sample, however, constitution length could plausibly have a different empirical relationship with inequality than reported here, though there is no reason to expect length to have a different relationship with income or unemployment.

5. Moreover, there is little to be gained from using random effects rather than fixed effects, since the efficiency gains of random effects wane in data sets as large as this one (Clark and Linzer 2015).
6. For this reason, chapter 3 could not include state fixed effects; including them would have precluded estimating the effects of procedural amendment variables.
7. State and year fixed effects are set to represent Ohio in the 2014–15 biennium, an observation that falls near the 2015 mean on all three economic indicators.
8. I refer here to each variable's overall standard deviation rather than its within or between standard deviation. References in subsequent paragraphs to standard deviations do the same.
9. Measures of fit have limited utility in any context, but they are especially flawed in fixed effects analysis, where the dozens of dummy variables used to address state and year fixed effects inflate statistics like R-squared tremendously. The R^2 statistics for the three models in Table 5.2 are 0.96, 0.88, and 0.95, respectively. For a somewhat better estimate of fit, an alternative approach is to demean each variable by year and state, then re-estimate each model without state or year dummies, yielding the same coefficients and standard errors given already. The resulting demeaned R^2 statistics are 0.50, 0.18, and 0.09, respectively. These models explain much of the variance in income per capita but only minimal variance in economic inequality, with unemployment falling in the middle.
10. Moving from one standard deviation below the mean to one standard deviation above the mean in the state economy's reliance on natural resources is associated with an increase of $11,788 in GDP per capita and a decline of 2.0 in the unemployment rate. By comparison, a corresponding change in the economy's reliance on manufacturing is associated with an increase of $3,931 in GDP per capita and a decrease of 0.9 in the unemployment rate. A corresponding change in the Hispanic share of the population is associated with a decrease of $10,785 in GDP per capita and an increase of 6.2 in the unemployment rate.
11. For observations included in this model, this movement in constitution length is from 14,343 to 48,145 words.

Chapter 6

1. Parts of this chapter appeared previously in Adam R. Brown and Jeremy C. Pope, "Measuring and Manipulating Constitutional Evaluations in the States: Legitimacy versus Veneration," *American Politics Research* 47 (5): 1135–61 (2019). Reprinted with permission.
2. The precise figures were 75 percent in September 2009, 74 percent in August 2010, 74 percent in August 2011, and 69 percent in August 2012; see National Constitution Center (2012).
3. From items placed by the author on the 2015 Cooperative Congressional Election Study (CCES).
4. Letter from Jefferson to Madison, September 6, 1789 (quoted in Boyd 1958, 392–98). Some sources state 34 rather than 19 years.
5. Letter from Jefferson to Maj. John Cartwright, June 5, 1824, Library of Congress, https://www.loc.gov/item/mtjbib025031/.
6. Letter from Jefferson to Adamantios Coray, October 31, 1823, Library of Congress, https://www.loc.gov/item/mtjbib024782/.
7. Letter from Jefferson to Samuel Kercheval, July 12, 1816, Library of Congress, https://www.loc.gov/item/mtjbib022494/.
8. Federalist 49 quotes drawn from Rossiter (1961). See also Manzer (2001).
9. Bailey (2015, 11) argues that we have "long overestimated the importance of stability for Madison," stressing that Madison's objection to conventions implied no objection to amendments. While true, Madison's endorsement of the onerous Article V amendment process does not imply an endorsement of the streamlined procedures and high amendment rates that have since emerged in many states.
10. Letter from Madison to Jefferson, February 4, 1790, Library of Congress, https://www.loc.gov/item/mjm023659.
11. On Madison's apparent preference for short constitutions, see Hammons (1999).
12. These are Chief Justice John Marshall's words from *McCulloch v Maryland*, 17 US 319 (1819).
13. More generally, Americans struggle with basic civic facts (Pew Research Center 2015).
14. The National Center for State Courts (2009) reported that only 53 percent answered affirmatively when asked whether their state has a constitution. A poll administered to respondents from a single state (Utah) found a slightly lower rate of 40 percent (Brown 2018b). Few respondents answer this question incorrectly; most answer either "yes" or "don't know." When I placed a similar question on the nationally representative 2015 CCES, 62 percent answered correctly—then again, only 79 percent answered that the United States has a constitution, which may reveal some confusion about what "constitution" means. The CCES question asked, "To the best of your knowledge, which of the following governmental bodies has its own written constitution—that is, a foundational document that describes its form, powers, and functions?" Combined, these studies suggest that around half of Americans know their state has a constitution.

15. From an item placed by the author on the 2015 CCES. In calculating each average, I omit the 1.1 to 1.5 percent of respondents who guessed 100 amendments or more for either document. The median guess for each constitution was 3 amendments. Only 10 percent of respondents correctly answered that the US Constitution had received one amendment, while 25 percent guessed that it had received none. Only 26 percent correctly guessed that their state constitution had received more amendments than the federal Constitution, while another 36 percent guessed that both had received the same number.
16. Calculated from data provided by the Comparative Constitutions Project, described in Elkins, Ginsburg, and Melton (2009), as downloaded from http://comparativeconstitutionsproject.org/ccp-rankings/. The CCP dates the United Kingdom constitution to 1215, when the Magna Carta was signed; I omit the UK from this comparison owing to the unique character of its constitution.
17. This may be a modest underestimate. Most of the rest chose "don't know" (44 percent) rather than "no" (5 percent). Unlike respondents on other platforms, MTurk respondents sometimes hide knowledge behind the "don't know" option (Brown and Pope 2021).
18. The page count estimate is the number of words divided by 550.
19. This comparison pools respondents from all conditions. Those in the full treatment and length-only treatment received this information; those in the full control and other partial treatments did not.
20. There is no evidence that respondents left the survey to search the internet for answers to these questions. Participants who took longer than the median (241 seconds) to complete the questionnaire fared no better on these checks than other participants.
21. Because all predictions tested in this chapter are directional, all probabilities are one-tailed. This finding persists even among the subset of respondents who correctly stated before starting the experiment that their state has a constitution. It is therefore clear that respondents are reacting to the specific information provided in the experimental treatment and not simply to the general fact that this study implicitly informed them of their state constitution's existence. The treatment effect for state constitutional evaluations depicted in Figure 6.1 is +0.14 ($p = 0.038$, $n = 605$) for the full sample and +0.20 ($p = 0.038$, $n = 314$) for those respondents who accurately stated on the survey's first screen that their state has a constitution. Prior knowledge is not randomly assigned, of course, but the latter treatment effect remains essentially the same at +0.19 ($p = 0.038$, $n = 314$) even after controlling for respondent gender, partisanship, education, and race.
22. This figure compares participants who received a particular type of information to participants in all other conditions (not only to participants in the full control), biasing the analysis against finding meaningful differences.
23. The constitutional evaluation battery includes two items mentioning the state's amendment rate, which may produce some circularity with respect to the amendment rate treatment. One solution is to omit these two items from the battery and recalculate the factor using the remaining five items, producing a factor that correlates

with the version used here at r = 0.91 (p < 0.01). The reported effects persist, though slightly attenuated, when using this modified factor.

24. Regressing the US Constitution factor on demographic characteristics produces these coefficients: Republican respondent (b = 0.60, p < 0.01), conservative respondent (b = 0.59, p < 0.01), male respondent (b = 0.22, p < 0.01), respondent age in years (0.013, p < 0.01), college-educated respondent (b = 0.0050, p = 0.93), constant (b = −0.88, p < 0.01). N = 999, R^2 = 0.30, adjusted R^2 = 0.29. Regressing the state constitution factor on respondent demographics produces these coefficients: Republican respondent (b = 0.50, p < 0.01), conservative respondent (b = 0.48, p < 0.01), male respondent (b = 0.12, p = 0.04), respondent age in years (0.0088, p < 0.01), college-educated respondent (b= −0.0063, p = 0.91), constant (b= −0.61, p < 0.01). N = 999, R^2 = 0.19, adjusted R^2 = 0.18.

Chapter 7

1. The Missouri constitution specifies filing deadlines and ballot language for judicial retention elections, as well as judicial nominating commissions' composition and procedures, while the Utah constitution leaves these details to statute.
2. See, for example, Natelson (2017).

References

Acemoglu, Daron, and James Robinson. 2012. *Why Nations Fail: The Origins of Power, Prosperity, and Poverty*. New York: Crown.

Adams, Willi Paul. 1980. *The First American Constitutions*. Chapel Hill: University of North Carolina Press.

Akaike, Hirotugu. 1974. "A New Look at the Statistical Model Identification." *IEEE Transactions on Automatic Control* 19 (December): 716–23.

Albert, Richard. 2019. *Constitutional Amendments: Making, Breaking, and Changing Constitutions*. New York: Oxford University Press.

Alt, James E., and David D. Lassen. 2008. "Political and Judicial Checks on Corruption: Evidence from American State Governments." *Economics & Politics* 20 (1): 33–61.

Alt, James E., and David D. Lassen. 2010. "Enforcement and Public Corruption: Evidence from US States." EPRU Working Paper Series No. 2010-08. Economic Policy Research Unit, University of Copenhagen.

Anckar, Dag, and Lauri Karvonen. 2002. "Constitutional Amendment Methods in the Democracies of the World." Paper delivered at the XIIIth Nordic Political Science Congress, Aalborg, Denmark, August 15–17.

Anderson, Benedict. 2006. *Imagined Communities: Reflections on the Origin and Spread of Nationalism*. Revised edition. New York: Verso.

Bailey, Jeremy D. 2012. "Should We Venerate That Which We Cannot Love? James Madison on Constitutional Imperfection." *Political Research Quarterly* 65 (December): 732–44.

Bailey, Jeremy D. 2015. *James Madison and Constitutional Imperfection*. New York: Oxford University Press.

Bakken, Gordon Morris. 1987. *Rocky Mountain Constitution Making, 1850–1912*. New York: Greenwood Press.

Baldwin, Simeon E. 1879. "Recent Changes in our State Constitutions." *Journal of Social Science, Containing the Transactions of the American Association* 9 (December): 136–51.

Bartels, Brandon L., and Chris W. Bonneau, eds. 2015. *Making Law and Courts Research Relevant: The Normative Implications of Empirical Research*. New York: Routledge.

Basman, Robert L. 1960. "On Finite Sample Distributions of Generalized Classical Linear Identifiability Test Statistics." *Journal of the American Statistical Association* 55: 650–59.

Beard, Charles. 1913. *An Economic Interpretation of the Constitution of the United States*. New York: Macmillan.

Benjamin, Gerald. 2006. "The Mandatory Constitutional Convention Question Referendum: The New York Experience in National Context." In *State Constitutions for the Twenty-First Century, Vol 1: The Politics of State Constitutional Reform*, ed. G. Alan Tarr and Robert F. Williams, 145–74. Albany: State University of New York Press.

Benjamin, Gerald, and Thomas Gais. 1996. "Constitutional Conventionphobia." *Hofstra Law and Policy Symposium* 1: 53–78.

Berinsky, Adam J., Gregory A. Huber, and Gabriel S. Lenz. 2012. "Evaluating Online Labor Markets for Experimental Research: Amazon.com's Mechanical Turk." *Political Analysis* 20 (Summer): 351–68.

Berkowitz, Daniel, and Karen Clay. 2005. "American Civil Law Origins: Implications for State Constitutions." *American Law and Economics Review* 7 (1): 61–84.

Berry, Frances Stokes, and William D. Berry. 1990. "State Lottery Adoptions as Policy Innovations: An Event History Analysis." *American Political Science Review* 84 (2): 395–415.

Besso, Michael. 2005. "Constitutional Amendment Procedures and the Informal Political Construction of Constitutions." *Journal of Politics* 67 (February): 69–87.

Beyle, Thad, and Margaret Ferguson. 2008. "Governors and the Executive Branch." In *Politics in the American States: A Comparative Analysis*, 9th edition, ed. Virginia Gray and Russell L. Hanson, 192–228. Washington, DC: CQ Press.

Bilder, Sarah. 2015. *Madison's Hand: Revising the Constitutional Convention*. Cambridge, MA: Harvard University Press.

Binder, Michael, Cheryl Boudreau, and Thad Kousser. 2011. "Shortcuts to Deliberation? How Cues Reshape the Role of Information in Direct Democracy Voting." *California Western Law Review* 48 (Fall): 97–128.

Binder, Michael, Vladimir Kogan, and Thad Kousser. 2011. "How GAVEL Changed Party Politics in Colorado's General Assembly." In *State of Change: Colorado Politics in the Twenty-First Century*, ed. Courtenay W. Daum, Robert Duffy, and John A. Straayer, 153–74. Louisville: University Press of Colorado.

Bjørnskov, Christian, and Stefan Voigt. 2014. "Constitutional Verbosity and Social Trust." *Public Choice* 161 (1): 91–112.

Blake, William D., and Ian G. Anson. 2020. "Risk and Reform: Explaining Support for Constitutional Convention Referendums." *State Politics and Policy Quarterly* 20 (3): 330–55.

Boehmke, Frederick J., Mark Brockway, Bruce Desmarais, Jeffrey J. Harden, Scott LaCombe, Fridolin Linder, and Hanna Wallach. 2018. "State Innovativeness: Dynamic Rate Scores from SPID v.1.0." Harvard Dataverse. https://doi.org/10.7910/DVN/GMVOI5.

Boehmke, Frederick J., and Paul Skinner. 2012. "State Policy Innovativeness Revisited." *State Politics and Policy Quarterly* 12 (3): 303–29.

Bonica, Adam, and Michael Woodruff. 2015. "A Common-Space Measure of State Supreme Court Ideology." *Journal of Law, Economics, and Organization* 31 (August): 472–98.

Bonneau, Chris W., and Melinda Gann Hall. 2009. *In Defense of Judicial Elections*. New York: Routledge.

Bonneau, Chris W., and Melinda Gann Hall, eds. 2016. *Judicial Elections in the 21st Century*. New York: Routledge.

Bouchard, Gérard. 2013. *National Myth: Constructed Pasts, Contested Presents*. New York: Taylor & Francis.

Boudreau, Cheryl, and Scott A. MacKenzie. 2014. "Informing the Electorate? How Party Cues and Policy Information Affect Public Opinion about Initiatives." *American Journal of Political Science* 58 (1): 48–62.

Boushey, Graeme. 2010. *Policy Diffusion Dynamics in America*. New York: Cambridge University Press.

Bowen, Catherine. 1966. *Miracle at Philadelphia*. New York: Little, Brown.

Bowler, Shaun, and Todd Donovan. 2004. "Measuring the Effect of Direct Democracy on State Policy: Not All Initiatives Are Created Equal." *State Politics & Policy Quarterly* 4 (3): 345–63.

Boyd, Christina L., Lee Epstein, and Andrew D. Martin. 2010. "Untangling the Causal Effects of Sex on Judging." *American Journal of Political Science* 54 (April): 389–411.

Boyd, Julian P., ed. 1955. *The Papers of Thomas Jefferson*. Vol. 12. Princeton, NJ: Princeton University Press.

Boyd, Julian P., ed. 1958. *The Papers of Thomas Jefferson*. Vol. 15. Princeton, NJ: Princeton University Press.

Brace, Paul, and Brent D. Boyea. 2008. "State Public Opinion, the Death Penalty, and the Practice of Electing Judges." *American Journal of Political Science* 52 (April): 360–72.

Brace, Paul, and Melinda Gann Hall. 1990. "Neo-institutionalism and Dissent in State Supreme Courts." *Journal of Politics* 52: 54–70.

Brace, Paul, and Melinda Gann Hall. 1993. "Integrated Models of Judicial Dissent." *Journal of Politics* 55: 914–35.

Brace, Paul, and Melinda Gann Hall. 1997. "The Interplay of Preferences, Case Facts, Context, and Structure in the Politics of Judicial Choice." *Journal of Politics* 59 (November): 1206–31.

Brace, Paul, and Melinda Gann Hall. 1999. "The State Supreme Court Data Project." *Law and Courts* 9 (Spring): 21–21.

Brace, Paul, and Melinda Gann Hall. 2001. "'Haves' versus 'Have Nots' in State Supreme Courts: Allocating Docket Space and Wins in Power Asymmetric Cases." *Law and Society Review* 35 (2): 393–413.

Brace, Paul, Melinda Gann Hall, and Laura Langer. 1999. "Judicial Choice and the Politics of Abortion: Institutions, Context, and the Autonomy of Courts." *Albany Law Review* 62: 1265–304.

Brace, Paul, Melinda Gann Hall, and Laura Langer. 2001. "Placing Courts in State Politics." *State Politics and Policy Quarterly* 1: 81–108.

Brace, Paul, Laura Langer, and Melinda Gann Hall. 2000. "Measuring the Preferences of State Supreme Court Judges." *Journal of Politics* 62 (May): 387–413.

Brennan, Timothy. 2017. "Thomas Jefferson and the Living Constitution." *Journal of Politics* 79 (3): 936–48.

Brennan, William J. 1977. "State Constitutions and the Protection of Individual Rights." *Harvard Law Review* 90 (3): 489–504.

Breslin, Beau. 2009. "Is There a Paradox in Amending a Sacred Text?" *Maryland Law Review* 69: 66–77.

Bridges, Amy. 2008. "Managing the Periphery in the Gilded Age: Writing Constitutions for the Western States." *Studies in American Political Development* 22 (Spring): 32–58.

Bridges, Amy. 2015. *Democratic Beginnings: Founding the Western States*. Lawrence: University of Kansas Press.

Brown, Adam R. 2011. "Wikipedia as a Data Source for Political Scientists: Accuracy and Completeness of Coverage." *PS: Political Science and Politics* 44 (2): 339–43.

Brown, Adam R. 2012. "The Item Veto's Sting." *State Politics and Policy Quarterly* 12 (2): 183–202.

Brown, Adam R. 2018a. "The Role of Constitutional Features in Judicial Review." *State Politics and Policy Quarterly* 18 (4): 351–70.

Brown, Adam R. 2018b. *Utah Politics and Government: American Democracy among a Unique Electorate*. Lincoln: University of Nebraska Press.

Brown, Adam R., and Jeremy C. Pope. 2018. "Measuring and Manipulating Constitutional Evaluations in the States: Legitimacy versus Veneration." *American Politics Research* 47 (5): 1135–61.

Brown, Adam R., and Jeremy C. Pope. 2021. "Mechanical Turk and the 'Don't Know' Option." *PS: Political Science and Politics* 54 (3): 416–20.

Bryce, James. 1888. *The American Commonwealth*. London: Macmillan.

Bueno de Mesquita, Bruce, Alastair Smith, Randolph M. Siverson, and James D. Morrow. 2003. *The Logic of Political Survival*. Cambridge, MA: MIT Press.

Burnham, Kenneth P., and David R. Anderson. 2004. "Multimodel Inference: Understanding AIC and BIC in Model Selection." *Sociological Methods and Research* 33 (November): 261–304.

Butterfield, L. H., ed. 1961. *The Adams Papers: Diary and Autobiography of John Adams*. Vol. 3. Cambridge, MA: Harvard University Press.

Cain, Bruce E. 2006. "Constitutional Revision in California: The Triumph of Amendment over Revision." In *State Constitutions for the Twenty-First Century, Vol. 1: The Politics of State Constitutional Reform*, ed. G. Alan Tarr and Robert F. Williams, 59–72. Albany: State University of New York Press.

Cann, Damon M. 2007. "Justice for Sale? Campaign Contributions and Judicial Decisionmaking." *State Politics and Policy Quarterly* 7 (Fall): 281–97.

Cann, Damon M., and Jeff Yates. 2016. *These Estimable Courts: Understanding Public Perceptions of State Judicial Institutions and Legal Policy-Making*. New York: Oxford University Press.

Canon, Bradley C., and Dean Jaros. 1970. "External Variables, Institutional Structure, and Dissent on State Supreme Courts." *Polity* 3: 175–200.

Chhibber, Pradeep K., and Ken Kollman. 2004. *The Formation of National Party Systems: Federalism and Party Competition in Canada, Great Britain, India, and the United States*. Princeton, NJ: Princeton University Press.

Clark, Tom S. 2009. "The Separation of Powers, Court Curbing, and Judicial Legitimacy." *American Journal of Political Science* 53 (October): 971–89.

Clark, Tom S., and Drew A. Linzer. 2015. "Should I Use Fixed or Random Effects?" *Political Science Research and Methods* 3 (May): 399–408.

Coan, Andrew. 2020. "The Dead Hand Revisited." *Emory Law Journal* 70: 1–12.

Cogan, Neil H. 1994. "Review: Moses and Modernism." *Michigan Law Review* 92 (May): 1347–63.

Connor, George E., and Christopher W. Hammons. 2008. *The Constitutionalism of American States*. Columbia: University of Missouri Press.

Cooley, Thomas M. 1868. *A Treatise on the Constitutional Limitations Which Rest Upon the Legislative Power of the States of the American Union*. Boston: Little, Brown, and Company.

Cornwell, Elmer E., Jr. 1981. "The American Constitutional Tradition: Its Impact and Development." In *The Constitutional Convention as an Amending Device*, ed. Kermit L. Hall, Harold M. Hyman, and Leon V. Sigal, 1–36. Washington, DC: American Historical Association and American Political Science Association.

Council of State Governments. 1990–2016. *Book of the States*. Lexington, KY: Council of State Governments.

Curtis, Charles P. 1950. "A Better Theory of Legal Interpretation." *Vanderbilt Law Review* 3 (April): 407–37.

Dahl, Robert A. 2003. *How Democratic Is the American Constitution?* New Haven, CT: Yale University Press.

Damore, David F., Shaun Bowler, and Stephen P. Nicholson. 2012. "Agenda Setting by Direct Democracy: Comparing the Initiative and the Referendum." *State Politics and Policy Quarterly* 12 (4): 367–93.

Dawes, Christopher T., and James R. Zink. 2021. "Is 'Constitutional Veneration' an Obstacle to Constitutional Amendment?" *Journal of Experimental Political Science* http://doi.org/10.1017/XPS.2021.29.

Dealey, James Quayle. 1915. *Growth of American State Constitutions from 1776 to the End of the Year 1914*. Boston: Ginn.

Dinan, John J. 2006. *The American State Constitutional Tradition*. Lawrence: University Press of Kansas.

Dinan, John J. 2016. "Twenty-First Century Debates and Developments Regarding the Design of State Amendment Processes." *Arkansas Law Review* 69 (2): 283–315.

Dinan, John J. 2018. *State Constitutional Politics: Governing by Amendment in the American States*. Chicago: University of Chicago Press.

Dixon, Rosalind. 2011. "Constitutional Amendment Rules: A Comparative Perspective." University of Chicago Public Law and Legal Theory Working Paper No. 347.

Dixon, Rosalind, and Richard Holden. 2012. "Constitutional Amendment Rules: The Denominator Problem." In *Comparative Constitutional Design*, ed. Tom Ginsburg, 195–218. New York: Cambridge University Press.

Druckman, James N., Erik Peterson, and Rune Slothuus. 2013. "How Elite Partisan Polarization Affects Public Opinion Formation." *American Political Science Review* 107: 57–79.

Durbin, James. 1954. "Errors in Variables." *Review of the International Statistical Institute* 22: 23–32.

Dziak, John J., Donna L. Coffman, Stephanie T. Lanza, and Runze Li. 2012. "Sensitivity and Specificity of Information Criteria." Technical Report Series #12-119. State College: Methodology Center at Pennsylvania State University.

Eckles, David L., Cindy D. Kam, Cherie L. Maestas, and Brian F. Shaffner. 2014. "Risk Attitudes and the Incumbency Advantage." *Political Behavior* 36: 731–49.

Ehrlich, Isaac, and Richard Posner. 1974. "An Economic Analysis of Legal Rulemaking." *Journal of Legal Studies* 3 (January): 257–86.

Eidelman, Scott, Jennifer Pattershall, and Chris Crandall. 2010. "Longer Is Better." *Journal of Experimental Social Psychology* 46 (6): 993–98.

Elazar, Daniel J. 1966. *American Federalism: A View from the States*. New York: Thomas Y. Crowell.

Elazar, Daniel J. 1982. "The Principles and Traditions Underlying State Constitutions." *Publius* 12 (Winter): 11–25.

Elazar, Daniel J. 1988. *The American Constitutional Tradition*. Lincoln: University of Nebraska Press.

Elkins, Zachary, Tom Ginsburg, and James Melton. 2009. *The Endurance of National Constitutions*. Cambridge: Cambridge University Press.

Elster, Jon. 1979. *Ulysses and the Sirens*. New York: Cambridge University Press.

Emmert, Craig F. 1992. "An Integrated Case-Related Model of Judicial Decision-Making: Explaining State Supreme Court Decisions in Judicial Review Cases." *Journal of Politics* 54: 543–52.

Emmert, Craig F., and Carol Ann Traut. 1992. "State Supreme Courts, State Constitutions, and Judicial Policymaking." *Justice System Journal* 16 (1): 37-48.

Epstein, Lee, and Jack Knight. 1998. *The Choices Justices Make.* Washington, DC: Congressional Quarterly Press.

Epstein, Lee, and Thomas G. Walker. 1995. "The Role of the Supreme Court in American Society: Playing the Reconstruction Game." In *Contemplating Courts*, ed. Lee Epstein, 315-46. Washington, DC: CQ Press.

Eskridge, William N., Jr. 1991. "Overriding Supreme Court Statutory Interpretation Decisions." *Yale Law Journal* 101: 825-41.

Eskridge, William N., Jr., and John Ferejohn. 2001. "Super-Statutes." *Duke Law Journal* 50 (5): 1215-76.

Eskridge, William N., Jr., and John Ferejohn. 2010. *A Republic of Statutes: The New American Constitution.* New Haven, CT: Yale University Press.

Farkas, Steve, Jean Johnson, and Ann Duffett. 2002. *Knowing It by Heart: Americans Consider the Constitution and Its Meaning.* Philadelphia, PA: National Constitution Center.

Ferejohn, John. 1997. "The Politics of Imperfection: The Amendment of Constitutions." *Law and Social Inquiry* 22 (2): 501-30.

Fino, Susan. 1987. "Judicial Federalism and Equality Guarantees in State Supreme Courts." *Publius* 17: 51-67.

Ford, Paul Leicester, ed. 1905. *The Writings of Thomas Jefferson.* Vol. 12. New York: G. P. Putnam's Sons.

Friedman, Lawrence. 2014. "The Endurance of State Constitutions: Preliminary Thoughts and Notes on the New Hampshire Constitution." *Wayne Law Review* 60 (Spring): 203-18.

Fritz, Christian G. 1994. "The American Constitutional Tradition Revisited: Preliminary Observations on State Constitution-Making in the Nineteenth-Century West." *Rutgers Law Journal* 25 (Summer): 945-98.

Gardner, James A. 1992. "The Failed Discourse of State Constitutionalism." *Michigan Law Review* 90 (February): 761-837.

Gelman, Andrew. 2008. "Scaling Regression Inputs by Dividing by Two Standard Deviations." *Statistics in Medicine* 27: 2865-73.

Gerber, Elisabeth R. 1996. "Legislative Response to the Threat of Popular Initiatives." *American Journal of Political Science* 40 (February): 99-128.

Gersen, Jacob E. 2013. "Unbundled Powers." *Virginia Law Review* 96 (2): 301-58.

Gill, Rebecca D. 2013. "Beyond High Hopes and Unmet Expectations: Judicial Selection Reforms in the States." *Judicature* 96 (May): 278-93.

Gill, Rebecca D, Michael Kagan, and Fatma Marouf. 2019. "The Impact of Maleness on Judicial Decision Making: Masculinity, Chivalry, and Immigration Appeals." *Politics, Groups, and Identities* 7 (3): 509-28.

Ginsburg, Tom. 2010. "Constitutional Specificity, Unwritten Understandings, and Constitutional Agreement." In *Constitutional Topography: Values and Constitutions*, ed. Andras Sajo and Renaita Uitz, 69-94. The Hague: Eleven International.

Ginsburg, Tom, and James Melton. 2015. "Does the Constitutional Amendment Rule Matter at All? Amendment Cultures and the Challenges of Measuring Amendment Difficulty." *International Journal of Constitutional Law* 13 (3): 686-713.

Glaeser, Edward L., and Raven E. Saks. 2006. "Corruption in America." *Journal of Public Economics* 90 (6): 1053-72.

Goel, Rajeev K., and Daniel P. Rich. 1989. "On the Economic Incentives for Taking Bribes." *Public Choice* 61 (3): 269–75.

Goelzhauser, Greg, and Damon M. Cann. 2014. "Judicial Independence and Opinion Clarity on State Supreme Courts." *State Politics and Policy Quarterly* 14 (2): 123–41.

Gordon, Sanford C., and Gregory A. Huber. 2007. "The Effect of Electoral Competitiveness on Incumbent Behavior." *Quarterly Journal of Political Science* 2 (2): 107–38.

Grad, Frank P. 1968. "The State Constitution: Its Function and Form for Our Time." *Virginia Law Review* 54 (June): 928–80.

Grad, Frank P., and Robert F. Williams. 2006. *State Constitutions for the Twenty-First Century. Vol. 2: Drafting State Constitutions, Revisions, and Amendments.* Albany: State University of New York Press.

Granger, C. W. J. 1969. "Investigating Causal Relations by Economic Models and Cross-Spectral Methods." *Econometrica* 37 (August): 424–38.

Gray, Virginia. 1973. "Innovation in the States: A Diffusion Study." *American Political Science Review* 67 (4): 1174–85.

Griffin, Stephen M. 1996. *American Constitutionalism: From Theory to Politics.* Princeton, NJ: Princeton University Press.

Grofman, Bernard, and Timothy J. Brazill. 2002. "Identifying the Median Justice on the Supreme Court through Multidimensional Scaling: Analysis of 'Natural Courts' 1953–1991." *Public Choice* 112: 55–79.

Haggard, Stephan, and Mathew D. McCubbins, eds. 2001. *Presidents, Parliaments, and Policy.* New York: Cambridge University Press.

Hall, Matthew E. K. 2014. "The Semiconstrained Court: Public Opinion, the Separation of Powers, and the US Supreme Court's Fear of Nonimplementation." *American Journal of Political Science* 58 (April): 352–66.

Hall, Melinda Gann. 1992. "Electoral Politics and Strategic Voting in State Supreme Courts." *Journal of Politics* 54: 427–46.

Hall, Melinda Gann. 2008. "State Courts: Politics and the Judicial Process." In *Politics in the American States: A Comparative Analysis*, 9th edition, ed. Virginia Gray and Russell L. Hanson, 229–55. Washington, DC: CQ Press.

Hall, Melinda Gann. 2014. "Representation in State Supreme Courts: Evidence from the Terminal Term." *Political Research Quarterly* 67 (2): 335–46.

Hall, Melinda Gann, and Paul Brace. 1989. "Order in the Courts: A Neo-Institutional Approach to Judicial Consensus." *Western Political Quarterly* 42: 391–407.

Hammons, Christopher W. 1999. "Was James Madison Wrong? Rethinking the American Preference for Short, Framework-Oriented Constitutions." *American Political Science Review* 93 (December): 837–49.

Hammons, Christopher W. 2001. "State Constitutional Reform: Is It Necessary?" *Albany Law Review* 64 (4): 1327–53.

Hausman, Jerry A. 1978. "Specification Tests in Econometrics." *Econometrica* 46: 1251–71.

Henretta, James A. 1991. "Foreword: Rethinking the State Constitutional Tradition." *Rutgers Law Journal* 22 (Summer): 819–39.

Herron, Paul E. 2017. *Framing the Solid South: The State Constitutional Conventions of Secession, Reconstruction, and Redemption, 1860–1902.* Lawrence: University Press of Kansas.

Hershkoff, Helen, and Stephen Loffredo. 2011. "State Courts and Constitutional Socio-Economic Rights: Exploring the Underutilization Thesis." *Penn State Law Review* 115 (Spring): 923–82.

Hibbing, John R., and Elizabeth Theiss-Morse. 1996. "Civics Is Not Enough: Teaching Barbarics in K–12." *PS: Political Science and Politics* 29 (March): 57–62.

Holmes, Stephen. 1993. "Precommitment and the Paradox of Democracy." In *Constitutionalism and Democracy*, ed. Jon Elster and Rune Slagstad, 19–58. New York: Cambridge University Press.

Hopkins, Daniel J. 2018. *The Increasingly United States: How and Why American Political Behavior Nationalized*. Chicago: University of Chicago Press.

Howard, A. E. Dick. 1996. "The Indeterminacy of Constitutions." *Wake Forest Law Review* 31 (Summer): 383–410.

Huber, Gregory A., and Sanford C. Gordon. 2004. "Accountability and Coercion: Is Justice Blind When It Runs for Office?" *American Journal of Political Science* 48 (2): 247–63.

Huber, John D., and Charles R. Shipan. 2002. *Deliberate Discretion? The Institutional Foundations of Bureaucratic Autonomy*. Cambridge: Cambridge University Press.

Huff, Connor, and Dustin Tingley. 2015. "Who Are These People? Evaluating the Demographic Characteristics and Political Preferences of MTurk Survey Respondents." *Research & Politics* 2 (September): 1–12. doi:10.1177/2053168015604648.

Hunt, Galliard, ed. 1904. *The Writings of James Madison*. Vol. 5. New York: G. P. Putnam's Sons.

Jackson, Vicki C. 2015. "The (Myth of Un)amendability of the US Constitution and the Democratic Component of Constitutionalism." *International Journal of Constitutional Law* 13 (July): 575–605.

Jaros, Dean, and Bradley C. Canon. 1971. "Dissent on State Supreme Courts: The Differential Significance of Characteristics of Judges." *Midwest Journal of Political Science* 15: 322–46.

Jillson, Calvin C. 2002. *Constitution Making: Conflict and Consensus in the Federal Convention of 1787*. New York: Agathon Press.

Jillson, Calvin C., and Cecil L. Eubanks. 1984. "The Political Structure of Constitution Making: The Federal Convention of 1787." *American Journal of Political Science* 28 (August): 435–58.

Jones, Matt Bushnell. 1939. *Vermont in the Making, 1750–77*. Cambridge, MA: Harvard University Press.

Kahn, Paul W. 1993. "Interpretation and Authority in State Constitutionalism." *Harvard Law Review* 106 (March): 1147–68.

Kahneman, Daniel, Jack L. Knetsch, and Richard H. Thaler. 1991. "The Endowment Effect, Loss Aversion, and Status Quo Bias." *Journal of Economic Perspectives* 5 (1): 193–206.

Kam, Cindy D. 2012. "Risk Attitudes and Political Participation." *American Journal of Political Science* 56 (4): 817–36.

Kam, Cindy D., and Elizabeth N. Simas. 2010. "Risk Orientations and Policy Frames." *Journal of Politics* 72 (2): 381–96.

Kam, Cindy D., and Elizabeth N. Simas. 2012. "Risk Attitudes, Candidate Characteristics, and Vote Choice." *Public Opinion Quarterly* 76 (4): 747–60.

Kane, Jenna Becker. 2017. "Lobbying Justice(s)? Exploring the Nature of Amici Influence in State Supreme Court Decision Making." *State Politics and Policy Quarterly* 17 (December): 251–74.

Karch, Andrew, Sean C. Nicholson-Crotty, Neal D. Woods, Ann O'M. Bowman. 2016. "Policy Diffusion and the Pro-Innovation Bias." *Political Research Quarterly* 69 (1): 83–95.

Keller, Morton. 1977. *Affairs of State: Public Life in Late Nineteenth-Century America.* Cambridge, MA: Harvard University Press.

Keller, Morton. 1981. "The Politics of State Constitutional Revision, 1820–1930." In *The Constitutional Convention as an Amending Device*, ed. Kermit L. Hall, Harold M. Hyman, and Leon V. Sigal, 67–86. Washington, DC: American Historical Association and American Political Science Association.

Kiewiet, D. Roderick, and Mathew D. McCubbins. 1991. *The Logic of Delegation: Congressional Parties and the Appropriations Process.* Chicago: University of Chicago Press.

Kincaid, John. 1988. "State Constitutions in the Federal System." *Annals of the American Academy of Political and Social Science* 496 (1): 12–22.

Kogan, Vladimir. 2010. "The Irony of State Constitutional Reform." *Rutgers Law Journal* 41: 881–905.

Kousser, Thad, Mathew D. McCubbins, and Ellen Moule. 2008. "For Whom the TEL Tolls: Can State Tax and Expenditure Limits Effectively Reduce Spending?" *State Politics & Policy Quarterly* 8 (4): 331–61.

Kousser, Thad, and Justin H. Phillips. 2012. *The Power of American Governors: Winning on Budgets and Losing on Policy.* New York: Cambridge University Press.

Kurland, Philip B., and Ralph Lerner. 1987. *The Founders' Constitution.* Vol. 5. Chicago: University of Chicago Press.

Langer, Laura. 2002. *Judicial Review in State Supreme Courts: A Comparative Study.* Albany: State University of New York Press.

Lascher, Edward L., Jr., Michael G. Hagen, and Steven A. Rochlin. 1996. "Gun behind the Door? Ballot Initiatives, State Policies, and Public Opinion." *Journal of Politics* 58 (August): 760–75.

Lau, Richard R., and David P. Redlawsk. 2006. *How Voters Decide: Information Processing in Election Campaigns.* New York: Cambridge University Press.

Lax, Jeffery R., and Justin H. Phillips. 2012. "The Democratic Deficit in the States." *American Journal of Political Science* 56 (January): 148–66.

Leonard, Meghan E., and Joseph V. Ross. 2014. "Consensus and Cooperation on State Supreme Courts." *State Politics and Policy Quarterly* 14: 3–28.

Leonard, Meghan E., and Joseph V. Ross. 2016. "Understanding the Length of State Supreme Court Opinions." *American Politics Research* 44: 710–33.

Lerner, Hannah. 2011. *Making Constitutions in Deeply Divided Societies.* New York: Cambridge University Press.

Levinson, Sanford V. 1988. *Constitutional Faith.* Princeton, NJ: Princeton University Press.

Levinson, Sanford V. 1995. "Introduction: Imperfection and Amendability." In *Responding to Imperfection: The Theory and Practice of Constitutional Amendment*, ed. Sanford Levinson, 3–12. Princeton, NJ: Princeton University Press.

Levinson, Sanford V. 2006. *Our Undemocratic Constitution: Where the Constitution Goes Wrong (and How We the People Can Correct It).* Oxford: Oxford University Press.

Levinson, Sanford V. 2012. *Framed: America's 51 Constitutions and the Crisis of Governance.* New York: Oxford University Press.

Levinson, Sanford V., and William D. Blake. 2016. "What Americans Think about Constitutional Reform: Some Data and Reflections." *Ohio State Law Journal* 77: 211–36.

Lewis, Daniel C., Frederick S. Wood, and Matthew L. Jacobsmeier. 2014. "Public Opinion and Judicial Behavior in Direct Democracy Systems: Gay Rights in the American States." *State Politics and Policy Quarterly* 14 (4): 367–88.

Lijphart, Arend. 1969. "Consociational Democracy." *World Politics* 21 (January): 207–25.
Lijphart, Arend. 2012. *Patterns of Democracy: Government Forms and Performance in Thirty-Six Countries*. 2nd edition. New Haven, CT: Yale University Press.
Lind, Michael. 2011. "Let's Stop Pretending the Constitution Is Sacred." *Salon*, January 4.
Lorenz, Astrid. 2004. "Stabile Verfassungen? Konstitutionelle Reformen in Demokratien." *Zeitschrift für Parlamentsfragen* 35 (3): 448–68.
Lorenz, Astrid. 2005. "How to Measure Constitutional Rigidity: Four Concepts and Two Alternatives." *Journal of Theoretical Politics* 17 (3): 339–61.
Lorenz, Astrid. 2012. "Explaining Constitutional Change: Comparing the Logic, Advantages, and Shortcomings of Static and Dynamic Approaches." In *New Constitutionalism in Latin America: Promises and Practices*, ed. Detlef Nolte and Almut Schilling-Vacaflor, 31–50. Farnham, U.K.: Ashgate.
Lupia, Arthur. 1994. "Shortcuts versus Encyclopedias: Information and Voting Behavior in California Insurance Reform Elections." *American Political Science Review* 88 (March): 63–76.
Lupia, Arthur, Yanna Krupnikov, Adam Seth Levine, Spencer Piston, and Alexander von Hagen-Jamar. 2010. "Why State Constitutions Differ in Their Treatment of Same-Sex Marriage." *Journal of Politics* 72 (4): 1222–35.
Lupia, Arthur, and Mathew D. McCubbins. 1998. *The Democratic Dilemma: Can Citizens Learn What They Need to Know?* New York: Cambridge University Press.
Lutz, Donald S. 1980. *Popular Consent and Popular Control: Whig Political Theory in the Early State Constitutions*. Baton Rouge: Louisiana State University Press.
Lutz, Donald S. 1988. *The Origins of American Constitutionalism*. Baton Rouge: Louisiana State University Press.
Lutz, Donald S. 1994. "Toward a Theory of Constitutional Amendment." *American Political Science Review* 88 (June): 335–70.
Lutz, Donald S. 1998. "The United States Constitution as an Incomplete Text." *Annals of the American Academy of Political and Social Science* 496 (March): 23–32.
Manzer, Robert A. 2001. "A Science of Politics: Hume, the Federalist, and the Politics of Constitutional Attachment." *American Journal of Political Science* 45 (July): 508–18.
Marshfield, Jonathan L. 2018. "The Amendment Effect." *Boston University Law Review* 98 (January): 55–126.
Marshfield, Jonathan L. 2022. "America's Misunderstood Constitutional Rights." *University of Pennsylvania Law Review* 170.
Martin, Andrew D., and Morgan L. W. Hazelton. 2012. "What Political Science Can Contribute to the Study of Law." *Review of Law and Economics* 8 (2): 511–29.
Martin, Andrew D., and Kevin M. Quinn. 2002. "Dynamic Ideal Point Estimation via Markov Chain Monte Carlo for the US Supreme Court, 1953–1999." *Political Analysis* 10: 134–53.
May, Janice C. 1992. "State Constitutions and Constitutional Revision, 1990–1991." In *Book of the States*, 20–28. Lexington, KY: Council of State Governments.
Mazzone, Jason. 2017. "Amendmentphobia." *Italian Law Journal* 3: 133–37.
McConnell, Michael W. 1997. "Textualism and the Dead Hand of the Past." *George Washington Law Review* 66: 1127–40.
McDonald, Michael P. 2017. "Voter Turnout." United States Election Project. http://www.electproject.org/home/voter-turnout/voter-turnout-data.
Meier, Kenneth J., and Thomas M. Holbrook. 1992. "'I Seen My Opportunities and I Took 'Em: Political Corruption in the American States." *Journal of Politics* 54 (1): 135–55.

Miller, Nancy Martorano, Keith E. Hamm, and Ronald D. Hedlund. 2015. "Constrained Behavior: Understanding the Entrenchment of Legislative Procedure in American State Constitutional Law." *Albany Law Review* 78 (4): 1459–84.

Montenegro, Alvaro. 1995. "Constitutional Design and Economic Performance." *Constitutional Political Economy* 6: 161–69.

Morey, William C. 1893. "The First State Constitutions." *Annals of the American Academy of Political and Social Science* 4 (September): 1–32.

Morgan, Edmund S. 1988. *Inventing the People: The Rise of Popular Sovereignty in England and America*. New York: Norton.

Mutz, Diana C. 2011. *Population-Based Survey Experiments*. Princeton, NJ: Princeton University Press.

Nardi, Dominic J. 2013. "It's Not What You Say, It's How Much You Say it: Comparing Authoritarian and Democratic Constitutions Using Latent Text Analysis." Unpublished manuscript.

Natelson, Robert. 2017. "How Progressives Promoted the 'Runaway Convention' Myth to Save Judicial Activism." The Hill. https://thehill.com/blogs/pundits-blog/the-judiciary/332172-how-progressives-promoted-the-runaway-convention-myth-to.

National Center for State Courts. 2009. Separate Branches, Shared Responsibilities: A National Survey of Public Expectations on Solving Justice Issues. http://www.ncsc.org/Services-and-Experts/Court-leadership/Poll--Separate-Branches-and-Shared-Responsibilities.aspx.

National Conference of State Legislatures. 2010. NCSL Fiscal Brief: State Balanced Budget Provisions. http://www.ncsl.org/documents/fiscal/StateBalancedBudgetProvisions2010.pdf.

National Constitution Center. 2012. The AP-National Constitution Center Poll, August. http://constitutioncenter.org/media/files/data_GfK_AP-NCC_Poll_August_GfK_2012_Topline_FINAL_1st_release.pdf.

National Municipal League. 1963. *Model State Constitution*. 6th ed. New York: National Municipal League.

Nelson, Michael J. n.d. "Elections and Explanations: Judicial Retention and the Readability of Judicial Opinions." Working Paper.

Newey, Whitney K. 1987. "Efficient Estimation of Limited Dependent Variable Models with Endogenous Explanatory Variables." *Journal of Econometrics* 36: 231–50.

Nicholson-Crotty, Sean C. 2009. "The Politics of Diffusion: Public Policy in the American States." *Journal of Politics* 71 (1): 192–205.

Nicholson-Crotty, Sean C., Neal D. Woods, Ann O'M. Bowman, and Andrew Karch. 2014. "Policy Innovativeness and Interstate Compacts." *Policy Studies Journal* 42 (2): 305–24.

North, Douglass C., and Barry R. Weingast. 1989. "Constitutions and Commitment: The Evolution of Institutions Governing Public Choice in Seventeenth-Century England." *Journal of Economic History* 49 (4): 803–32.

Okun, Arthur M. 1975. *Equality and Efficiency: The Big Tradeoff*. Washington, DC: Brookings Institution Press.

Owens, Ryan J., Alexander Tahk, Patrick C. Wohlfarth, and Amanda C. Bryan. 2015. "Nominating Commissions, Judicial Retention, and Forward-Looking Behavior on State Supreme Courts: An Empirical Examination of Selection and Retention Methods." *State Politics and Policy Quarterly* 15 (2): 211–38.

Patterson, Steven E. 1981. "The Roots of Massachusetts Federalism: Conservative Politics and Political Culture before 1787." In *Sovereign States in an Age of Uncertainty*, ed. Ronald Hoffman and Peter Albert, 31–61. Charlottesville: University Press of Virginia.

Perrson, Torsten, and Guido Tabellini. 2003. *The Economic Effects of Constitutions*. Cambridge, MA: MIT Press.

Pew Research Center. 2015. "What the Public Knows in Pictures, Words, Maps, and Graphs." http://www.people-press.org/2015/04/28/what-the-public-knows-in-pictures-words-maps-and-graphs/.

Pope, Jeremy C., and Shawn Treier. 2020. *Founding Factions: How Majorities Shifted and Aligned to Shape the US Constitution*. Ann Arbor: University of Michigan Press.

Prakash, Saikrishna B., and John C. Yoo. 2003. "The Origins of Judicial Review." *University of Chicago Law Review* 70 (3): 887–982.

Przeworski, Adam, Michael E. Alvarez, Jose Antonio Cheibub, and Fernando Limongi. 2000. *Democracy and Development: Political Institutions and Well-Being in the World, 1950–1990*. New York: Cambridge University Press.

Raftery, Adrian E. 1995. "Bayesian Model Selection in Social Research." *Sociological Methodology* 25: 111–63.

Randazzo, Kirk A., Richard W. Waterman, and Michael P. Fix. 2011. "State Supreme Courts and the Effects of Statutory Constraint: A Test of the Model of Contingent Discretion." *Political Research Quarterly* 64 (4): 779–89.

Rasch, Bjorn Erik, and Rodger D. Congleton. 2006. "Amendment Procedures and Constitutional Stability." In *Democratic Constitutional Design and Public Policy: Analysis and Evidence*, ed. Rodger D. Congleton and Birgitta Swedenborg, 319–42. Cambridge, MA: MIT Press.

Reutter, Werner, and Astrid Lorenz. 2016. "Explaining the Frequency of Constitutional Change in the German Länder: Institutional and Party Factors." *Publius: The Journal of Federalism* 46 (1): 103–27.

Roberts, Andrew. 2009. "The Politics of Constitutional Amendment in Postcommunist Europe." *Constitutional Political Economy* 20 (2): 99–117.

Rossiter, Clinton, ed. 1961. *The Federalist Papers*. New York: New American Library.

Samuelson, William, and Richard Zeckhauser. 1988. "Status Quo Bias in Decision Making." *Journal of Risk and Uncertainty* 1: 7–59.

Sargan, John Denis. 1958. "The Estimation of Economic Relationships Using Instrumental Variables." *Econometrica* 26: 393–415.

Sartori, Giovanni. 1994. *Comparative Constitutional Engineering: An Inquiry into Structures, Incentives, and Outcomes*. London: Macmillan.

Segal, Jeffrey A., and Albert D. Cover. 1989. "Ideological Values and the Vote of U.S. Supreme Court Justices." *American Political Science Review* 82 (2): 557–65.

Segal, Jeffrey A., and Harold J. Spaeth. 1993. *The Supreme Court and the Attitudinal Model*. Cambridge: Cambridge University Press.

Shipan, Charles R., and Craig Volden. 2006. "Bottom-Up Federalism: The Diffusion of Anti-Smoking Policies from US Cities to States." *American Journal of Political Science* 50 (4): 825–43.

Shor, Boris, and Nolan McCarty. 2015. "Aggregate State Legislator Shor-McCarty Ideology Data, June 2015 Update." Harvard Dataverse. http://doi.org/10.7910/DVN/K7ELHW.

Siddali, Silvana R. 2015. *Frontier Democracy: Constitutional Conventions in the Old Northwest*. New York: Cambridge University Press.

Sinclair, Barbara. 2016. *Unorthodox Lawmaking: New Legislative Processes in the US Congress*. 5th edition. Washington, DC: CQ Press.

Sink, Michael. 2004. "Restoring Our Ancient Constitutional Faith." *University of Colorado Law Review* 75: 921–62.

Snijders, Tom A. B. 2005. "Power and Sample Size in Multilevel Modeling." In *Encyclopedia of Statistics in Behavioral Science*, ed. B. S. Everitt and D. C. Howell, Vol. 3, 1570–73. Chichester, U.K.: Wiley.

Sorauf, Frank J. 1981. "The Political Potential of an Amending Convention." In *The Constitutional Convention as an Amending Device*, ed. Kermit L. Hall, Harold M. Hyman, and Leon V. Sigal, 113–30. Washington, DC: American Historical Association and American Political Science Association.

Spaeth, Harold J., Lee Epstein, Andrew D. Martin, Jeffrey A. Segal, Theodore J. Ruger, and Sara C. Benesh. 2016. "Supreme Court Database, Version 2015, Release 03." http://supremecourtdatabase.org.

Squire, Peverill. 2007. "Measuring State Legislative Professionalism: The Squire Index Revisited." *State Politics and Policy Quarterly* 7 (June): 211–27.

Staiger, Douglas, and James H. Stock. 1997. "Instrumental Variables Regression with Weak Instruments." *Econometrica* 65 (May): 557–86.

Stephanopoulos, Nicholas O., and Mila Versteeg. 2016. "The Contours of Constitutional Approval." *Washington University Law Review* 94 (1): 113–90.

Stevens, Joe B. 1993. *The Economics of Collective Choice*. Boulder, CO: Westview Press.

Stumpf, Harry P. 1998. *American Judicial Politics*. San Diego, CA: Harcourt Brace Jovanovich.

Sturm, Albert L. 1982. "The Development of American State Constitutions." *Publius* 12 (Winter): 57–98.

Sutton, Jeffrey S. 2018. *51 Imperfect Solutions: States and the Making of American Constitutional Law*. New York: Oxford University Press.

Tarr, G. Alan. 1991. "Constitutional Theory and State Constitutional Interpretation." *Rutgers Law Journal* 22 (Summer): 841–61.

Tarr, G. Alan. 1994. "The Past and Future of the New Judicial Federalism." *Publius* 24 (2): 63–79.

Tarr, G. Alan. 1996. "State Constitutional Politics: An Historical Perspective." In *Constitutional Politics in the States: Contemporary Controversies and Historical Patterns*, ed. G. Alan Tarr, 3–23. Westport, CT: Greenwood.

Tarr, G. Alan. 1998. *Understanding State Constitutions*. Princeton, NJ: Princeton University Press.

Tarr, G. Alan. 2006a. "Introduction." In *State Constitutions for the Twenty-First Century, Vol. 1: The Politics of State Constitutional Reform*, ed. G. Alan Tarr and Robert F. Williams, 1–18. Albany: State University of New York Press.

Tarr, G. Alan. 2006b. "Introduction." In *State Constitutions for the Twenty-First Century, Vol. 3: The Agenda of State Constitutional Reform*, ed. G. Alan Tarr and Robert F. Williams, 1–6. Albany: State University of New York Press.

Tarr, G. Alan. 2014. "Explaining State Constitutional Change." *Wayne Law Review* 60 (1): 9–30.

Tarr, G. Alan, and Robert F. Williams, eds. 2006a. *State Constitutions for the Twenty-First Century. Vol. 1: The Politics of State Constitutional Reform*. Albany: State University of New York Press.

Tarr, G. Alan, and Robert F. Williams, eds. 2006b. *State Constitutions for the Twenty-First Century. Vol. 3: The Agenda of State Constitutional Reform*. Albany: State University of New York Press.

Thelen, Kathleen Ann. 2003. "How Institutions Evolve: Insights from Comparative Historical Analysis." In *Comparative Historical Analysis in the Social Sciences*, ed. James Mahoney and Dietrich Rueschemeyer, 208–40. Cambridge: Cambridge University Press.

Thomson, H. Bailey. 2006. "Constitutional Reform in Alabama: A Long Time Coming." In *State Constitutions for the Twenty-First Century, Vol 1: The Politics of State Constitutional Reform*, ed. G. Alan Tarr and Robert F. Williams, 113–44. Albany: State University of New York Press.

Townsend, Nancy J. 1985. "Single Subject Restrictions as an Alternative to the Line-Item Veto." *Notre Dame Journal of Law, Ethics, and Public Policy* 1 (2): 227–58.

Tsebelis, George. 2002. *Veto Players: How Political Institutions Work*. Princeton, NJ: Princeton University Press.

Tsebelis, George. 2017. "The Time Inconsistency of Long Constitutions: Evidence from the World." *European Journal of Political Research* 56: 820–45.

Tsebelis, George. 2021. "Constitutional Rigidity Matters: A Veto Players Approach." *British Journal of Political Science* 51 (1): 280–99.

Tsebelis, George, and Dominic J. Nardi. 2016. "A Long Constitution Is a (Positively) Bad Constitution: Evidence from OECD Countries." *British Journal of Political Science* 46: 457–78.

Tversky, Amos, and Daniel Kahneman. 1991. "Loss Aversion in Riskless Choice: A Reference-Dependent Model." *Quarterly Journal of Economics* 106 (4): 1039–61.

Velasco-Rivera, Mariana. 2021. "Constitutional Rigidity: The Mexican Experiment." *International Journal of Constitutional Law* 19 (July): 1042–61.

Vermeule, Adrian. 2006. "Constitutional Amendments and Common Law." In *The Least Examined Branch: The Role of Legislatures in the Constitutional State*, ed. Richard W. Bauman and Tsvi Kahana, 292–72. Cambridge: Cambridge University Press.

Versteeg, Mila, and Emily Zackin. 2014. "American Constitutional Exceptionalism Revisited." *University of Chicago Law Review* 81: 1641–707.

Versteeg, Mila, and Emily Zackin. 2016. "Constitutions Unentrenched: Toward an Alternative Theory of Constitutional Design." *American Political Science Review* 110 (4): 657–74.

Voigt, Stefan. 2009. "Explaining Constitutional Garrulity." *International Review of Law and Economics* 29: 290–303.

Walker, Jack L. 1969. "The Diffusion of Innovations among the American States." *American Political Science Review* 63 (3): 880–99.

Washington, Henry Augustine. 1859. *The Writings of Thomas Jefferson*. New York: Derby and Jackson.

Wattenberg, Martin P., Ian McAllister, and Anthony Salvanto. 2000. "How Voting Is Like Taking an SAT Test: An Analysis of American Voter Rolloff." *American Politics Research* 28 (2): 234–50.

White, Jean Bickmore. 1996. *Charter for Statehood: The Story of Utah's State Constitution*. Salt Lake City: University of Utah Press.

White, Jean Bickmore. 2011. *The Utah State Constitution*. New York: Oxford University Press.

Williams, Clifton. 1931. "Expressio Unius Est Exclusio Alterius." *Marquette Law Review* 15 (June): 191–96.

Williams, Robert F. 1988. " 'Experience Must Be Our Only Guide': The State Constitutional Experience of the Framers of the Federal Constitution." *Hastings Constitutional Law Quarterly* 15 (Spring): 403–28.

Williams, Robert F. 2009. *The Law of American State Constitutions*. New York: Oxford University Press.

Williams, Robert F., and G. Alan Tarr. 2004. "Subnational Constitutional Space: A View from the States, Provinces, Regions, Länder, and Cantons." In *Federalism, Subnational Constitutions, and Minority Rights*, ed. G. Alan Tarr, Robert F. Williams, and Josef Marko, 3–24. Westport, CT: Praeger.

Wilson, Sven E., and Daniel M. Butler. 2007. "A Lot More to Do: The Sensitivity of Time-Series Cross-Section Analyses to Simple Alternative Specifications." *Political Analysis* 15 (2): 101–23.

Windett, Jason H., Jeffrey J. Harden, and Matthew E. K. Hall. 2015. "Estimating Dynamic Ideal Points for State Supreme Courts." *Political Analysis* 23 (3): 461–69.

Wood, Gordon S. 1969. *The Creation of the American Republic, 1776–1787*. Chapel Hill: University of North Carolina Press.

Woodward-Burns, Robinson. 2021. *Hidden Laws: How State Constitutions Stabilize American Politics*. New Haven, CT: Yale University Press.

Wu, De-Min. 1974. "Alternative Tests of Independence between Stochastic Regressors and Disturbances: Finite Sample Results." *Econometrica* 42: 529–46.

Young, Ernest A. 2007. "The Constitution outside the Constitution." *Yale Law Journal* 117 (3): 408–73.

Zackin, Emily. 2013. *Looking for Rights in All the Wrong Places: Why State Constitutions Contain America's Positive Rights*. Princeton, NJ: Princeton University Press.

Zink, James R., and Christopher T. Dawes. 2016. "The Dead Hand of the Past? Toward an Understanding of 'Constitutional Veneration.'" *Political Behavior* 38 (September): 535–60.

Index

For the benefit of digital users, indexed terms that span two pages (e.g., 52–53) may, on occasion, appear on only one of those pages.

Tables and figures are indicated by *t* and *f* following the page number

Adams, John, 26
Alabama, 7–8, 10–12, 14, 22–23
amendments to state constitutions
    and economic performance, 106–7, 111, 115, 117–18
    initiated, 59–60, 65–67
    and judicial interpretation, 31–32, 75–76, 81–85
    limits, 58, 61–62, 66, 67, 96–97, 107
    procedural difficulty, 17, 23, 45, 49–50, 52, 56–60, 146 (*see also* legislative complexity)
    rates, 12, 15, 22, 49–50, 52, 67, 112, 146–47
    ratification, 64–67
    and revision, 14, 22, 24, 37–43, 130–31
    voter support for, 127, 130–31, 135–36
appellate courts, 2
Arizona, 79
Arkansas, 54, 58
attitudinal approach, 77

balance-of-powers approach, 76–77, 84–85
Bill of Rights, 27, 56
Book of the States, 21–22, 68, 74, 93–94
Brennan, William, 28–29
Bryan, William Jennings, 39

California
    amendments, 54, 64
    constitutional limitations of legislature, 7–8, 35, 79, 108–9
    supreme court, 80
Civil War, 34–35, 38–39, 43
Colorado, 43–44, 54, 79
Constitution. *See* US Constitution

constitutional conventions
    state conventions, 3–4, 31, 35, 37, 39–41
    1787 federal convention, 3–4, 24, 41–42, 56
Continental Congress, 25
Cooley, Thomas, 28
corruption, 46, 107, 113–14, 118

dead hands problem, 2, 146
Declaration of Independence, 51
democracy
    attitudes towards, 11–12, 26
    stability and, 51–52, 60, 128
    state constitutions and, 34, 127
    types of, 4
Democratic Party, 23, 66
Dorsey, Volney, 130

economic performance
    constitutional age, 111
    constitution length, 104–5, 110, 114*f*, 116, 143
    constitutional specificity, 108–9, 117, 148
enumerated power, 9, 17, 24, 32. *See also* plenary power
expressio unius est exclusio alterius, 33
extraconstitutional structures, 7 (easier to modify)

Federalist Papers. *See* Hamilton, Alexander, *and* Madison, James
firearm policy, 5, 13
Florida, 7–8, 55
Folsom, James, 12
framework provisions, 9–10, 46*f*, 79, 109–10

Gardner, James, 29–31

Georgia, 37, 55
governor, 6–7
Gray, Andrew, 130
Great Depression, 16–17
Gulliver's Travels, 1, 2, 12, 20–21

Hamilton, Alexander, 75, 78, 91
House of Representatives, 6

Idaho, 55
Illinois, 35, 58
Indiana, 55

Jefferson, Thomas
   on constitutional longevity, 20, 43, 50–51, 128–30
   legacy of, 131, 138
Jim Crow provisions, 11–12
judicial invalidations, 2, 79–81, 84, 88, 92–103
jurisprudential approach, 78, 85–86

Kansas, 55, 58
Kentucky, 58
Knox, John B., 10–11

legislative complexity, 58, 62f, 62–63, 64
Lilliputians. *See* Gulliver's Travels
Louisiana, 37, 54, 55, 80

Madison, James
   Federalist 10, 35–36
   Federalist 43, 50
   Federalist 49, 129
   Federalist 51, 1, 3
   Madison's dilemma, 1–2
   views on constitutional change, 128–31, 138
Maine, 55
Marshall, John, 50
Massachusetts, 26
Meredith, William, 130
Missouri, 54, 55, 79–80, 144–45
Montana, 55

National Municipal League (National Civic League), 28
neo-institutional approach, 76–77, 93–94

Nevada, 54, 55
New Hampshire, 39, 52
New Judicial Federalism, 24, 28–29
New Mexico, 54
New York, 8, 79
North Dakota, 54, 55

Oklahoma, 7–8, 54
omnibus statute, 83
Oregon, 54
originalism, 31, 81, 139–40

Pennsylvania, 26, 35
plenary power
   constitutional specificity and, 48, 75, 108
   foreign constitutions, 17
   interpretation and, 32–33
   scope of, 9, 24
policy provisions, 9–10, 46f, 79, 109–10
positive rights, 7–8, 17, 27–28, 33–34, 35, 138
precedent, judicial adherence to, 31–32, 78, 82–83, 90

race/racism, 10–11, 35
Republican Party, 23, 45t, 63
revision, 15, 22, 24, 34, 36, 37–43, 56, 66–67, 75–76, 82–83, 127, 147–48
Rhode Island, 67
Riley, Bob, 12
Roosevelt, Theodore, 130–31

slavery, 30
South, American
   amendments, 63
   comparability of regions, 29
   constitutional reform, 35, 37f, 38f, 38–39
   constitution length, 44f, 45t
   duration of constitutions, 43t
South Carolina, 52
South Dakota, 54, 55
stare decisis, 31–32. *See also* precedent
state supreme courts
   amendment process, 32
   constitutional revision, 42
   constitutional specificity, 75, 79–81
   federal constitution, 90
   judicial review, 76–77

Texas, 8

US Constitution
   amendment process, 31–32, 52, 56, 81
   attitudes toward, 127–28, 130–38, 140*t*, 155n.8
   brevity of, 78, 79, 81
   Commerce Clause, 78
   differences from state constitutions, 24, 32
   Fourteenth Amendment, 108
   global effects of, 16
   House of Representatives, 6
   Necessary and Proper Clause, 78
   origins of, 5, 25, 30
   presidential authority, 6–7
   supreme court, 7
   uniqueness of, 3, 26–28

US Supreme Court
   Congress, 7
   New Judicial Federalism, 24, 28–29
   US Constitution, 31–32, 56

Utah, 13, 54, 79, 109, 144–45

Vermont, 7–8, 14, 43–44
veto, 5–6, 7, 18
Virginia, 55
voter ratification, 61–62, 64–67

Washington state, 79
World War II, 16–17
Wyoming, 54